THE ART OF WINE
FROM THE VINE TO THE TABLE

a good nose & great legs

Robert Geddes
Master of Wine

MURDOCH BOOKS

Contents

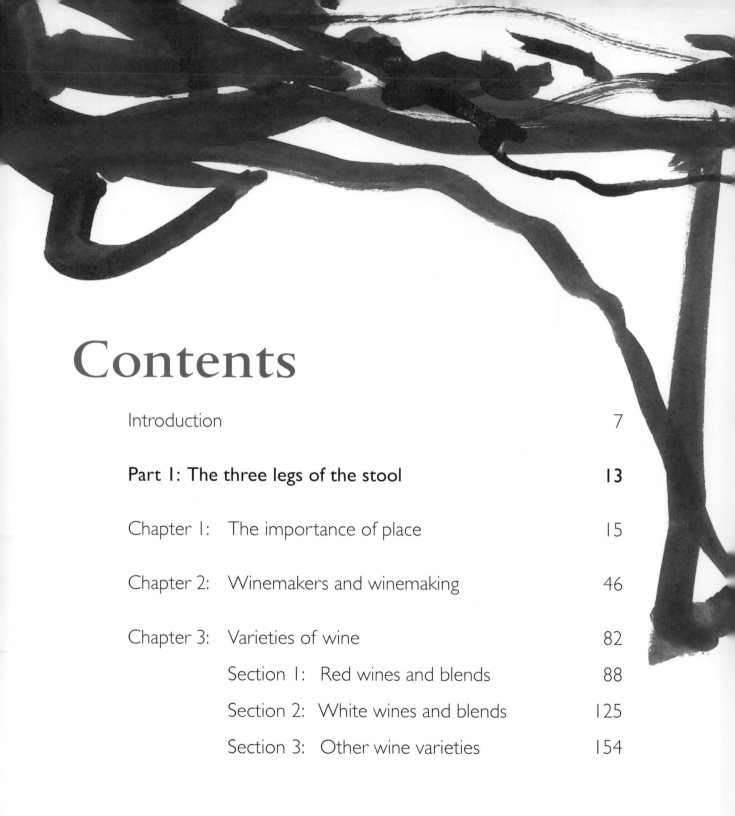

Introduction

It was a hot, dusty, smelly day in the sheep yards of our farm in the Clare Valley; flies were clinging furiously onto any bit of moisture that was about. My mind was racing and the hairs on my arms tingling with excitement as my back strained to hold the young ram that was bucking about while my father and I examined its fleece.

As Dad parted the fleece he talked about its quality and explained how this sheep produced wool that suited the environment where it was raised. It dawned on me that if the wool responded to the climate, then we could identify and select specific sheep for a particular region to produce the wool we wanted. We could use adaptation beneficially.

It was not long after this event when a revelation came to me while I was drinking homegrown Clare riesling, that environmental adaptation could equally be applied to grapes and wine. I could taste differences between bottles of the same variety from different vineyards due to subtle variances that the soil and climate had on the grape. It was a magical moment. A door opened—wine became the land talking to me.

It was my headmaster who started me off. I had always seen the trucks laden with purple grapes disappearing into the winery, and now it was my turn to follow them in. I was a bookish boy who loved geology, hence the headmaster linked it to wine; so in my final days of Year Four at Clare Primary School he did something parents would hate today, and gave me a note for permission to visit the local winery for a look around. Guided by family friend Mick Knappstein, my senses came alive to the smells, the noise and the sense of industry with humour. I loved every minute of it.

My teenaged friends in the early 1970s also had access to a vast cellar of Clare Valley wines from the 1950s to the mid-1960s, so we discovered the joys of wine appreciation. Our random wine selections, often sampled in outrageous locations, gave us a rough-and-ready knowledge of the local styles and varieties and considerable experience with old wines.

In 1950, in the company of some winemaking students at Roseworthy College, I found myself very earnestly tasting and discussing a dozen bottles placed in brown paper bags so that we couldn't see the labels. As I tasted three of the wines I was reminded of the wines of Clare. The taste seemed so familiar to me that without fear I volunteered that they were from the Stanley Clare Valley Bin 56 Cabernet Malbec, the Stanley Clare Valley Bin 49 Cabernet Sauvignon, and the Stanley Bin 61 Shiraz. To me it didn't seem such a remarkable thing to do, but as I was leaving one of the winemakers put a very brotherly arm around my shoulder and said, 'You've got a talent—don't waste it.' Those words changed my life.

I was studying agriculture at the time and knew that I was not going to embrace a passion for sheep farming like my father. Instead I began to study wine socially, making a pest of myself with any winemaker who would chat while I was completing the course. Thankfully many did, such as Scott Collet, Don Bird, Darren De Bortoli, Neil McGuigan, Graham Buller and Keith Mugford. The Roseworthy wine courses were held in high regard and continue to be under the aegis of the University of Adelaide. The students there were willing to be my teachers. I learned a lot.

Over two summers I managed to acquire work in wineries during vintage in the Clare and Hunter Valleys, in between sandwiching a job as an extra in a motion picture. What followed was a period of eight years running the Wine and Brandy Producers Wine Information Bureau in Adelaide. Then a phone call from my brother Jim, who described a bottle of very ancient wine in the window of Berry Brothers & Rudd in London, persuaded me to visit (in what would eventually become an extended stay) the United Kingdom. A kindly employee from the Australian Embassy alerted me to a tasting in London and I met David Gill, a Master of Wine. A job followed, as did David's comment: 'If you can write the way you speak, you could make a Master of Wine.'

Several years of study, accompanied by many bottles of wine, boon companions and much help from older Masters of Wine, and many lonely kilometres visiting European growers on a shoestring budget, fostered my winemaking education. Walking among (and occasionally sleeping in) various European vineyards, tasting their wines and eating their food crystallised in 1992 when I passed the Masters of Wine theory exam. Later that year I moved my family to Griffith in New South Wales, courtesy of the Riverina Grape Growers and Winemakers when I became their first regional public relations officer.

In 1993 I passed the Masters of Wine tasting exam, becoming only the third Australian to do so. This position introduced me to Griffith's rich Italian traditions and the laconic De Bortoli family. Through Darren De Bortoli and his wonderful Noble One wine, I learned that every place has its own story and reaffirmed for myself that wines do come from a unique set of circumstances.

One of the greatest lessons I have learned from this is that, contrary to its image, the wine industry is one of the toughest in which to survive. No matter how skilled winemakers may be, they are at the mercy of nature's elements and in recent times the retail markets. Wine production is moving away from a large group of families in an industry to a few corporations in a business. It is transforming from the limited production of a farmer's product to endless flows controlled by multinational corporations. Winemakers still get one shot to show their stuff each year but the environment in which they operate is more challenging.

More astronauts have visited space and returned than people have passed the Masters of Wine exam.

DAVID STEVENS MW

Masters of Wine

The Institute of Masters of Wine (IMW) was founded in 1955 and for many years members were drawn from the English wine trade. During the late 1980s the IMW shifted from a UK trade body to an international organisation with regular activities in the United States, Australia and continental Europe, as well as maintaining their original operations in the United Kingdom.

The IMW undertakes a wide range of activities, including a symposium every four years, annual study courses with accompanying exams conducted across three continents, and classic tastings each year in London. Presently there are 255 Masters of Wine in 16 countries. Members of the institute travel widely to keep abreast of technical issues and new developments in the industry, as well as purchasing wine. It is an important way to gain insights into the producers, vineyards and wines of the world. There have been more than 19 official visits to various countries, including the celebrated 1985 Australian visit, which was a turning point for the recognition of the quality and diversity of our wines, especially in the United Kingdom. Australia and California in the United States are the only places to have hosted a return visit.

The Masters of Wine qualification is gained through seven exams undertaken over four days. Exams test knowledge and expressions in wine tasting, and different aspects of the wine industry from the vineyard to the market place. The three tasting exams use wines of representative quality and style from anywhere in the world and demand a reasoned explanation and description of their quality. A very small pass rate reflects the exams' standards and the expectation that the IMW's graduates understand the world of wine, in particular fine wine.

THE BOOK

This book was written for its own sake. It was born during a mid-life period of unemployment, and continued through to my current position where I am running my own media relations and marketing services firm for the wine industry.

It's a moot point whether a deeply knowledgeable person is able to write or adhere to a code of honour and impartiality when writing. I could quite easily have turned my back on the project and walked away, but wine for me is as much about the people I know as what I know.

I found myself drawn to completing the book because the more you do the more you learn, and in wine you learn by tasting and listening. There were debts to be repaid. The journey has given me a great opportunity to test and measure what I know and what I have learned. I hope my efforts within these pages increase your knowledge.

To me a bottle of wine is a coded message from another place, and I hope to give you the key to the code that unlocks the message. I want to share with you the mystery in every sip of wine, so that you can understand the leaps of imagination created by honest men and women of the soil who keep refining the code every year, giving us better and better wines. That code in every bottle of wine has three stories:

- where it comes from—the place
- who made it—the person
- what it is made from—the grape varietal or varieties.

The first part of this book introduces you to these three elements: the place where the vine is grown, the process of making wine, and lastly the vine varieties that go into wine and their special properties.

In the second part I will concentrate on you, the consumer of the wine. You will learn to discern what you like in a wine so you can purchase with confidence, as well as learning to appreciate the nuances that go with the wine lifestyle, in particular matching food with wine. Part of this process is learning to discern wines of high quality. That is, that they are well made, possibly award winning and low-volume produced, often from a single vineyard, hand-picked and privately owned. These are wines made with passion and extraordinary commitment, wines which have a worthy place on a table or in the cellar of any wine collector anywhere in the world.

So how do you unlock the information about these good wines and bring your level of understanding up? That is the challenge set here.

MEMORABLE WINE

I want to illuminate for you the fundamentals that go into making the many varieties of wines so that you can enjoy them all the more.

Rather than simplify what happens in winemaking and tasting I want to take you straight to the core—the defining, essential part of wine that is memorable.

Wine is a living, changing expression of life itself. It has a birth, it reflects the places it is raised, it matures in its making and declines with time. Wandering through the art and science that makes this delectable drop, you will find a rich tapestry of human existence.

Wine is a marvel. While it is not essential, it gives such pleasure and has been a part of human existence for thousands of years. It has travelled with civilizations, inserting itself where the climate is suitable for viticulture, creating its own rich history. In many ways, its expansion around the world is the story of humankind's diaspora—wine has gone where we have and evolved as we have. Today, wine provides us with tastes and tasting opportunities that have never existed before. Wine gets complex in its antiquity, flavour, diversity, colour and quality—it is at once simple but, oh, so complicated.

Telling the story of wine allows the wines to speak to you, especially those that have a special quality which you savour and remember. Even if you don't recall a wine's name or its exact flavour, you'll remember the occasion and how much you enjoyed drinking it. These are wines that enhance the occasion they celebrate and make them memorable, and they help shape our own, individual stories.

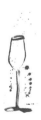

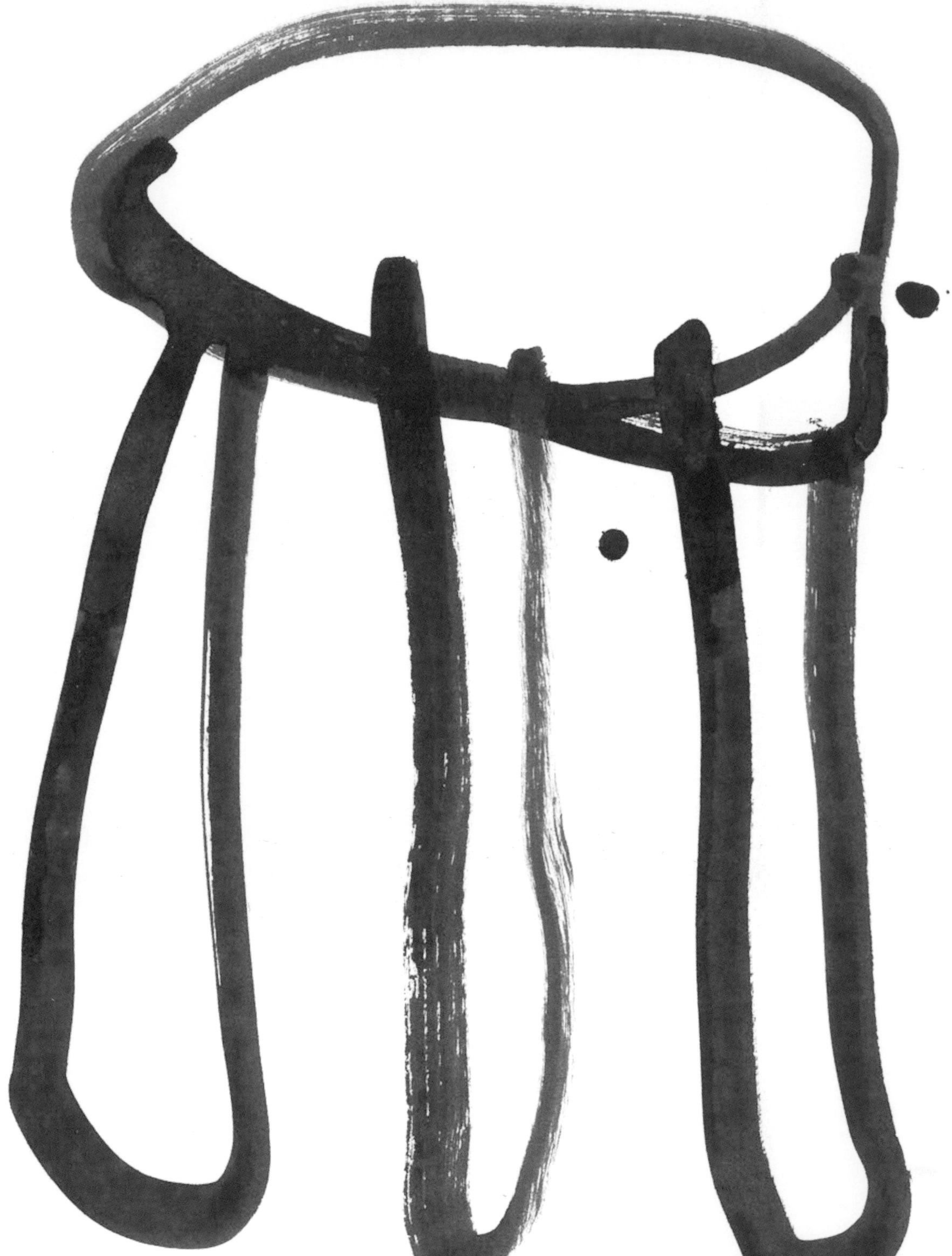

part one

The three legs of the stool

When a discussion arises about a **memorable wine** the first thing many people try to do is to **define it**—we try to nail the experience.

Winemakers and wine experts have come up with a whole range of baffling expressions to describe the sum awareness of wine. But all that rhetoric boils down to three main aspects of winemaking:

- the place where the grape was grown and its climate
- the people who grow wine and the process of winemaking
- the grape variety itself.

We call these elements the 'three-legged stool of wine' to evoke an image of stability and interconnectedness. A stool is also an age-old item, somewhat rustic, and it is used here as a metaphor for the timeless nature of wine. Examining these three legs and placing you, the wine drinker, on top of the stool, can tell the story of each memorable bottle of wine. Take away one leg and there is no support. Shorten or lengthen one leg and the balance tilts, tipping you off the chair of enjoyment. But when constructed with artistry, you have a wine that works perfectly—three legs with a seat, all perfectly balanced.

These components are inextricably interconnected and interdependent, and need to be looked at together. The same grape variety grown in different places will taste different; the same grape variety grown in the same place by different people making different decisions will also taste different. Each of these elements adds its own layer of complexity to the final product.

And you, of course, have a part to play in this complex process. For it's your decision—whether you try and buy based on your tastebuds and preferences or based on current market trends—that affects what is grown and continues to be grown.

In this first part we will be looking at these three legs. Understanding how it all fits together goes a long way to understanding wine. But remember, there is always a mystery at the heart of memorable wine, which we will hopefully never be able to pin down. It's like personality development. We may understand more and more about the various facets of growth and development but there is always an 'X' factor that contributes to the 'art' component of winemaking.

chapter 1

The importance of place

If the only story you have got is where you come from,
you need a new story

BILLY CONNOLLY

PLACE DOES MATTER

Put simply, place matters because the relationship of the vine and the environment dictates the characteristics of the wine.

It's true to say that every wine carries the characteristics of the place it comes from, some broadly and others more subtly. In some instances it's actually possible to taste-track memorable wines back to their individual vineyard origins. The degree to which origins are revealed depends on all the people in the chain: the understanding of the local scientists, the intentions of the grape grower and the winemaker, and the abilities of the marketers to negotiate the marketplace.

According to Rob Gibson, winemaker and vigneron, moving vines from their traditional European homelands is similar to moving Australian eucalypts to other countries, where they achieve extraordinary growth beyond what they are capable of in their native situation. Moving grape vines from the vineyards of Europe to the Southern Hemisphere greatly increases their vigour (energy) due to different ecological balances. This requires grape growers to learn new vineyard tools and strategies to decrease the vines' vigour in their vineyards.

Human understanding is often the limiting factor in the new equation. For example, it has taken generations of observation for winemakers and grape growers to understand that key ripening processes dependent on water depletion of soil in Bordeaux are triggered in the same way in different soils of the Barossa Valley in December with the correct vine training.

There is little doubting the ingenuity of humanity. In this age of cheap energy and boundless enthusiasm, almost anything can be, and is, done to grow and develop new vineyards. We continue to enjoy the efforts of pioneer vignerons who led the way, thanks to better fungicides, into new winegrowing areas in cooler and wetter environments. Vignerons pushed the boundaries of the vine into regions that formerly were impossible. They even irrigated deserts or moved millions of tonnes of rocks to overcome nature and plant their crops. Vines planted in climatically challenging sites add to the drama of winemaking as we know it today, as does the fascinating battle by winemakers to challenge both the vine and themselves to produce a memorable drop.

A key difference between the new and old world lies in the use of irrigation to manage a vineyard site. Additional water coupled with our abundant sunlight affects the vigour of the vines. Irrigation can be an emotional topic, but there is no doubt that in places where the soils are low in moisture and water-holding capacity irrigation works. Great examples are Washington State, Chile and many regions of Australia.

Legend for winegrowing regions in Australia

Adelaide Hills	45	Hastings River	3	Pemberton	53
Adelaide plains	47	Heathcote	21	Perricoota	10
Alpine Valley	27	Henty	16	Perth Hills	58
Ballarat	19	Hilltops	11	Pyrenees	18
Barossa Valley	48	Hunter Valley, lower	1	Queensland, coastal	61
Beechworth	27	Hunter Valley, upper	2	Riverina	9
Bendigo	20	Kangaroo Island	43	Riverland	49
Blackwood Valley	54	King Valley	26	Rutherglen	25
Canberra district	12	Langhorne Creek	41	Shoalhaven	15
Clare Valley	50	Macedon Ranges	33	South Burnett	60
Coonawarra	37	McLaren Vale	42	Southern Eyre Peninsula	51
Cowra	6	Manjimup	53	Southern Fleurieu	44
Eden Valley	46	Margaret River	55	Sunbury	32
Geelong	31	Mornington Peninsula	29	Swan district	59
Geographe	56	Mount Benson	39	Swan Hill	7
Gippsland	28	Mount Gambier	36	Tasmania, northern	34
Glenrowan	25	Mudgee	4	Tasmania, southern	35
Goulburn Valley	22	Murray Darling	8	Tumbarumba	14
Grampians	17	Nagambie Lakes	23	Upper Goulburn	24
Granite Belt	62	Orange	5	Wrattonbully	38
Great Southern	52	Padthaway	40	Yarra Valley	30
Gundagai	13	Peel	57		

Winegrowing regions of Australia

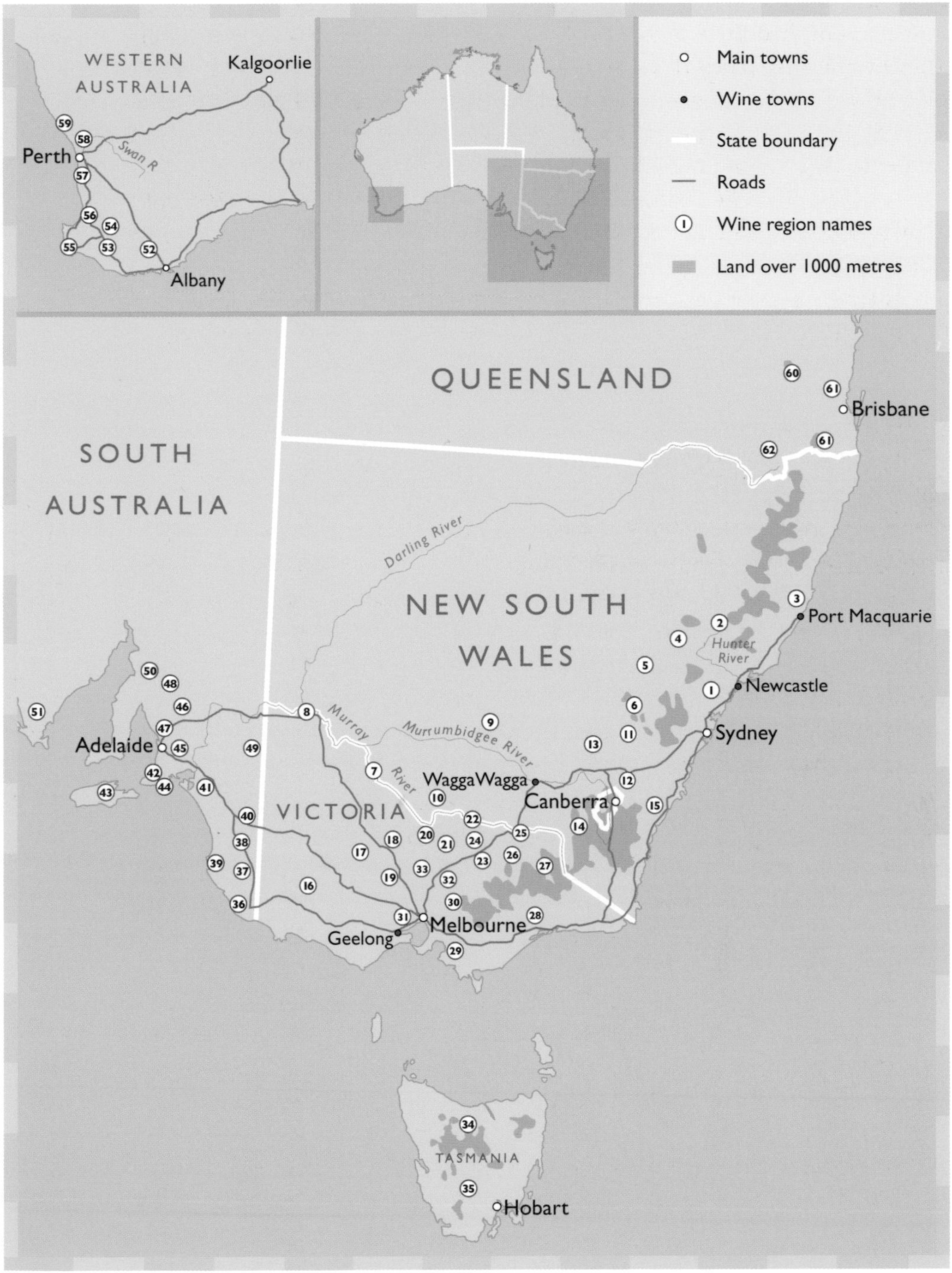

ADAPTED FROM: 'WINE REGIONS OF AUSTRALIA' FROM JAMES HALLIDAY, *AUSTRALIAN WINE COMPANION*, 2007 EDITION

Such is the culture of wine and the fabric of human nature that the wine industry always tries to make the best it can from what is on offer. Winegrowers are nominally in charge by choosing where and what to plant, but after that the DNA of the vines and the local weather patterns put pressure on those decisions. It's almost masochistic that winemakers pioneer cooler areas for growing grapes and run the risks in such climates of frost, rain at critical periods, cool summers and under-ripeness of the fruit, and then challenge themselves to make varietal wines that faithfully reflect their origins. In other words, they start trying to make great wines from their place similar to the great wines of other places. Over subsequent generations, and with added knowledge, these wines are then further developed and refined, adding to the constant evolution of wine.

Memorable wines can also come from gentler places more in keeping with the vines' ancient origins. These areas naturally possess the mix of climatic conditions that favour their genetic heritage; therefore the vines deliver a natural richness of flavour, structure and an ability to age even when they were never really destined to grow there. In these chosen environments the vines are happy because their demands are met without excessive nurture, and this is reflected in the wine that is produced.

In the battle for memorable wine, vines are rarely planted in easy-to-manage flat, sun-drenched, irrigated fields. Fine wine today comes from vines that prosper in areas where the warm sun and cool air provide enough energy without excessive heat; this is quite different from the warm Mediterranean origin of most vines. Grape growers explore the make up of the soil and change it if necessary; or they choose the soil to match the varieties they are wanting to plant. They will seek friable, well-drained soils with a clay content that allows the vines to take up water gradually. They are unlikely to be the same soils or places that can grow cereal crops, being less fertile or more sloping.

For vines to satisfactorily grow and ripen grapes, they require adequate light and heat, among other inputs. If the soils fail to warm up enough, the roots do not reach a temperature sufficient to set off the hormones that drive their biological clocks, causing the plant to fail to flower and set fruit.

In juggling these growth limits two factors can be used by the grape grower to manipulate the plant. Foremost, the site's location within a cool climate to provide a longer ripening period, preserving acidity. At the same time the vine's attempts to survive and reproduce sees it pour as much energy as it can into the production of flavour by creating compounds that evaporate from the skin of the fruit. So memorable wines can be produced from the climatic limits of vine growth—above 30° latitude north in the Northern Hemisphere and south in the Southern Hemisphere, and where the annual mean temperature is above 10°C. In Australia, wines in these regions show finer fruit flavours with fresh zingy acidity, subtle small berry fruits, a delicacy in the mouth and with no sense of overripeness; it is a tender structure as opposed to warmer climate fruit that produces a greater force of ripe flavours.

The second factor is the choice of trellis and vine training to maximise light and warmth. When the vines in European regions are in balanced growth, very small and quite simple trellises are used. In Australia, however, we need larger structures and more complex training and management approaches to accommodate the vigour of the vines driven by the abundant sunlight, warmth and water.

Often there is a margin of risk from climate events on the fringes of growing areas where vines are challenged, such as the chilling frosts of 2006 in the Yarra Valley and Coonawarra. Generalisations are dangerous but memorable wine requires warm sunshine, the appropriate mix of rainfall and drought, and soils without great fertility. The human management of memorable wines focuses on modest crops, carefully made by winemakers competing to find the elusive path to maximise varietal flavour without sacrificing the taste of the place the wines come from.

It's a struggle on one side to overcome the challenges of place and a celebration on the other when we achieve the range of characters from delicacy to strength that can define memorable wine. Place of origin is so closely associated with quality in the public mind that it is very common for people to seek out regional information when they buy a wine. New Zealand and Australian winemakers are blessed with a great many regions that favour our imported vines. It's an exciting unfolding story, as yet we do not have all the answers or all the knowledge.

PLACE OVER VARIETY

The importance of place comes from the vine as its relationship to the environment dictates the range of flavours available.

This has always been recognised by the Europeans who named their wines after the places where they were grown and produced distinctive flavours. Developments, particularly in the selection of specific grape varieties for growing in different parts of Europe started in the sixteenth century; thus building regional reputations that are still famous today.

Varietal wine—one named after the variety in the bottle—can come from anywhere in the world where the vine grows. But Margaret River, Coonawarra, the Hunter Valley, and select vineyards within these regions, are some of the special places with special flavours that cannot be copied. In the Australian context, for example, if I grow my sauvignon blanc in the cool, damp, elevated Adelaide Hills, or in Tumbarumba, or in the south of Western Australia, I'm going to end up with a wine that has a fresh grassiness with ripe passionfruit flavours and a lovely, zippy acidity. But if I take the same

grape out of its element, to the hot, sweaty, baking plains of the inland, I will wind up with a wine that is low on the pungent green herbaceous characteristics of sauvignon blanc and broader in texture. It's also going to be less flavourful because much of the delicate aromas would have evaporated even before the grapes were harvested and the vines would have spent less time producing at their most biologically efficient rate. A smart winemaker may pick early and get a limited version of the fruit flavours available. A smarter one will plant the grape where it does best.

Many varietal wines are grown in conditions to suit ripening large crops while maintaining low costs in production. At their fundamental (cheap) level these wines have

Varietal pyramid

Quality and quantity are inversely related. Within wine the highest qualities are associated with reduced volumes.

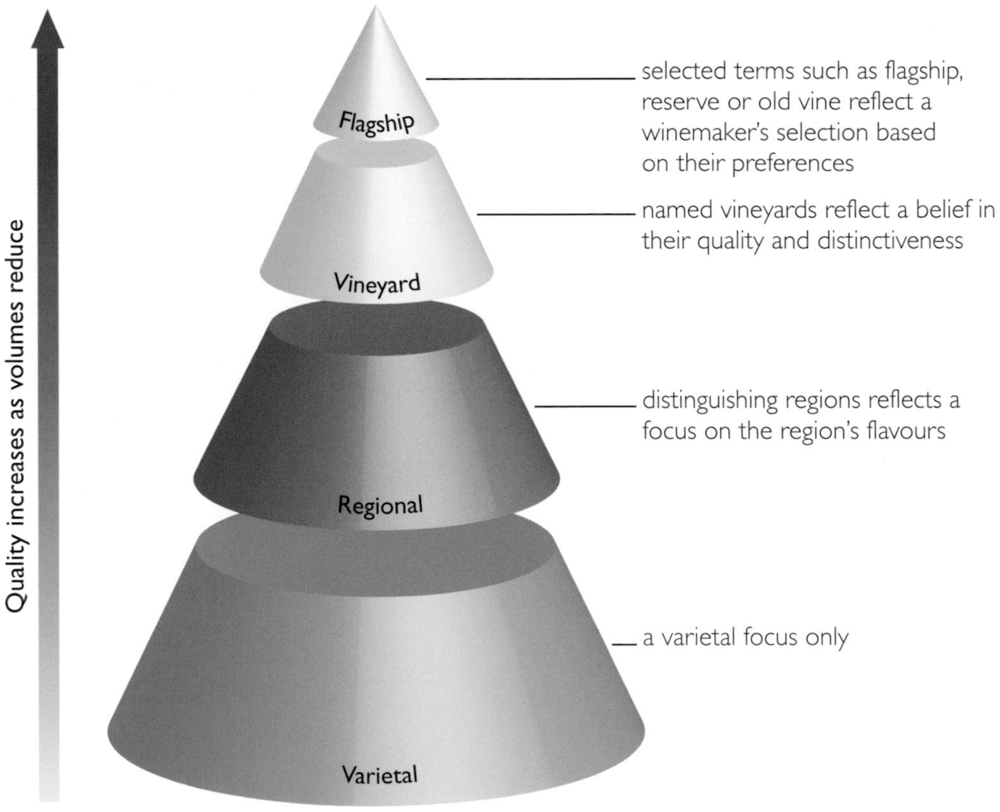
Quality increases as volumes reduce
Flagship
Vineyard
Regional
Varietal
selected terms such as flagship, reserve or old vine reflect a winemaker's selection based on their preferences
named vineyards reflect a belief in their quality and distinctiveness
distinguishing regions reflects a focus on the region's flavours
a varietal focus only

little to identify them beyond the variety and brand. They are often sound and reliable but anonymous to taste and their regional origins hard to distinguish. Wine sold by its variety is easy to duplicate by planting more of the same in different places. With nothing more to its heritage than its brand and variety they are everyday wines made and sold on price. Varieties quickly lose their uniqueness with the drinker unless they come from somewhere within a climate that suits the variety and elevates the wine. It is where the grapes are grown that gives wine its uniqueness.

The Europeans have learned about the importance of place over centuries of viticulture. This has served us very well in Australia and other places that are called the 'new world'. For example, we have been able to predict, to a relative degree, where cabernet sauvignon will grow well by examining the conditions under which it grows well in France. This grape grows beautifully in Bordeaux, where the variation in day–night temperature is not too great, thanks to the Gulf Stream current. The gravel soils and clay subsoils also manage the water requirements of the vines by storing heat and re-radiating the warmth at night—conditions suitable for ripening small crops.

We do not completely understand all the factors involved in the process. When we take cabernet sauvignon to cool places that are often statistically similar with cold nights, such as Chile or Marlborough in New Zealand, a weedy, herbal, capsicum character can appear. Even when ripe flavour and aroma are mastered there still remains the challenge of mastering the hard astringent tannins that are common in these climates—neither a good taste nor texture in this variety. Yet sauvignon blanc thrives in the same environment.

Chardonnay, on the other hand, seems unbelievably tolerant to different climates although historically it was grown a long way from the coast in temperate climates. Chardonnay grapes typically have an early budburst, which means that the flowers and fruit come out early in the season. This makes it an extremely risky grape to grow in cold climates, where late spring frosts can wreak havoc. This exact scenario occurred in Australia in 1998, and even more disastrously in late 2006, when we had chilling frosts across south-eastern Australia from Canberra to the Coonawarra region and across to Melbourne. The French worked this one out long ago and most northern European chardonnay is planted on slopes that drain cold frosty air away.

We often find that conditions adverse to vines, aside from cool temperatures, can help create conditions for making quality wines. In the Margaret River region, chardonnay flowers as the cool spring winds of the district start, dispersing its pollen, making it difficult for pollination to take place. Not a good thing for a grape grower but a delight for the winemaker picking these naturally yield-reduced precious berries.

Some varieties are more fickle than others. Riesling is native to Germany and France, and does well in hilly, cool, inland sites with low fertility soils and cool nights. Following this pattern, the great Australian rieslings come from areas that are removed from excessive heat and enjoy the cool, often maritime influence of places such as Central

Victoria, Western Australia and South Australia. Riesling is not a happy traveller like chardonnay and does not handle warmer regions well, losing its floral aromas quickly in these less ideal conditions. All of this experience leads to you being able to predict the character of the wine you are choosing if you know a bit about where it comes from.

Soils can play an important role. Merlot vines can throw a complete hissy fit if deprived of water or over-heated during the ripening process. The fruit flavour disappears in part because merlot has a less robust root system and stresses easily, so vignerons have to be very aware of the water balance of the soil. The clay subsoil in the cool Pomerol and St Emilion appellations in Bordeaux has the ability to hold water and not dry out quickly; hence the soil has proved to be an excellent host to merlot. In the new world some vignerons use sophisticated irrigation systems to overcome such such limitation.

The place a wine grows leaves various hints of its origin: low (warm climate) or high (cool) acidity; medium- or full-bodied alcohol; ripe, raisin, jammy fruit, or a cooler, ripe, fresh berry fruit. Taken collectively all these clues can lead you to where a wine originated by recognising and identifying the characteristics. A big mouthful of high-alcohol red with a soft acidity that smells of super-ripe berries or even raisins and prunes will come from a hot climate while a chardonnay, for example, from a cool climate will have fresh acidity and an elegant long flavour with subtle notes of citrus and pear. In short, wines can speak to you across time and distance by showing their origins if we know how to interpret the tastes of the places from which they were grown.

WHERE TO PLANT

Historically, winemakers choose **grape varieties** with regard to **experience and tradition** within the climate and possibly the soil.

Winemakers in the new world look at the market, then the soil's water-holding capacity and the climate—whether maritime with risk of excessive rainfall, Mediterranean with threat of drought, or continental with winters so cold that the vine's wood freezes and splits, leading ultimately to the death of the vine. Winemakers look carefully at the range of temperatures, including the likelihood of frost, water availability, humidity, as well as the heat of the warmest months (January and February in the Southern Hemisphere). For example, if the preference is for red-wine grapes, then January and February need to be hot; if these months are cooler then the temperature would be advantageous for more aromatic white wines.

Winemakers would also look at the diurnal (night and day) temperature variation. The cool nights of the Clare Valley make for a large diurnal range and this seems to create a singularly happy marriage with the riesling grape. The cooling evening breezes from Gulf St Vincent help cool McLaren Vale and the Barossa Valley, aiding the vines to develop flavour.

Latitude also makes a big difference because of its effect on the total hours of sunlight the vines receive. By looking at all these factors and more, the winemaker can save many years of trial and error. The data of 'terroir' (all the factors, such as soil and climate and aspect that go into making a wine) do not replace the winemaker's art, but provide a useful matrix for getting started.

But first they look at the hill, the slope on which to plant their vines.

Terroir—towards a definition

Terroir (pronounced tehr-wahr) has come to mean so many things to winemakers and wine experts that defining it has become essential. Terroir derives from the French word which technically means 'soil'.

As Bordeaux observer Bruno Pratts has said, 'The very French notion of the terroir looks at all the natural conditions which influence the biology of the vinestock and thus the composition of the grape itself. The terroir is the coming together of an infinite number of factors within the climate, the soil and the landscape. These include temperatures by day and night, rainfall distribution, hours of sunlight, soil acidity, presence of minerals, depth, water retention, exposure to sunlight, slope and drainage to name but a few. All these factors react with each other to form in each part of the vineyard what the French growers call a terroir.'

Great terroir comes from consistent performance over time creating respect for it due to its similar style and flavour over successive vintages. This is why the French don't like to do too much to the basic facts of terroir. Believers in terroir hold strongly to the view that the unique sense of place should always be evident in the wine. It's like the basic personality of an individual: you work with it, not against it, and encourage its natural characteristics to come charging out. Hence there is a growing pocket of vignerons using organic or biodynamic techniques and their results are often significantly more interesting than their neighbours'.

The defining factors of terroir can be modified somewhat if need be, such as additions to the soil and the planting of windbreaks. Sometimes this happens accidentally, for example, the building of a railway line destroying the drainage of some famous vineyards in the Margaux commune and reducing the quality of the wines. This is where the winemaker can take a very active role in the terroir—because terroir can be created. An excellent example is the Medoc region around Bordeaux, home of the greatest cabernet merlot blends in the world. If it hadn't been for the Dutch in the late 1700s, with their experience in draining marshlands and reclaiming soil, much of what the wine world holds great would still be a swamp. Removing the limitation of the terroir in this way allowed other stunning characteristics—personality traits, if you like—to come through. Paradoxically, careful interference can unlock a superior expression of the land.

Evolutions in style on a particular terroir tend to be focused around gently improving the soil, refining the vine variety and its growth, small changes which allow the winemaker to create more detailed wines. Winemakers may experiment with vine row width, vine spacing and yields, and change management techniques, such as pruning. Where terroir is respected, growers have learned by trial and error how to micro-manage specific factors within the whole—by experimenting with the constraints they find out what the boundaries are.

Terroir is a dynamic system that exists within intellectual and time constraints; it has to be respected to exist. While it has commercial implications, terroir exists despite money, and almost to spite money. Wines from terroirs are rare, limited in production, and more money cannot make more of them, unlike some other wines. It is the matching of grape varieties, viticulture and winemaking to the particular parameters of a place by people who respect the traditions. It lays a foundation for the pursuit of quality in that place.

The recognition of tradition within terroir is a key point to understanding its meaning. The most refined terroirs are those that have been utilised the longest, with Burgundy showing the way over seven centuries, starting with monastic management. New countries have traditions, obviously, but they are younger and the application of new technology could be described as their tradition. Large landholdings and sparse populations get in the way, with the large vineyards wielding the scythe of mechanical harvesting, levelling the differences that hand-picking would otherwise reveal. Then the bewildering choice of techniques winemakers have—such as pressing methods for grapes; skin contact time, when the white skins are left in contact with the juice to extract extra flavour at the cost of additional tannins and a heavy mouthfeel; use of different yeast, length and time of fermentation, to oxidise or not, to add oak or not—all blur terroir with technological possibilities.

Australia is blessed in the general sense by having a well-organised, philosophical approach to wine, which is best described as 'the wine show' system, an agreed philosophy of quality, expanded by consensus and tempered by experience gathered over time. This has given a brilliant snapshot of our varieties and how they fit jigsaw puzzle-like within the countryside, even with the chill winds of the marketplace blowing the pieces away. Len Evans, one of Australia's great wine judges, commentators and raconteurs, pointed out that what is interesting in Australia is that we may not have found or even planted our very best regions or terroirs yet, so there is still opportunity for development. The vast cooler climate hinterland on the western side of the Great Dividing Range from Canberra to Bathurst and beyond is rich with possibilities.

The long evolution of Australian wines has seen many phases. While regions are broadly recognised we have tended to reach for the power-packed crescendo rather than the subtle song of place. Winemakers in the 1980s and 1990s started labelling their distinctions in fruit intensity and concentration rather than vineyard differences. An explosion of wines labelled as 'reserve' explained the graduations to consumers and it became commonplace for winemakers to issue entire ranges of varietal and reserve editions. The argument ran that reserve meant lower yields for greater fruit intensity and often more expensive oak with more ripe fruit and alcohol, overlooking whether the variety really was suited to the region.

After a period of holding their breaths at the reserve logic, our Northern Hemisphere critics responded that the differences between more expensive reserve bottlings and the normal ones were often meaningless in their terroir-trained eyes. In the United States the opulence of our shiraz became a benchmark. What was needed, according to the United Kingdom, was not more wines, but fewer wines with more refinement and interest thanks to their regional character, less ripeness and more refined use of oak. The reserve concept came a cropper, with many of the wines possessing excessive alcohol and oak, and our inability to answer their challenging question of how the same region can produce reserve wines across a number of varieties. Especially when the European understanding is that varieties produce their best in quite different climates.

In Australia the docile workhorse shiraz helped regionality become accepted through the magnifying glass of wine show successes, as this marvel can perform strongly across many regions and produce distinctive flavours. A useful step forward was the exploration and refinement of varieties such as gewürztraminer and cabernet sauvignon, which did not respond well to many regions and as a consequence required more fine-tuning.

Australia's mix of regional varietal success stories continue to rise through the wine show system in the broad sense, with further development coming from individual producers' respect for the philosophy of terroir and its limitations. Winemakers only get to make and experiment with wine once a year and the terroir of their vines rolls on in its own timely fashion, encouraging the winemaker to develop the perfect elixir within its folds.

The slippery slope

One aspect that some winemakers talk about when planting is choosing 'the right side of the hill'. This is important because the correct side of the hill will be the side that gets the most sunlight for vine development.

Until recently most plantings were to maximise sunshine—that is, a northern aspect in the Southern Hemisphere. But a recent trend has been to plant on the cooler southerly side to keep temperatures down, retain more flavour, reduce alcohol and save the vine's natural acidity. Planting on slopes where the water drains away from the vine's roots and on thinner, less fertile soils also reduces the amount of vigour a vine can extract from the soil and help balance its growth.

The other issue associated with planting on hills is altitude. You lose 0.5°C to 1.0°C in temperature for every hundred metres of altitude you climb. So if you are in a cooler climate you don't want to go too high for fear that cool temperatures will prevail rather than sunlight. Under these circumstances the leaves will not reach their biologically efficient temperatures for photosynthesis, especially if the area is windy. But growers around the world also exploit the effect of altitude. They plant higher altitude vineyards combined with the cooler air to give them cooler temperatures than the lower valley floors so that the fruit develops better acidities.

Where and for how long the sun shines will determine the grape quality. So if we imagine two hills with a gully in between, then the vines in the gully are going to get less light than the vines on the hills. We can see this in two adjacent Burgundian wines, where the wine made from the grapes in the gully, Pernand Vergelesses, is a thinner, less attractive wine than the produce from the hill of Corton, which produces a rich and fantastic wine.

Place is really about having happy vines. When conditions are optimum or nearly optimum and the vines aren't held back by environmental pressure, we get a balanced vine. They produce well both in terms of quality and quantity. Remarkably, a great vintage will often see the vines producing larger crops in conditions so good that they allow the vines extra time to trap even more sunlight and turn the grapes into flavours with the finest edge to them; and thus the crop is then ready for harvest earlier than normal.

In many ways vines are like people. Give them the right conditions and they'll generally do well. Add a bit of stress here and there and it will bring out different strengths and weaknesses, and possibly lead to greatness or ruin, depending on how hard you push or how harsh the deprivation you subject them to.

Too hot, too cold ... just right

Climate refers to the long-term averages of temperature, rainfall, humidity, wind and frost in a region; whereas weather is the day-to-day localised variations and events that constitute climate. The vine can grow nearly everywhere and is on all the continents with the exception of Antarctica. Its best homes are located between 30° and 50° North and between 30° and 44° South, but vines can grow in other areas too, including tropical climates. With special management they can crop year round if temperatures permit. In places like Thailand they deliver five crops in succession before dying (most likely of exhaustion).

Grape growers have learned to divide climate into three different zones:

- macroclimate (the regional climate)
- mesoclimate (the climate of the actual site)
- microclimate (the climate within the vine canopy).

Flowover world map of temperatures

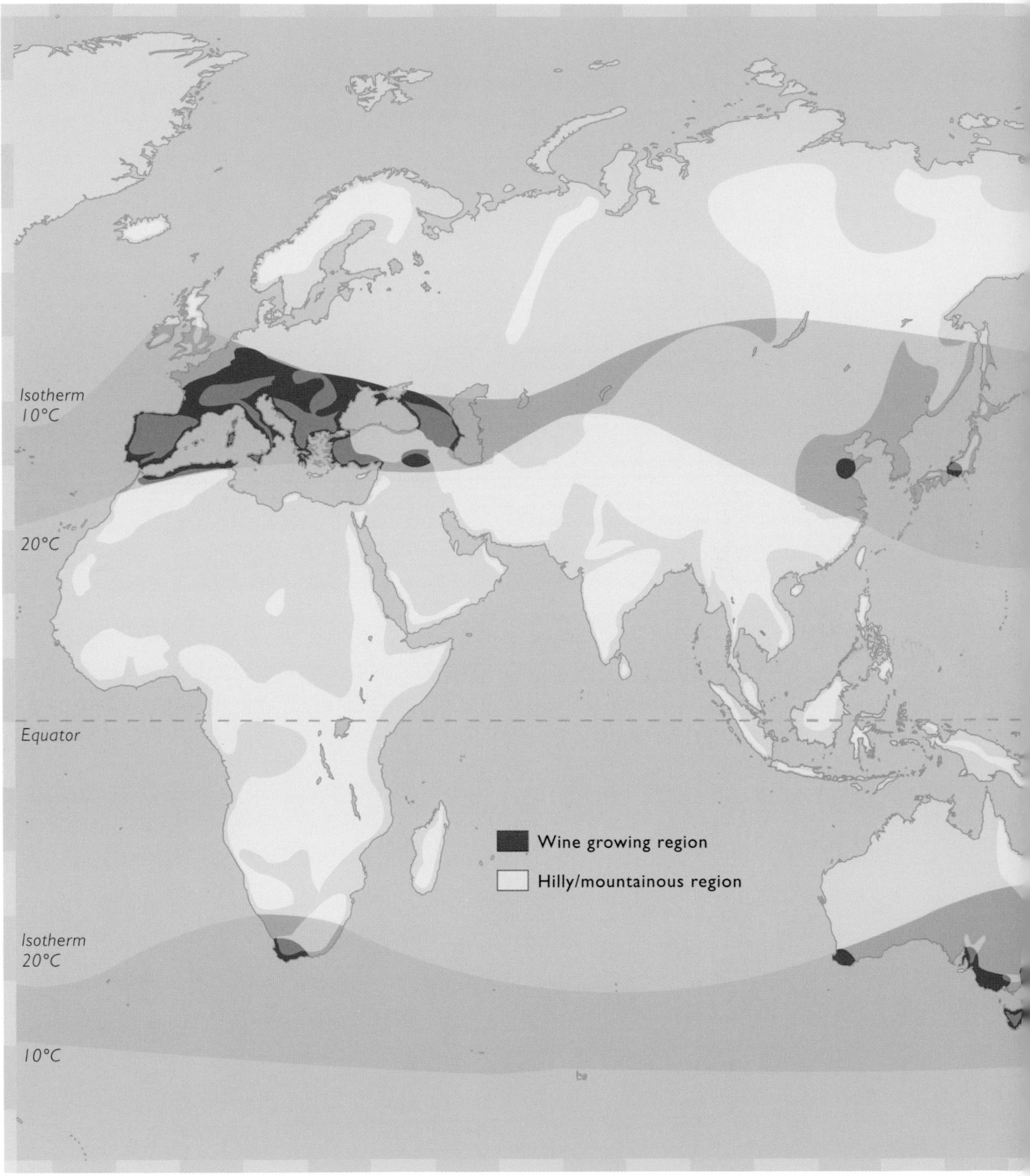

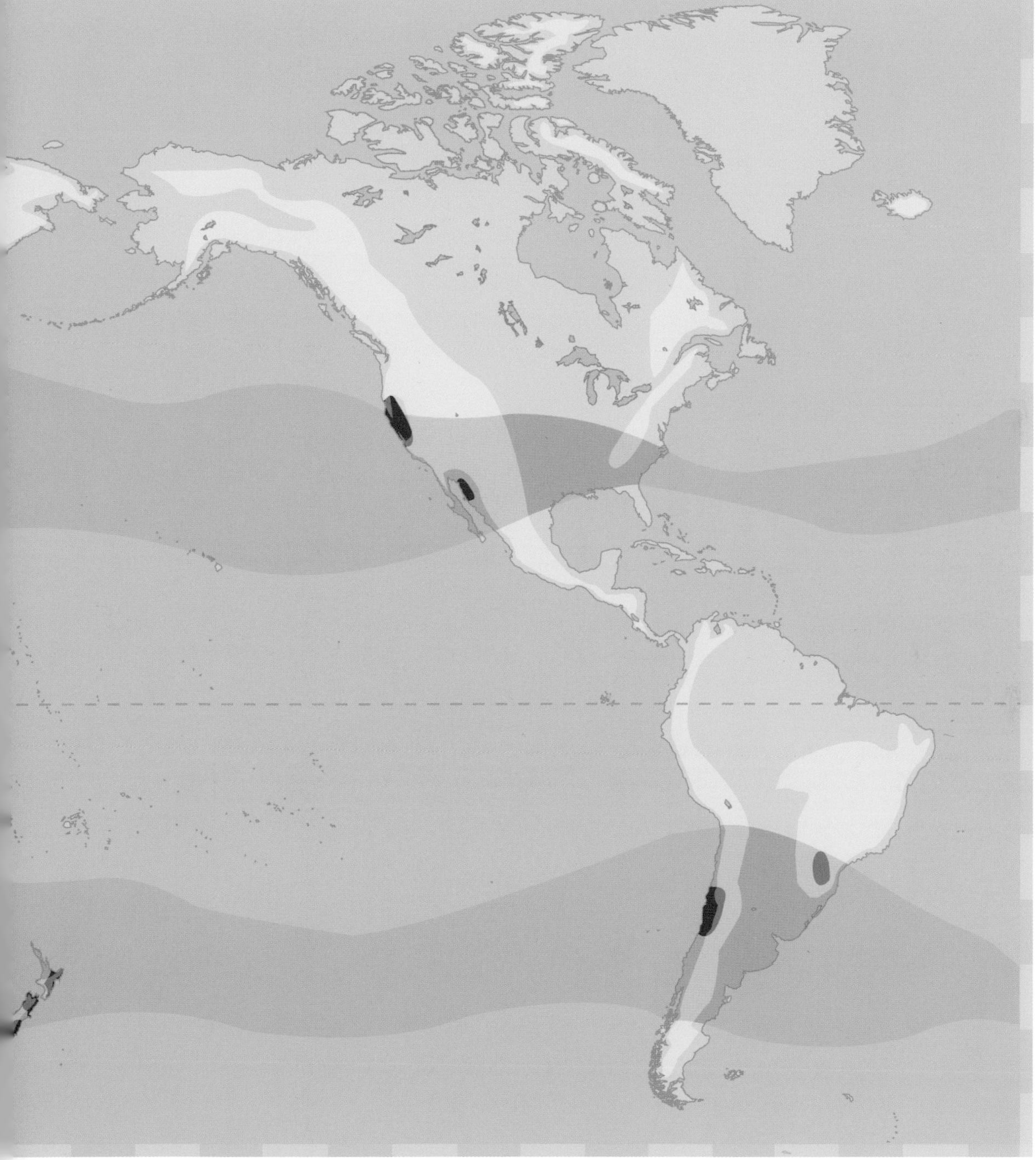

Macroclimate

To grow successfully wine grapes require dry autumns, and the most important climates for this condition are maritime or temperate, the latter having two subtypes: continental or Mediterranean. Each climatic type brings a mix of triumph and challenges and some are indeed blessed with additional, extraordinary natural advantages.

Maritime climates produce many extraordinary wines, often against significant challenges, as they are climates with no real dry season. The sea plays a nurturing role in keeping the temperatures in these regions even, and when the soil and the site work together—for example, in Bordeaux, Margaret River or Marlborough for sauvignon blanc and Tasmania for pinot noir or sparkling wine—the results can produce extremely memorable wines.

Temperate regions are responsible for the majority of the world's wine. Many areas have distinctly cold winters with spring frosts and hot summers. These areas exist away from the influence of sea or lakes, and the characteristic day–night temperature range increases the further inland you go. These climates are where the summers can be warm to hot to ripen the grapes, but the typical cold winters pose significant challenges to vines, including possible freezing.

Within the temperate zones continental climates have large temperature swings from day to night that can be an advantage when they slow down the ripening of the vines until cooler autumn months, after the fastest growth in the hottest summer months have passed. But not all temperate continental climates are suitable for grape growing as those more inland continental regions will have freezing winters and run the risk of vines freezing and splitting, then eventually dying.

Mediterranean climate areas are parts of large landmasses close to the sea. Traditionally these conditions belong to countries bordering the Mediterranean Sea with hot and dry summers and the effects of cooling sea breezes. Grapes do well in these regions as the wet winters, hot summer weather and cooling maritime breezes suit them.

The cooler, more humid regions within this climate range in Australia are southern Western Australia and most of southern coastal South Australia, such as Coonawarra and the Limestone Coast, not surprisingly home to some of our finest wines.

'Vineage'

Economically most vineyards are pulled out around 33 years of age unless something special is happening and their life gets extended. However there is no legal recognition or industry definition of what constitutes 'old vine'. Creating an Australian register of vine age, allowing the 'vineage' to be recorded for these significant vineyards, would be a useful classification; it will help extend the life and value of good, old vineyards through controlled use of terms and by creating market awareness, reputation and value.

Mesoclimate

Bacchus amat colle (Bacchus loves the hills) is an old Roman saying about their god of wine. As mentioned earlier, when it comes to picking a site within a region to grow their vines, winegrowers traditionally chose hills for their superior drainage, air, water and cold temperatures, and their increased ability to trap sunlight and warmth. Most Australians would be aware that the grass on north-facing hills browns and dies first because it receives more sunlight and therefore more heat. The actual difference in sunlight between flat areas and hills has been measured in Europe (applying to south-facing hills) and the results are a stunning insight into the role of the slope for improving light, heat and wine quality at high latitudes. A 30 per cent south-facing slope in northern Germany gets 70 per cent more light in October; while a northern slope gets 10 per cent of the light a flat surface would get in the same month.

The ability of vines to give you memorable wine ultimately comes down to the vineyard site and the fact that subtle differences exist in the vines' interception of its effects within a mesoclimate. Sites differ in fine ways and this gives us the fascination of a wine. The old world, particularly the French, have a highly refined system of understanding small vineyards and this has been applied through the new world's filter of experience.

Microclimate

Grape growers have learned to modify microclimates and therefore grape flavours by changing their vine-training systems to allow more light into the leaves, and by plucking leaves near the berries to allow for better fruit exposure. Also, leaving grass or bare earth between rows helps to increase or decrease temperatures as necessary.

Optimum climate for growing grapes

This would have to depend on the variety and could be the classic temperate climate: cold winters to kill any lurking fungus and insects and plenty of winter rainfall.

It's around 180 days from budburst to leaf fall, during which we would like a not very windy yet reasonably warm spring with light rainfall. Then we'd order the rain (and wind) to stop around late spring for flowering time so that the plant can go through the reproductive phase smoothly; this is followed by bright sunshine with some cloud in the warmer regions in the last 20 days before and through to harvest. During this time we'd order a bit of rain, but not too much, and hopefully not at harvest. Too much rain means great big, watery bunches of grapes with diluted sugar and flavour.

The trend towards extended summers and overall warmer conditions seems to be changing the vines' growth cycle and we are seeing a revision of the time frame for growth, resulting in earlier harvests. We are also seeing vines moving through their cycles faster and shortening the periods between flowering and harvest. Earlier harvests are occurring in many regions of the world. In Burgundy, for example, flowering is occurring 14 days early than the 50-year average harvest, and ripening is coming earlier also, sometimes by as much as 10 to 14 days, due to the way the vines are responding to today's overall warmer conditions.

You want the plants' vegetative growth to slow right down at harvest time. Mostly, you want a dry four to six weeks so that the vines' activity is to focus on creating flavour.

General growing season in the Southern Hemisphere

Budburst	onset varies according to warmth of season
Budburst to flowering	8 weeks
Flowering	occurs over 2 weeks
Flowering to veraison*	9 weeks
Veraison to harvest	6 weeks but varies extraordinarily according to prevailing conditions
Total	**22–25 weeks**

** when the grape swells and changes in colour and texture*

Here comes the sun

It seems a bit obvious to stress that grapes are affected by the sun, but for wine-producing vines the relationship with sunlight is critical, especially the red and blue spectrum light colours which some wit has suggested reflects on the logic (blue) and passion (red) that it takes to make great wine! Warm to hot sun is perfect.

Grape vines like to live within 15°C and 30°C. Intermittent days of 40°C are okay, but weeks of them are not. The red grape varieties prefer a mean average temperature of 21°C and the whites 19°C. Leaf temperatures above 30°C leave vines unable to photosynthesise, sucking up vital stores of water and causing thirsty, hot and stressed vines that are unable to use the light to create flavour or sugar.

The combination of the water and sunlight within the ideal temperature range is efficiently converted into sugar through photosynthesis, which ultimately dictates the level of flavour in the grapes. The ideal temperature for leaves is 25°C. This is when the plant, along with the water it draws up through the roots, uses sunlight most effectively. With the help of water, sunlight creates carbohydrate, which is the basic building block of flavour in a grape. The grape intercepts sunlight and turns it into sugar.

If we take a vine and grow it in the high hills behind Kosciuszko, the number of hours each day that those leaves are at the optimum temperature is going to be greatly reduced. Similarly, if we take that vine to the plains of the Riverina the same situation occurs, but in reverse. In the high Alpine climate, the grape vine is going to take a long time just to warm up; while in the Riverina the vine is going to warm up way past the optimum temperature for most of the day. A four-year-old, cool-climate chardonnay can look in broad terms like a one-year-old from a hotter climate and live for another six to eight years when its hotter cousin is fat and flabby and dead in the glass at three.

Sugar and sunlight

Photosynthesis occurs when the leaves of the vine use the energy from the sun to produce sugar, which the plant in turn uses as fuel to continue growing. Carbon dioxide plus water plus sunlight give off oxygen, with carbohydrate to the vine, and ultimately sugar when the vine is fruiting. Mathematically, the equation looks something like:

$$6H_2O + 6CO_2 \longrightarrow C_6H_{12}O_6 + 6O_2$$

This roughly translates to six molecules of water plus six molecules of carbon dioxide to produce one molecule of sugar plus six molecules of oxygen.

General changes in the composition of grapes as they ripen

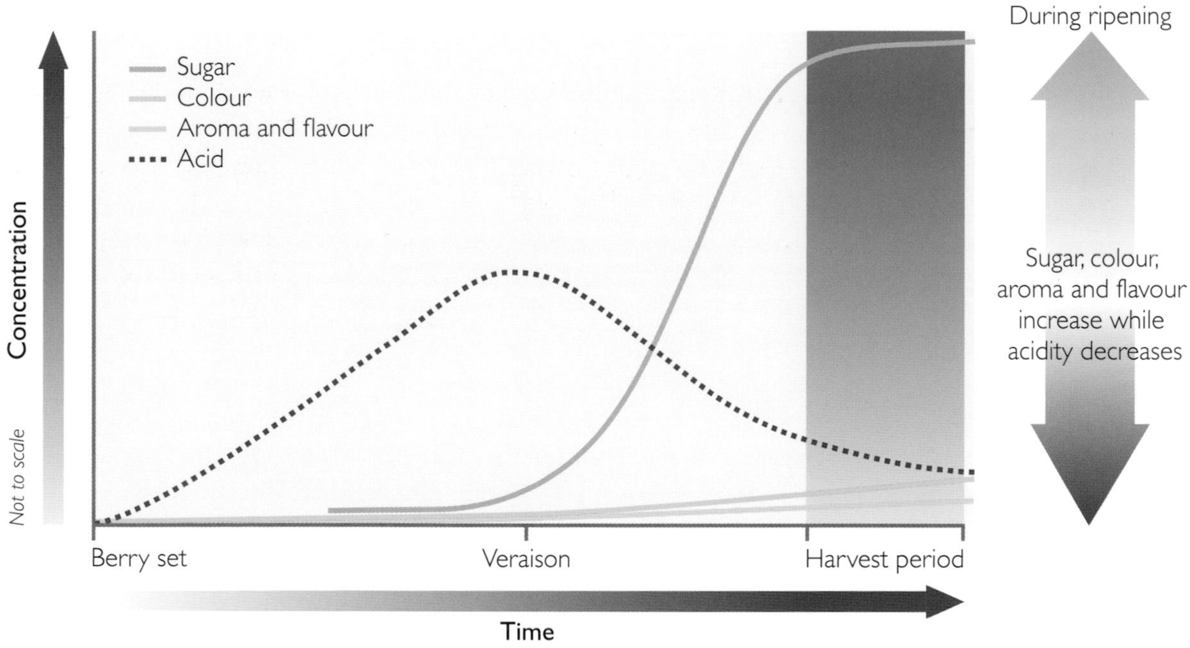

Europe's sunny advantage

Earth's angle of tilt is 23.5° as it orbits the Sun, putting the Southern Hemisphere closer to the Sun than the Northern Hemisphere. This angle of tilt creates summer and winter by its annual rotation around the Sun. Twice a year an equinox occurs, when the Sun is directly overhead at midday local time on the equator.

In the Southern Hemisphere, the autumn equinox is 20 to 21 March and spring is 22 to 23 September, and vice versa for the Northern Hemisphere. The date variation is a result of leap years and the relative differences of 179 days from March to September and 186 days from September to March, due to the elliptical nature of Earth's revolution—it spins slower as it gets further away from the Sun.

Conveniently for the Northern Hemisphere, the period between their spring and autumn equinoxes ensures they receive nearly seven extra days during which they get more than 12 hours of sunlight for spring and summer than the Southern Hemisphere.

In addition, perihelion (when Earth is closest to the Sun) also occurs in Europe's warmer months and results in the greater landmass absorbing more heat than it radiates back into the air; this further increases the warmth of air over continental Europe. The average temperature of the planet is 16°C in July yet only 13°C in January. Aphelion (when Earth is furthest from the Sun) results in 7 per cent less energy received in Australia.

What this amounts to is that the temperatures involved allow the vine to grow in a wider range of regions in the Northern Hemisphere of generally temperate to Mediterranean climates, between 30° and 50° North as against the 30° and 44° South.

Wind, drought and frost

Vines don't like wind. It closes the stomata (the breathing pores on the underside of the leaves), shutting down the process of photosynthesis and therefore slowing down the ripening process. The vine shuts down to its basic survival level; however, like most constraints, this can sometimes be an advantage. Take that bottle of Margaret River chardonnay mentioned earlier. The region is windy, especially during chardonnay flowering time, but the beauty of being windy is that it reduces the crop yield so that the vignerons end up getting very small crops and concentrated wines with enormous appeal.

Droughts make for tougher conditions for grape growers as the water balance between soil and air that usually buffers us from extremes is missing. Droughts are often times when we have larger than normal gaps between day and night temperatures. Why? Well, with the dry air that replaces the moist air of wetter times we lose the warm blanket of moisture-rich air that by day reflects heat back into the atmosphere and at night acts as cover for keeping heat in.

Dry soils fail to decay the vegetable matter lying on them, which adds to the fire risk. Soil moisture also plays a part in modifying climatic conditions by creating mists and fog that help retain heat as warmth leaks out of the soil back into the air at night. During 2006 the cool Coonawarra region had seven frosts; this was many more than a normal wet year, in part because loss of soil moisture means no heat is trapped for latter release. Clear cloudless days mean that the soil heats as there is no moisture in the atmosphere to protect it from the full blast of the midday sun or provide a blanket of moist air at night.

Soil ain't soil

Few wine people in Australia talk a lot about the importance of soil but there is an emerging local understanding of it. Does soil count for much? For most wine drinkers, it won't make a huge deal of difference to the enjoyment of memorable wine—until they start to wonder about pinot noir and see Burgundy in action with its precise vineyard and taste delimitations.

Most people won't necessarily be able to identify soil as a factor in a memorable wine, but there is a significant debate at high levels of the wine industry about its importance. One camp says that soil is a very small part of what matters and the climate affects growing conditions much more directly. Most Australian winemakers would accept this view, but then we live in a warm, dry climate where there are many ideal places to grow grapes. And we are still sorting out what and where to grow things. A smaller group believe we should make wine that has a strong sense of place and push to identify those places. Many others see the vineyard as the important factor, especially if they have 100-plus-year-old vines to work with.

Interestingly, the old vine phenomenon has a twist. Most of the soils that have sustained the vines to old age are deeply fertile and not great soils for table wine. They were planted for large crops of fortified (port-like) wine. Today, as these vines sway and slow and their crops are reduced to a few bunches with essence-like qualities, it is only those on the deeply fertile soils that have survived.

Soils and slopes particularly matter in areas where the climate is cold and marginal. If the climate is not ideal, then the soil and slope can become the most important factor in creating a happier, more nurturing environment for the vine. Apart from northern France, regions that bear this out include Victoria and Tasmania, the South Island of New Zealand and northern Germany, and no-one would dispute that all these regions produce very memorable wines. In fact, the results can be spectacular.

If you are a northern French vigneron (in Champagne, for example) who battles frost and damp weather, then you have to make the most of what you've got—terrific soil from which you can coax terrific wines. Perhaps that is the reason why the French word for soil, terroir, is so often pronounced with a reverent, guttural growl.

Globally, many great wines come off a limestone-base soil. In fact vignerons have come to select them, planting on the chalk of Champagne, the limestone of Burgundy, St Emilion, the Clare Valley and Coonawarra. This is because limestone holds the ideal amount of water, creating the optimal humidity for roots to grow and expand to infiltrate every aspect of the soil.

Limestone holds a biologically useful amount of water to nurture the vine and also warms quickly in the spring, giving the vine roots enough heat to start off the cycle.

A highly personal view of the happiest marriage of vines and regions

New South Wales and Canberra	
Hunter Valley	shiraz, chardonnay, semillon
Orange	merlot, chardonnay, sauvignon blanc
Shoalhaven	semillon
Griffith	botrytis semillon, durif, petit verdot
Canberra	shiraz viognier
South Australia	
Adelaide Hills	sauvignon blanc, shiraz in locations
McLaren Vale	shiraz, grenache
Barossa Valley	shiraz, mourvedre, grenache
Barossa Hills and Eden Valley	shiraz, riesling
Langhorne Creek	shiraz, cabernet sauvignon
Coonawarra	cabernet sauvignon
Clare Valley	riesling, shiraz, grenache, semillon
Victoria	
Rutherglen	muscat à petite grains rouge as liqueur muscat, durif, muscadelle
Mornington Peninsula	pinot noir, pinot grigio
Yarra Valley	shiraz, shiraz viognier, sauvignon blanc
Macedon	sparkling wine
Tasmania	sparkling wine, pinot noir, riesling
Western Australia	
Margaret River	cabernet, merlot, chardonnay, semillon, sauvignon blanc
Great Southern	shiraz, cabernet sauvignon, merlot, riesling semillon, sauvignon blanc

Roots are sluggish in spring when the soil is too water-retentive (and thus cold and wet). The cold means that they are unable to perform their function of sending hormonal messages to the leaves to grow. As explained earlier, when the vine starts to grow at the beginning of a season, the roots have to warm up to certain temperatures before they are able to secrete key chemical messages via growth hormones. Put simply, the first hormone, gibberellin, tells the vine to grow leaves and tendrils. As the root warms up further, the second hormone, cytokinin, is secreted, which tells the vine to move from vegetative to reproductive growth—flowers are produced and then the berries grow.

The white chalky soils of Champagne and the dark slaty soils of northern Germany are legendary because, despite the exigencies of the climate, they provide a marvellous crucible for warming up the roots. In Champagne the water content of the white chalks allows for the heat of the sun to be rapidly transmitted to the roots, while the dark slates perform the function via their dark colour capturing the heat and preserving it in the ground and radiating it back at night.

In many of Germany's finest river vineyards, such as the Mosel of the Rhine, the vines hold on with all their might to the slaty, steep, terraced slopes. The age-old stories of vignerons falling down cliffs and dying in the service of their wines is the sad side of the fact that these slopes intersect much more sunlight than a flat surface would and therefore provide the vines with ideal conditions in such northerly (49° and 50° North) latitudes.

Centuries of dirty work

How soil develops flavour over time is best observed in places like Burgundy in France, although the day is not too far away when the soils of the Clare and Barossa Valleys will be in the spotlight.

The attributes of the soil in France are magnified by a long and patient tradition backed up with a stable political background and stable grape varieties. The Burgundians have had 800 years or so of continuous viticulture and in this we can see a degree of specialisation in the quality of the soil that achieves distinctive and remarkable wines. They have simply had time to work it out by trial and error.

The system of classifying wines has grown out of winemakers observing these vineyards and working out the very intimate relationship between soil and flavour. The Cru system in Burgundy puts a name and a rating to often tiny parcels of hillside vineyards with differing altitude, soils, aspect and subsoils that regularly express a distinctive and particular character and flavour in their wines.

The system in Bordeaux names the wines after the chateau and gives them a classification, yet the vineyards may be scattered across the gently rolling countryside in proximity to the Gironde River. Bordeaux has flexibility with its definitions of name, quality and vineyard, which suggests that each chateau is as much a style as a reflection of a terroir.

OF HISTORICAL IMPORTANCE

The other defining characteristic of place is its history and the traditions resulting from this.

The history of wine development starts in the era when sugar was rare and sweetness was valued highly. We roll back the fabric of time to the Middle Ages when an extensive maritime wine trade existed around the Mediterranean and with Europe. Exporting wine could only be justified if it first, was worth money, and second, if it travelled well. Intensely sweet wines fitted the bill on both counts. So growers around the Mediterranean often dried their grapes on the ground to concentrate the sweetness. Essentially, those ancient wines were very sweet wines.

Another vital step in this process was the conquest of Spain by the Moors, who brought with them the science of distillation. This involved boiling the wine and trapping and condensing the alcohol as it evaporated. Much later the Spanish evolved fortified wines by adding spirit into unfermented or partly fermented grape juice to produce wines that were strong, sweet and stable; this idea later spread to Holland. This meant that it was possible for wines to travel safely over long distances but the general rule was that locals drank local wine. Of course the local wine developed side by side with the local food and this provided the traditional rule of matching food and wine: if it grows there it goes there.

Interestingly, the Rioja region on the coast of Spain became a prominent wine-producing region when some French winemakers settled there in the late 1800s. Their own vines back in France had fallen victim to the vine louse phylloxera.

As time went on, many of the great wine regions of Europe flourished on the Atlantic seacoast because transport between ports was easy and cheap. 'Cheap' is relative, of course. To a mediaeval winemaker the wine had to be very good and very much in demand to justify the cost of the road and then sea transportation. The Burgundian wines made from chardonnay and pinot noir were prized enough to justify the long road transport; they were worth the premium and customers would pay for it.

One of the big losers in proximity to urban non-winegrowing markets was Italy. Italian wines had to travel further and were therefore more expensive. Hence there was not the same opportunity to develop the sort of wines the market wanted—so I would argue that the Italians remained more regionally diverse and distinct with over 2000 varieties in use. Their style was keeping the grape flavours in the background and suiting the food. The personality was built on refreshment with subtle, dry, firm white wines and restrained tannic reds. Italian wine is a great delight and the edges of different styles

have not been smoothed out by the commercial demands of history. They escaped the amplification of international trade and maintained the magnifying glass on regional wines and styles.

By contrast, the French had time (or intuitively selected) to separate out and refine those varieties that contained sweet fruit, because the 'ripe fruit' sweetness was valued. Nowadays, you can still see the legacy of these two approaches. So if you blend, say, 5 or 10 per cent of a French varietal, such as cabernet sauvignon, merlot or shiraz, into sangiovese the result would be the introduction of sweet fruit flavours to round, smooth and sweeten the intense tannins of their local varieties.

And of course there are other European countries that produced wines for the locals—Romania, Bulgaria, Yugoslavia and Russia produce wines with character and personality, but are just murmurs in the songbook of global viticultural history. They only sang for a while according to politics in international markets before the locals went back to drinking them. Perhaps their day will come if transport costs or fashion gives them market advantages.

Key to tradition was the knowledge and mindset passed from one generation to another, and one of the biggest of these received wisdoms is the very French notion of terroir.

NATURE VERSUS NURTURE

You only have to drink wines from specifically different vineyards to know that terroir is true.

You can sense this from the term used in Burgundy to describe their individual vineyard sites: climat, which refers literally to the vineyard site and its unique climate, not just the land. Their ability to map individual wine quality in well-established districts, and then rank individual vineyards' wine quality, has led to the view that it is the individual chemical constitution of the soil and its immediate climate, or its terroir, that is the essential quality factor. Taken to heart by years of experience, the French have used as the basis of their wine law the Appellation Controlée system of regulations that protect vineyard names.

The new world use of clever brands for identity versus the old world use of regional rules for identity and to regulate wines, especially where names have become international styles, sets the scene for one of the great debates in wine. Clare Valley winemaker Jeffrey Grossett has found an Australian word for the idea of terroir:

'pangkarra', from the original inhabitants of the Adelaide plains. While it refers to the soil and the local topography it does also come some way to explain their relationship with the land and highlights the fact that the English language does not really have a similar word to the French terroir. English, it seems, is a good language for engineering or law but lacks subtlety of phrasing when it comes to food or wine.

Terroir is a touchy subject for Australian winemakers who were taught that climate, not soil, is the most important determinant of quality. You can measure temperature, sunshine and rainfall and their relationship to ripeness and quality, but how do you measure soil's contribution to flavour? It is also touchy at another level because if terroirs are unique, then you can't make any more of them—an idea at odds with the corporate winemaking ethos that feeds shareholder dividends.

There are many differences in wine, some deeply important and others less so, but they all depend on what you are seeking. The commercially important ones, such as labelling and name, are less important taste-wise compared to the affinity of a grape variety for a certain soil, climate or region. There is no doubt that the best wines are in short supply and that our ability to make more of these highly praised tastes is limited. Why? Well, we don't really know.

Terroir comes from the conditions of the physical environment; expression of terroir is the human aspect

ROB GIBSON, WINEMAKER, VIGNERON AND CONSULTANT

How far have we come with terroir?

The French system arose at a time when vignerons did not all have a lot of technology at their disposal and were culturally close knit. They would pick on the same day, and use the same winemaking approaches, and where the terroir was favourable they learned to respect it. Later legal moves ensured the system protected the growers so that other regions could not pass off their wines for more famous names.

The explosion of technological opportunities in the twentieth century, such as high-strength nitrogen fertilisers, tractors, leaf plucking, mechanical harvesting, and cold maceration (storing picked grapes, sometimes in cool rooms, to allow breakdown of the inside of the skins by the juice), have challenged traditional practices and influenced the expression of terroir and market acceptance.

Terroir believers have chosen to restrict their use of soil-modifying technology, but the challenges of rising labour costs are forcing them to accept such things as mechanical harvesting. Terroir tests the limits of science, it is never precise, it's essentially an untellable story, because like children peeking through the door to listen to the discussions of their parents, we never quite get the whole language with its context and riches.

Few have opened the book of wine at the terroir page in Australia, for a variety of reasons, including a lack of small vignerons, young vines and an overall short wine history, and the use of mechanical harvesters. One of the first who did so in my experience is Michel Dietrich at the then Quelltaler in the Clare Valley in the mid-1980s. He could show us riesling on limestone hill tops and clay soil valleys and we could taste the difference. I became a believer overnight. Increasingly now, the recognition of genuine terroirs is growing from a few to many striving to expound its meaning.

Science can often tell us what has happened, but struggles to explain why. It can measure outcomes and effects and give us data which can help us understand the reasons behind the effects, but with something as diverse as grape growing, and as wide as the regions cropped, we simply remain peeking through the door.

Terroir can be measured when it applies to the scientific variables of a climate and decisions can be made from that on a reliable basis. Terroir cannot be measured when one tries to explain the taste of wine in terms of its soil—such is our inability to finger every aspect of the influences of soil and aspect on vines, grapes and wines.

The human (both maker and marketer) elements of terroir claim it is 'the land speaking to us' or 'the taste of the land' that makes it unique, yet rationally no two humans make the same decisions and hence wines from the same terroirs taste different despite the power of nature and soil to influence the flavour. In short, terroir is part of the magic of wine—nearly glimpsed when restrained by the bonds of science and a wild poetry when left to the hands of humankind.

The dark side of terroir lies when successful marketing creates recognition and riches that blunt the winemaker's desire to strive to keep improving a wine because the vineyard or appellation is widely recognised and guarantees high prices based solely on the reputation of the land rather than what is in the bottle.

Additional challenges lie ahead with the increase in the world's carbon dioxide levels, which influence vine growth. Global warming changes the historic performance of vineyard sites. Market challenges include the rise of serious rivals in the new world and, to me, their half-baked response by encouraging quality improvements and giving growers more freedom to be independent (good), but allowing cross-blending of sites without due recognition (bad) and cross-blending vintages.

The notion that better wines come from certain regions is in the mind of many drinkers and to me it is a fact. Time will tell how far and to what degree terroir will become a feature of modern wines. The broad understanding of place is being taken by a number of pioneering vignerons and winemakers to a higher level with finer vineyard-driven distinctions, so it seems that the importance of a sense of place can only grow in step with drinkers' understanding. As they say, 'winemakers provide and markets decide'.

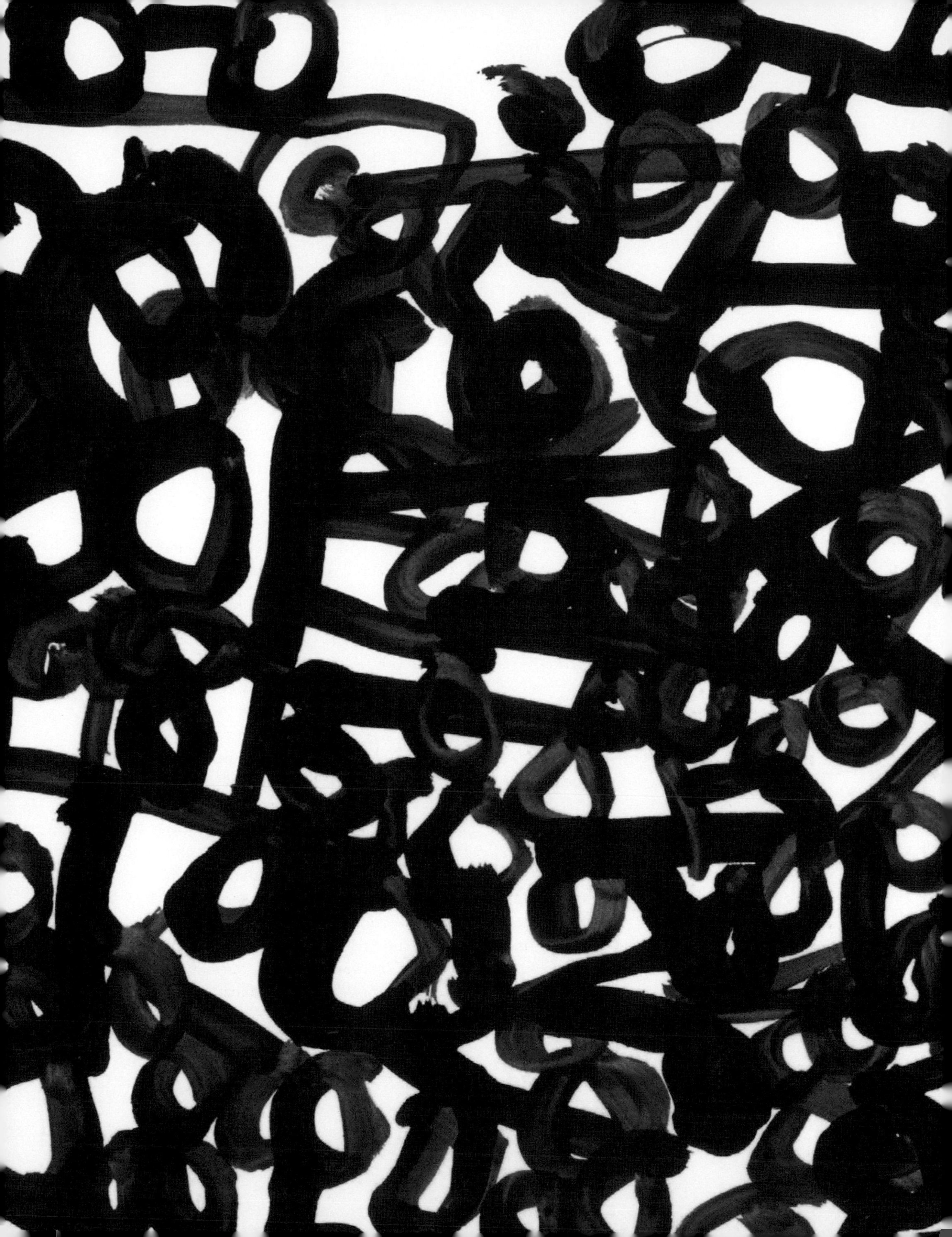

chapter 2

winemakers and winemaking

If you look to the reputation of the great chefs . . .
does the public remember the quality of the produce they select
or the quality of the dishes they produce?

PHILIP SHAW, GRAPE GROWER AND WINEMAKER

RISE OF THE WINEMAKER

The second leg of the stool of memorable wine is the people who grow the grapes and make the wine.

The cult of personality is strong in our modern era, and as most wine drinkers live far from vineyards, market forces play a strong role in what they drink, for better or worse. One of the elements of market forces is the 'fashion' of wine variety; the popularity of some and not others. The other element that's critical here is personality, and the personality I'm talking about here is that of the people behind the winemaking.

Interest in the growers of the grapes and the makers of the wine (and they are not always the same person) started to happen in a small way as far back as the mid-seventeenth century. The English nobility of the seventeenth century showed great interest in wines, and the winemakers in Bordeaux targeted those customers. One of the first examples is Monsieur Arnaud de Pontac, the powerful head of the Bordeaux parliament as well as the wealthy owner of the renowned Château Haut-Brion in Bordeaux. The historic record is blurred but it may have been a son or other relative who ran the London pub where de Pontac stocked and promoted his wines and sold expensive food (some things never change!). The pub was patronised by all the luminaries of the time, including the writer Mr Samuel Pepys, who recorded in his diary how he tasted delicious French food and also 'drank a sort of French wine called Ho Bryan that hath a good and most particular taste I never met with'. This is perhaps one of the earliest records of wine described by where it came from, and knowledge of its owner's nobility, wealth and status would have provided it with an extra cachet.

The profession of specialised winemaker, or *régisseur*, began to take form in Bordeaux around this same era. The wealthy families of Bordeaux, perhaps taking a leaf from de Pontac's marketing approach, wanted to glorify, or at least dignify, the production of wines on their properties to raise their profile. So they built grand chateaux on their vineyards, gave their product defined brand names, employed the best Dutch irrigation engineers to drain the gravel soils of the Medoc (the newest region in Bordeaux, developed in the last third of the seventeenth century), and employed winemakers and staff with particular skills to do specialised jobs.

Who does what?

grape grower: person responsible for the quality of the fruit; a term used in the new world for the carer of the vines

régisseur: French term for winemaker, borrowed from its theatrical meaning of the person who stages the show

vigneron: French word for the grape grower

winemaker: person responsible for overseeing logistics and making of the wine, often highly qualified to do such

wine producer: an interchangeable term (in this book) for the person doing all the jobs listed above—think impresario!

The vigneron effect on grapes

You can have ten good wine producers in the same district and there will always be somebody who is the best. It's like any other achievement in life and art—there's an indefinable quality to it. I am of the opinion that the people who make the best wines reduce the risks to a minimum. They start with the right vineyard, and then follow certain consistent principles. The best vignerons know every vine on their land as opposed to those that buy in the grapes to make the wine. As has recently become fashionable to observe: the best thing a winemaker can put on a vineyard is his own two feet.

Good winemakers begin the work of producing memorable wine by coaxing the vine and not expecting their vines to produce big crops. They proceed carefully, they're not in a hurry, they're stoic, and they systematically reduce the range of threats to their vines. Good winemakers know how to coax the best out of what they've got.

Since the 1990s there's been a definite tendency to reduce the ego associated with winemaking—or should that be wine marketing? These days the vineyard is the focus and the vigneron is far more likely to say 'we' rather than 'I'. The 'we' being all inclusive of those who work on the vineyard and of the berry produced; that is, the vine. The main response of vignerons to biological constraints or economic change is to manipulate their vines to produce the quality they seek by applying intense, expensive and/or refined management techniques.

CULTIVATING THE VINE

The vine family, *Vitis vinifera*, is extensive, with relations in Asia and the United States.

The American cousins are very important as they are, to varying degrees, phylloxera resistant, and also climatically diverse. They love deserts, limestone, cold winters and wet conditions among other characteristics. The flavours of the fruit are strong, and different to European fruit, making an interesting diversion should you be in the eastern states of the United States. Virginia Dare and Concorde wines will give a taste of the unique expression of native north American fruit.

The European vine, *Vitis vinifera sativa*, in its wild state was a forest dweller. There are thousands of distinct types within the *Vitis vinifera* family, further confused today by selections within varieties, called clones, with strong general similarities and subtle differences in habit—often to do with berry size or bunch weight, growth habits or freedom from disease. The vines we are interested in come from temperate climates (continental or Mediterranean) and don't tolerate very cold winters.

The European vine probably ranged from western Asia to the European woodlands and it is by nature a climber. Its adaptation to its original habitats provides us with two major features that we exploit while growing the vines today: hardiness and its climbing ability. Competition in a forest meant the vine developed a competitive streak to tolerate temporary water shortages and infertile soils, making it a good plant that travels well across the globe. As a climber fighting for sunshine it relies on other plants for support, which we exploit to manage its leaf and crop volumes by creating purpose-built frames or trellising systems upon which it can wander at our will. Its need for sunlight we put to our advantage by training the growth to receive enough light to control its fertility and crop size.

This tendril-climbing plant requires pruning or trimming each year to produce its crop because only the buds from the previous year are fertile, the older ones having lost their vitality. The number of fruiting buds and their exposure to light and air needs to be managed to produce the best relationship between quantity and quality in terms of the flavour and balance of the key elements that create our wines: acidity and sugar. For this to happen a suitable site for the chosen variety or clone would have been selected with regards to its climate and soil and, in Australia, availability of water. This is why some wines grow better in some places than others; careful selection is crucial.

Australia got a great start with the raw material brought in and cultivated by James Busby in the 1830s. He conscientiously selected 680 varieties but other importations were already underway by John Macarthur and ships' captains trying to make a quick quid from South African stock. The industry today has a thorough vine identification system and rigorous improvement schemes to raise the best varieties and clones for our environment. But people still talk of the occasional illegal importation to get a new variety underway.

Traditional European viticulture used small vines grown low on soil of little fertility. Caring for these tiny vines was a matter of tradition and offered little advice for those growing vines on the more fertile sunny sites of the new world, where we often have much more vigorous vines to deal with. As a consequence, bigger trellises and more management, such as shoot positioning and shoot thinning, are required.

The basic tool of the vigneron is pruning, the annual removal of old growth in preparation for the following year's growth in an organised fashion. This shapes the vine and controls the new growth so that a canopy of leaves can be nurtured to expose the vine and its fruit to sunlight and meet the grower's expectations of the produce. The new growth emerges from the vine's buds and the stem grows vigorously towards the sun, shooting a group of lateral leaves that form the vine's canopy, which in turn shades the fruit. Quality of fruit is largely linked to yield, which is controlled by pruning and dictated by the trellis design.

What constitutes an old vine?

Though no formal rules exist anywhere at present, in France generally any vine under 18 years old is considered young, 18 to 45 is classed as mature, and everything else is old vine. It would be a great opportunity for Australia to formalise this in a register as we have sufficient old vine vineyards to make the job worthwhile.

At the viticulture session at the 2006 Shiraz Alliance in the Barossa, Prue Henschke gave us three examples of 2006 Hill of Grace, taken from the barrels they had resided in for two months. All the examples had been made in the same way to show how the fruit from young, mature and old vines has distinctly different flavours and structures. The tasting illustrated the benefits of fruit from old vines.

Wine 1: Hill of Grace nine-year-old vines—watery rim, obviously very youthful, straightforward floral, confectionery blackberry, raspberry fruit aromas, upfront fruit flavours and a short length of palate.

Wine 2: Hill of Grace 18-year-old vines—solid colour to the rim, greater depth of fruit with liquorice, red fruit, cinnamon and clove spice, longer palate length, showing much more fruit and length and texture.

Wine 3: Hill of Grace 146-year-old vines—finer aromas with spices, anise, liquorice, blackberry and gaminess, much more density and texture in the mouth, full, even across the palate, weighty and silky showing increased depth of fruit and palate length.The increasing length and density with the very old vine material was most noticeable by the mouthfeel—more even textured, and matched with an increase in the depth of fruit and palate length.

Nurturing the berry

Grape growing is active in that the process involves everything from site selection through to soil preparation, drainage, trellis selection, pruning and canopy management. The interaction the grower has with the site—including such decisions as fertilisers, cover crops, mulches, weed control, irrigation, managing fungus, insects and viruses that can threaten vines—deeply affects the vine's life and its produce. Each year the grower needs to balance the vines' activities with the growing season, as the crop quality and quantity is affected by pruning (vine trimming), leaf removal, crop thinning to control yield as well as harvest methods.

The heart of a grape

Stalks contain bitter tannins and are only rarely used in winemaking
Bloom, or waxy coating on the outside of the skin, contains natural yeasts
The skin is the source of colouring agents, tannins, and flavouring compounds, which give wine its character
The pulp makes up most of the grape and comprises water, sugar, acids plus flavour compounds
The pips contain bitter tannins and will generally be removed during the winemaking

The process of nurturing the vines has changed over the centuries. In Australia, the effect of rainfall on vines is variable, from thirst quenching in high precipitation areas through to irrigation dependence in hotter regions to none at all. Irrigation has given us the equivalent of steroids for the vines. As our understanding of irrigation has improved,

previously dry land vineyards have enjoyed improved vine health during dry spells. The use of fungicides have enabled the grape grower to grow vines in humid or wet areas, where fruit rot would have ruined such crops in the past.

'Dry grown', that is without irrigation, is a buzz-word term with several meanings. Before the 1960s it covered all our quality wine regions, as irrigation outside the Murray River system was not the formalised process it is today. Most of the vineyard regions established without supplementary water—Langhorne Creek being the notable exception—now have irrigation, as the carefully measured use of supplementary water is seen to help in bringing better wines through reliable vine growth.

Irrigation has resolved many dilemmas for growers concerned with vine health. Much of the vine's fruit produced in hot regions is the source of value-for-money wines, grown by efficient, thoughtful winemakers who really know their stuff and excel within the climate they have chosen, as in Griffith or the Sunraysia region. Growers are mindful to seek varieties with the appropriate performance to match their climates, such as high acid and Italian varieties. This is where the most exciting development in grape growing has come from in recent times.

Sometimes just one family is associated with a particular variety, such as the Morris family of Rutherglen and their French-crossed durif imported some 50 years ago. This selection was based on their assessment of its suitability for Victoria's north-east. More recent selections have been made by taking into account the historic origins and the inherent DNA of the vines for their ability to hold their acidity and their growth under hot conditions. These vines positively shine in hot or irrigation-dependent regions. The drive for better hot climate wines is opening the door to a range of regional wines that we could not have imagined a decade ago. Many such as vermentino and lagrein have been pioneered and imported by Chalmers nursery.

A word on vintage

Vintage is strictly the harvesting and processing of grapes that gives the wine its birth year. The year becomes the reference on the wine label—the grapes harvested in 2006 have that date on the bottle. The use of vintage as a reference is most common in champagne, with vintage champagne coming from a particular year's harvest. Non-vintage wines are a mix of fruit from various years. The value of non-vintage is that it can be made in order to provide a consistent style of wine.

Vintage is the most important time of year for winemakers and grape growers alike. For grape growers it's getting the delicate fruit at optimal ripeness, intact and disease-free, to the winemaker on time. For winemakers it's about applying a gentle, guiding hand to the process in which grape juice becomes wine.

Each year, the inevitable vagaries of vintage—the sum total of the growing conditions of the year including wind, rain, temperature—remind us that wine is, first and foremost, an agricultural product. Every harvest returns a unique crop, and each region bears a different set of challenges.

Annual life cycle of Australian grape growing

In terms of value, grapes are the most important fruit crop in the world with considerable variation in their growth habits, due to differing variety, climates and availability of water. It is a surprise to many that vines are not propagated from seeds but come from cuttings of existing vines. Vines take about eight months to go through their annual cycle and what follows is a 'grown-in Australia' explanation of the vine's (or wine's) annual cycle.

June

The first month of winter is when new vines are planted and decisions that affect vineyard layout are made. Red grape varieties are grown on northern slopes, while white varieties grow best on cooler, southern slopes. Although vines can be uprooted and moved later, the chance of surviving the process is less than 50 per cent, meaning it's not really commercially feasible. So selection and planning now are important.

A vineyard's crop and quality potential is primarily dictated in the Northern Hemisphere by the amount of sunshine it receives per unit of ground, but in the Southern Hemisphere it is dictated by the amount of water. So the vineyard manager's job is to judge the amount of sunshine, moderated by the available water and nutrients (through the soil's fertility and depth), and then to choose a planting density and trellis type that is suitable for the site. For example, the closer together vines are planted the more efficient they are at using the available light and heat from the sun, because of the competition for these between them. So apart from choice of vine variety, the key decision to be made before planting is to determine vineyard density—the number of vines planted in any one hectare—which impacts on the overall quality of the vineyard.

Low-density plantings give large amounts of soil and possibly water to the vines and depending on water availability, encourage highly vigorous vines and excessive leaf growth. This may translate to large crops or else lead to excessive leaf shading of the fruit and therefore reduce crop quality. While it is possible to grow small crops on low-density vineyards (1466 vines per hectare) by pruning hard to concentrate the vines' growth on a few buds, the trend is to higher densities (around 6000 to 8000 vines per hectare). As a consequence of the competition for soil nutrients and water, the vigour of the plant and thus the crop size per vine is reduced. The drive behind this is more intense flavours, as everything is concentrated onto fewer grapes—in other words, as vine density increases yield per vine decreases but yield per unit of land increases.

France followed this wisdom due mostly to the need to maximise the sun's energy and, originally, the traditional use of manpower and then horsepower, which allowed for rows to be planted closer together. In Australia, with large tracts of land, abundant sunshine and fewer people to hand-pick fruit, accommodating for tractors became a prime motivator for wider rows.

Trellising is another factor to be considered at planting stage as it involves the collective training of the vines to a shape that suits the vineyard management. Decisions on the planting density and the type of trellises to use go hand in hand, and are often determined by harvest method, final wine style, and commercial considerations such as land cost. Today, there are high-value, cool-climate vineyards that often use denser planting to maximise the vineyard's quality potential and yield as explained above.

Increasingly, winemakers make this commercial decision on the understanding that the use of higher-density planting and trellises will ensure that their vineyard will crop low per vine, providing better quality produce, yet will incur higher establishment and management costs.

July

During July the vines in established vineyards are at rest and the vineyards assume their skeletal winter appearance of gnarly wood amid chequerboard green pasture. July and August are when pruning and vine training take place. Pruning is one of the most skilled jobs in the vineyard, reducing the growth from the previous year by over 80 per cent and as a result the number of buds that can produce the next crop. Knowledge about the variety and the intended use of the fruit dictate the number of buds left on the vine, and hence the yield of fruit for that year.

Attempts to use machines to do this work have met with limited success and are being discarded by high-quality winemakers in favour of the judgment of the experienced human eye. July and into August can be quiet months in the vineyard especially once pruning has been completed. But there is plenty of work to be done in the cellars as the new wine matures.

August

It is in August that 'weeping' first starts to be seen in Australian grape vines, the first external sign that established vines are waking up after winter and its relative dormancy. As soon as the air temperature rises above 10ºC the roots start to collect water and the vine pushes sap up into the very limits of its branches. The sap starts to ooze out of the pruning cuts and this is what causes the vine to weep. It occurs quite suddenly and rapidly and could increase in intensity and then decrease gradually. Each vine can lose up to five litres of sap, depending on the location of the vineyard and the system of vine training. There is a challenge that any early growth, though, could be subject to frost, which can be frightening for a grape grower at any time.

September to early October

At the beginning of spring the vines begin to show the emergence of shoots followed by leaves, which start photosynthesis. Some 20 to 30 days after the vines stop weeping the buds left from winter pruning create the small shoots which become the new year's growth. This stage is known as 'bud break'. Different vine varieties bud break at different times. Chardonnay, for example, is a very early bud breaker, pinot noir is a mid-season one and cabernet is late.

Just when a vine variety goes through bud break can depend on how cold the winter has been. Different types of soil will also influence the timing. Some soils are quite cold, like clay versus loam—cold clays will delay bud break, while red loams will warm and encourage the process.

Spraying begins once the leaves and shoots start to emerge; this is a vulnerable time for the crop. Spraying occurs to minimise vine pests, diseases and other disorders and normally continues into November and December. Spraying operations are normally done by tractor and are very carefully monitored.

October to early November

The greatest risk from frost to a vineyard is during the 40 to 80 days it takes for the full leaf mass of the vines to grow. Many vineyard managers have sleepless nights trying to judge if the risk is real and potentially going to damage the tender growing vine tips by freezing and thus destroying them. The vines during this period begin to show the emergence of long shoots and really take off; foliage develops and further shoots start to be sent out, followed by the little embryo bunches.

By mid-October the fourth or fifth leaf has emerged and the miniature green clusters that will form this year's crop have been exposed to the world too. These are the vine's flowers and are often called embryo bunches as they have yet to bloom in order to be fertilised.

November

Flowering normally occurs somewhere around eight to ten weeks after bud break. This is a magical time to walk through the vineyard. Flowering takes place in mid-November driven by changes in soil temperature, this leads the roots to secrete enzymes that change the growth cycle of the vines from vegetative cycle through to reproductive cycle.

Starting with cap fall (the tops of budding flowers pop off), pollen is released and the fertilisation of the flowers occurs over a period of about two weeks, followed by fruit set. This is when you'll get the first indication of the potential crop size. Flowering normally lasts around ten days and winemakers cross their fingers that the weather will be dry, frost-free, windless, with temperatures between 20°C and 30°C.

December

After flowering vegetative growth slows and the embryo bunches rapidly evolve into true clusters. Each fertilised berry expands into a recognisable grape. The number of grapes per bunch will vary according to vine variety.

Vineyard spraying against insect infestations and fungal diseases continues at this time, up to about 40 days before harvest. Growers are very vigilant of this break between spraying and picking as wineries and importing countries test their wines for residual chemicals to ensure that the 'withholding period' has been observed.

Summer pruning in the form of canopy leaf trimming or bunch-area leaf stripping is done to improve the sunlight and air penetration into the canopy of the vines. This assists in concentrating the vine's energy on fruit ripening.

In most vineyards weeding, or ploughing of the winter cover crop (*see* 'May to June', page 62) back into the soil, provide the vines with excellent green manure at this time. This feeds the microbes in the soil and supplies mulch on the top for moisture retention.

January

There is no rest for an Australian grape grower when the rest of the country is on holidays. Depending on the success of flowering and subsequent fruit set, growers in cooler regions may remove bunches, called 'green harvesting', to reduce the crop to the desired level. Some may perform this apparently insane act more than once to reach optimum level for the wine style they are seeking. Alternatively, leaves can be removed to expose the fruit to dappled sunlight, allowing the vines to ripen the fruit and provide it with enough sunshine and warmth to help the development of flavours. This is sometimes called summer pruning.

The aim of summer pruning is to gauge the amount of leaf and fruit so that each vine gives an appropriate crop according to the wine style—by balancing the amount of sunlight through removing leaves the fruit receives appropriate exposure. Some growers choose to do nothing and others work to expose more fruit, particularly in the thick-skinned red varieties, or provide dappled light in the case of pinot noir and white varieties. This is largely a quality decision relating to the price the grower receives.

Removing leaves during January also allows air to circulate, which reduces the amount of humidity and thus discourages disease within the canopy. Judging the level of leaf removal is critical in red varieties, where red wavelength light helps develop the pigments and tannins that are the sources of red wine flavour. As winemakers understand and fine-tune this process they are becoming wiser at deciding the amount of leaves and exposure for the berries in the final six weeks before harvest; this is resulting in red wines, especially pinot noir, with additional finesse.

For white wines the reverse can happen. Fruit exposed to direct sunlight rather than dappled sunlight becomes 'suntanned' and grape skins turn from green to brown. This results in white wines with a more golden, less green colour and thicker, less fresh, more tannic textures, hence making for more weight in the mouth. Hot, dry spells that result in leaf loss or droughts rarely create the fine white wines of a cooler summer.

As mentioned above, some growers go much further than leaf plucking and do what the French call *vendage verte*, which translates as 'green harvest', removing a proportion of the potential crop in order to concentrate the vines' energies on just a few bunches. Once the vines have flowered, growers can assess the crop size and start to remove fruit that will yield an excessive crop. It seems ironic that in premium wine production the care of the vines and crops means killing off a significant percentage of the harvest close to picking, but it does produce the best crop in terms of flavour, acidity and sugar balance.

The architecture of the ripening fruit zone is decided via this pruning process each year, and in damper regions, even though 'green harvesting' is not being practised, some bunches will be removed so that no two bunches touch when the grapes are ripe, thereby reducing the risk of disease. Other weather conditions can threaten harvest—drought, in particular, can pose a danger to the ripening grapes. Likewise, heavy rain or even hail at this time of year may well damage fruit by breaking the berries and allowing mould, bees or wasps to get in.

Depending on the region, the weather conditions and the grape variety, grape harvest will generally begin en masse in February, though it has been known to begin in January in the Hunter Valley in warm years such as 2007, 1981 and 1900. The warm conditions speed up the vines' metabolism, creating early fruit ripening. In cooler regions vegetative growth will cease as the vines focus on reproductive growth, providing they are not irrigated too much. Paramount here is the encouragement of the vines' reproductive growth cycle.

For the rest of Australia, with later picking dates, bunches remain green and hard during January, going through the process of cell division with little appearance of change on the outside. During this period the vines develop their fleshy fruit but with very little chemical change taking place inside the berry until the colour changes at veraison.

Wine production and life cycle compared to other alcohols

Harvest	Production	Maturation	Shelf life
White wine	3 months to 1 year	3–12 years	5–8 years
Red wine	3 months to 1 year	1–2 years	10 months
Rosé	3 months to 1 year	3 months	2–3 years
Sparkling wine	3 months to 1 year	1–2 years	4–5 years
Mass market beer	all year round	up to 10 days	9 months
Bottled fermented beer	all year round	up to 3 months	6 months
Spirits	all year round	1–2 years	unlimited

Veraison is a series of the most important chemical changes, marked by the colouring, swelling with increased sugar, and softening of grape berries. It is about the rise in the fruit sugar levels and it is an important moment for the vines. Red grape skins will start to change colour at this time and the sugar content dramatically begins to increase, with the very hard-tasting malic acid diminishing and being replaced by the riper tartaric acid.

Although tartaric acid is the primary acid in grapes it will begin to decline after about two weeks. From a tannin build-up point of view, January is important for red grapes as it is after veraison that the tannins start to ripen (hydrolyse) within the berries. This is a critical moment because it is only hydrolysed tannins that are capable of softening as a wine matures.

The temperature at this time of year can have an effect on the grapes. The ideal temperature average seems to be at 21°C for reds and 19°C for whites. A few days of 40°C temperature is okay, but weeks are not. Temperatures above 30°C inhibit leaves to photosynthesise and use sunlight effectively to create flavour and sugar, while the vines suck up vital stores of water due to the thirsty, hot, stressing weather. How and when temperatures influence the final vintage quality is not really known but we do know it does. Considerable research is already underway to assess the factors that influence grape quality, such as tracking vineyard temperatures and then tasting the wine produced. Other activities that continue in the vineyard in January are weeding and clearing beneath the vines.

February

Early February really sees winemakers getting everything sorted out, particularly their winemaking equipment in readiness for the harvest. White grapes ripen before red grapes and so these have to be harvested early to achieve the necessary high acidity balance.

The harvest generally occurs in late February for early varieties and runs through into March. Harvesting can continue to as late as April, the timing being earlier for places closer to the equator and later for the more southerly regions. Factors which determine when the fruit is picked are the flavour, sugar, pH and acid levels, assessed against the type of wine—sparkling or table wine—to be made.

March

Depending on the region, this is the busiest harvesting time of year. The vineyard will require either many teams of hand-pickers or a number of harvesting machines to pick the grapes as quickly as possible. The choice of harvesting method will depend on labour availability, wine style, and how quickly the harvest needs to be done.

Grapes do not ripen once they have been picked so harvest timing is a big decision and a challenge for winemakers. It's a make or break time as flavour stops developing once the grapes are picked and could decline depending on handling and transit times. As grapes ripen their sugar levels rise while the acidity falls and the flavours kick in. Weather conditions often play a vital role in this, especially rain, which can leave the grapes vulnerable to rot or the water being picked up by the vines' roots and going into the bunches and diluting the juice.

Hand-harvesting is the most expensive but best way to produce memorable wines. However, in Australia the vast areas to be picked often dictate the use of mechanical method. Harvesting into small bins that are rapidly taken to the winery is ideal, as the bins can be moved before the fruit has a chance to warm up. For this reason, many winemakers choose to harvest between midnight and 9 am—the cooler the fruit the easier to handle, as many reactions affecting juice quality are dependent on temperature.

Then again, winemakers using the Italian *ripasso* or 'cordon cut' technique will be in the vineyards working with their grapes intentionally while they warm up. This method involves cutting the vines' long fruit-holding canes and leaving the fruit to shrivel for a few days in the sun before harvesters begin removing it. Cane-cutting to dry up the grapes' water supply has been used in the Clare Valley for nearly 30 years, and is becoming a popular technique with some vineyard owners of Italian origin in the King Valley. In red wine it is a modification of the process used for Amorone wines of Valpolicella.

Doubling your vintage

With only one chance a year to make wine, ingenious Australian winemakers in the 1980s hit upon a method to double their experience by making the journey to the Northern Hemisphere each year for harvest. The winemakers who made these excursions came to be called 'flying winemakers'. After the March to May harvest and vintage season was completed in Australia they would head overseas, eager to participate in the Northern Hemisphere harvest from September to October. As the skills and work ethics of the flying winemakers became widely understood, mutterings within the wine industry turned to discussions about their role in the globalisation of wine.

Those in opposition were concerned that flying winemakers were producing huge increases in volume for large supermarkets and threatening traditional expressions of European wine regionality by making new world styles. The Northern Hemisphere supermarkets which retained their services were seen to be blurring the lines of the then known flavours of Europe to guarantee vast quantities of homogenous wine for their customers.

As quality increased the critics decreased. The overall view now is that our winemakers learned more than they exported in terms of knowledge and their impact on lifting world wine quality is undoubted. Besides, it has already been observed that you could turn a winery around in one vintage but a vineyard took several years to change. Australia's outlook on vineyards started to change to being viewed as crops of regional flavour; overall, winemaking became more expressive and technically diverse, and the wines started to show more of the finer details of their varietal personality. The aims of winemaking in Australia are too diverse to ever be captured in one phrase but a lot of our

memorable wines are made from the point of view of encapsulating 'the most varietal flavour without losing regional character', while others with the opportunity are drilling down to highlighting the vineyard's character.

The Europeans have started to move as well and for the more quality-conscious estates the impact has been very exciting. European winemakers could be seen flying to Napa Valley, South America and South Africa to impart their thinking and knowledge of styles to local winemakers.

Globalisation continues for popular-priced wines with new levels of recognition of regional skills such as American expertise with blush (rosé) and pink wines to the extent that they virtually dominate the English market. We see the Europeans refining their traditional wine styles of subtle, fresh, regional wines in the new world climate, creating even more alternative styles and quality. Good examples can be found in the Sancerre-based Henri Bourgeouise making Marlborough Sauvignon Blanc or Bordeaux-bred Jacques Lurton with his vineyard on Kangaroo Island. Each makes a contribution based on their knowledge and beliefs demonstrating the importance of man in the three-legged stool of memorable wine.

April

By April, harvesting is winding down in warmer regions of Australia. During April and May vineyard managers will give their vines a last drink as the sap starts to retreat into the protection of the vine's root system. The characteristic autumn orange colours start to appear as leaves dry, having stored minimum carbohydrate. They have done their jobs.

May to June

With later harvests comes *Botrytis cinerea*. Some grapes are left on the vine to be deliberately affected by the fungus, which leads to the conditions for wines to be made using noble rot. This creates the sticky, dessert wines. Surprisingly, grapes can still be waiting on the vine to be infected with botrytis in the Riverina region. Semillon is deliberately left on the vine this late to wait for the autumn and winter mists so the infection can take hold.

From May to June winemakers also start making *eiswein*, which is really much more at home in the Northern Hemisphere during their winter months. Eiswein can be one of the world's most spectacular wines as it is only the water that freezes in the berries. This can be skimmed off once the grapes have been processed in order to leave behind a super-concentrated mass that is very sweet. Techniques employed in Australia to make it include freezing harvested juice in tanks to concentrate the sugars and skim off the frozen water.

This is the time when cover crops will be planted between the rows to improve soil fertility. In the case of legumes, nitrogen is taken in from the air and deposited in their roots. These often deep-rooted crops play a vital role in helping to manage soil fertility as their roots remain after the crops have been cut or died off from lack of water. The crops are often mown and left to rot on the surface to encourage the presence of earthworms, which will recycle the crop into water-soluble nutrients that the vine roots can find.

THE ART OF FERMENTATION

For the purpose of dividing memorable wine from 'popular-priced' wines the obvious needs to be stated. Some wines are made as a process with cost in mind to the style required, the so-called 'fit for the purpose'.

Many memorable wines are made by winemakers with a philosophy that they articulate through their wines such notions as organic, biodynamic, or respecting regional varietal styles, such as Hunter Valley semillon, McLaren Vale shiraz or Clare Valley riesling; or a house style, such as Penfolds Bin series reds or the detailed vineyard-driven Yarra Valley Estate-grown wines of De Bortoli. They seek to harness the most of the natural assets of the fruit and region according to their notion, experience and knowledge. Mercifully some of these wines are not very expensive but in general the maintenance of the style and standards does add to their costs and hence affects the consumer.

The overview below is a general guide only to the critical steps taken in making the wine, as winemakers have a number of techniques and tools at their disposal that reflect on their ingenuity as winemakers, such as:

- harvest timing, to capture the ultimate moment for grape flavour
- degree and timing of crushing
- fermentation onset, temperature, technique and timing
- use of pumps versus gravity draining
- ageing methods, particularly barrel size, age and type of oak.

White wine

Harvesting: D-day in a wine's life as essential attributes of the fruit and the season are captured either by hand as bunches or machine harvested and removed as a mix of whole and broken bunches. Larger vineyards rely on machines and the technology is well understood. Where labour is cheap or the wine is expensive hand-harvesting is a feature. It is seen at its pinnacle in sauternes where selection for the most botrytis-affected fruit requires skilled pickers to leave less affected bunches for the next 'tri' or passage through the vines. Some varieties benefit from spending time in a cool room before being pressed cold.

Crushing and de-stemming grapes: For juice to flow the berry needs to be gently squeezed without being torn and the stalks removed as they may release bitter tannins if they are bruised.

Pressing grapes: White varieties are pressed quickly before fermentation starts to remove the juice from the skins with a focus on clear juice for aromatic varieties and cloudier juices for some styles of chardonnay.

Clarification and cold settling: The juice, now called must, is treated differently according to grape variety. In aromatic varieties it is chilled to help settle debris, called solids, to quickly create clear, clean juice. It is racked (pumped) to another tank in a neat process that leaves a milky sea of solids at the bottom of each tank. The art with chardonnay is to judge the amount of fine solids to be included, as too much creates very undesirable aromas and phenolic or tannic finish; but when finely judged a little is extremely useful. The technical variants are slow and careful settling in cold temperatures (down to 5°C) then juice racked off solids, or the faster use of centrifuges to clarify must into cleaned tanks to be inoculated with yeast.

Cool (at 12°C to 16°C) for controlled fermentation: As yeast activity is temperature-dependent the advent of refrigerated cooling has forevermore changed winemaking to an industrial scale by providing winemakers with the ability to control ferments in large-capacity stainless steel tanks, thus replacing the smaller, more expensive vats which, according to winemaking legend, were often cooled with blocks of ice. Having tasted a few of these wines I can see nothing wrong with the practice, although modern standards dictate a more precise approach. Fermenting in barrels is generally done in cool rooms to help control the temperature, but less precisely.

Checking ferment daily: According to the grape variety ferments are monitored to check yeast activity, and aroma and flavour development. Techniques vary according to variety. Towards the end the temperature needs to be adjusted to assist in finishing ferment.

Racking off yeast: Once ferment is completed most styles require yeast lees to be removed (*see* 'Sur lies', page 73).

Fining: Most winemakers will add an animal or mineral protein to manage the clarity and texture of wines and prevent a brown protein haze forming later during maturation or if the wine is heated. Some have developed methods to avoid fining but they remain an exalted few. Fining aids clarity of flavour and texture of the finished wine.

Cold stabilisation (<2°C) for tartrate stability: Tartaric acid is the main acid in wine and is less soluble when temperatures are low and prone to forming crystals over time. To avoid this white wines are chilled to remove tartaric acid and make them stable for ordinary circumstances. The crystalline dust that does occasionally form in bottles is sometimes mistaken for ground glass but a simple visual examination will confirm it is not glass.

Filtration: The process of filtering or sieving out small particles of unstable compounds prevents cloudy wines developing, and can also be used to remove yeast cells and/or bacteria.

Bottling: When a winemaker decides that the wine is ready for bottling they will check stability and clarity (as described above) and bottle it.

Some components of wine

	approx % composition (by weight)
Flavour compounds	0.1%
Colour and tannins – in red wines	0.3%
Acids	1.0%
Sugar – dry wines	0.1%
– sweet wines	8.0%
Water	80–90.0%
Alcohol – table wines	normally 8–15.0%
– fortified wines	usually 15–21.0%

NOTE: *Alcohol content is normally expressed as % by volume, not weight. However, the values are similar to those given in this table*

Red wine

Harvesting: There are many definitions of ripeness in red grapes depending on variety, style and location, and winemakers will vary harvest timing according to the year as well. A feature of recent years has been the need to delay harvest until flavours catch up with the sugar in the grapes. High sugars are achieved as a by-product of the wait for flavour ripeness in the fruit, producing wines with corresponding high alcohols.

Crushing and de-stemming of grapes: Red grapes will be de-stemmed according to style with some producers, particularly of pinot noir, choosing to retain a percentage. They can contribute a vegetal flavour if they are green and crisp tannic complexity when well judged. Most of Australia's red wines are de-stemmed.

Yeast inoculation: Winemakers add yeast to help control fermentation. (*See* 'The yeast world', page 70.)

Fermentation/maceration: Ferment checks twice daily and plunging or pumping over includes tasting and eventually running off of skins—can involve anything from 12 to 24 hours for rosé to four to six days for many reds, and up to seven to 19 days for some types of high-quality shiraz and cabernet, according to the winemaker's quest for the right balance of tannin and colour. Extended skin contact past seven days generally produces very tannic wines, while extending the time further can hasten polymerisation and condensing of tannins yielding both fuller-bodied and silky tannins.

Pressing: Red wines are pressed after a period of maceration or skin contact time. The complex tannins and colour of red wines require various lengths of maceration to extract tannins and flavours in the skin and pressing ends this process. The harder the skins are pressed the more bitter the flavours and more disagreeable the mouthfeel. Timing and choosing the type of press to be used is an art of winemaking, particularly when the tannin structure of the fruit is suitable for building wine density and length. We have seen an increase in the use of older-fashioned technology, such as basket presses, for this process. Pressing often occurs before fermentation has been completed, with the wine finishing ferment in barrels—a style skilfully applied to Langhorne Creek shiraz by John Glaetzer at Wolf Blass to create marvellously soft and complex wines that in the mid-1970s heralded a new style of Australian wine.

Oak barrel or tank maturation: Rosé and light reds aside, red wines require a period for their tannins to polymerise and aromas, flavour and structure to build, chiefly due to small amounts of oxygen entering the wine, a process of which is well understood. Oak with its positive flavour contribution has been the traditional wood, although cherry wood and other more aromatic woods do make for interesting wines. Oak storage and maintenance is expensive, and includes monthly topping up and preservative testing. To monitor wines in barrels is a slow process and costly, which explains the rise of stainless steel variants to the traditional barrique of 225 litres or hogshead of 300 litres. Imports of oak have reduced dramatically in the last ten years as styles have sought more fruit expression and left the toasty, charry character of oak behind.

Topping wine: Incredibly, by putting wine in oak it evaporates—in humid environments losing more alcohol and in dry environments more water. Thus the volume is reduced and allows in air, which is normally excluded. Topping up with the same wine avoids oxidation or infiltration by yeasts that could spoil the wine. For example, a 225-litre barrel can lose up to 25 litres of wine in a year.

MLF: Malolactic fermentation lowers the acidity and softens the palate of red wines; this is a good thing as tannins taste more bitter in higher acid situations. The formation of a tiny amount of aromas by the bacteria during the conversion of malic acid to lactic acid gives complexity.

Blending: Tasting to identify the relevant qualities in young wines is the great art of winemaking and a considerable point of difference to the tasting skills of most wine journalists, whose experiences lie with bottled wines. In concept the sum of the blend should be greater than its components and give consumers more pleasure. In reality there are as many ways to blend as there are winemakers. The full matrix of blending differences that can come from small changes at any stage in a wine's production can be aimed at producing a consistent style from year to year, or a blend of varieties, most commonly and commercially a blend of regions. At its peak in Bordeaux the assemblage of a blend of different varieties, ages of vines, soils and years can yield structured wines with complexity and balance that are unsurpassed in their consistent style and character.

Fining of wine: Many red wines are not as filtered or tartrated, or stabilised to the same extent as white wines, thus forming a crust that requires decanting.

Filtration: This is done to ensure stability of colour, clarity and flavour; as a generalisation, less expensive wines will receive more management to ensure stability to avoid customer unease due to variation. Many reds go to bottle without filtration based on the electrostatic properties of fining agents, which can be used selectively to modify the mouthfeel and tannin structure. A range of animal and mineral products have been used in the past 200 years and are well understood. The absence of their use is held by some wine writers to mean superior quality, but the variation in ageing, both between the same bottling and different vintages, casts doubts on these claims. Australian food regulations outlaw the use of the anti-microbial Velcorin, which is used by a significant number of US winemakers, to claim that the wine is 'unfined and unfiltered' on the label.

Bottling: Methods for bottling vary, from the winemaker's grandmother using gravity to fill bottles in Burgundy with such care and precision that she did not spill a drop, to fast production line equipment. But in both cases the wine is hygienically filled into a bottle with the right amount of sulphur dioxide to preserve it and then sealed. Many now see bottling as 'packaging', a crucial distinction as marketing becomes more important.

Building blocks of wine

Fermentation occurs when yeast converts sugar into alcohol, creating heat and giving off carbon dioxide. Building balanced wines relies on the basic elements of a place's climate to provide the building blocks for the produce, and the winemaker coordinating the elements of creating wine from grapes. The elements which experts analyse when trying to assess wine quality are sugar, acidity, tannin and alcohol.

Grape sugar is fermented into alcohol and this gives wine its richness and a degree of fleshiness in the mouth. The riper the grapes generally the higher the fruit flavours and the higher the level of sugar, although leaving grapes for too long on the vine, depending on the site, can see flavours expire rather than increase due to heat from the sun and the vine's own metabolic rate. Various methods such as cutting the canes that grapes grow on and leaving them to dry on the vine in the vineyard, and the *ripasso* method of drying grapes as bunches in sheds, are fascinating techniques to increase sugar.

Acidity is part of what balances alcohol and keeps the fruit lively on the palate, especially in white wine; it also gives freshness and encourages you to have another mouthful. White wines without acidity become very bland, flat and quite featureless, while reds seem to be fat, fleshy and unexciting, and with low acidity lack the structure to age. The balance of acidity to tannin is critical, too high an acidity makes tannins taste bitter. Many Australian winemakers accept acid levels in reds that leave our international rivals gasping as they settle for less acidic and more mouthfilling if shorter-lived wines.

Tannin, which comes from the grape skins, pips and oak, should not be noticeable in white wines even though it is there. A white wine with excessive tannin would be described as 'phenolic', and it will have a dry or an astringent finish. In wine, tannin is what gives a red wine its all-important structure, enabling length and complexity of flavour to develop—the personality of the wine.

In Australia our wines tend to have a lot of ripe, rich fruit characters which often overtake the weight of tannin so the wine will seem quite soft and easy, even though there

F

will be tannins underneath. Tannins also help the life of the wine and for it to mature with age, as they are at the frontline in the battle with any oxygen that comes in contact with the wine via the cork or closure. Oak tannins are used to flavour and structurally enhance wines and can be counted on to help build body on the front palate and flavour and body to the finish.

Recent work with screw caps suggests that oxygen is not needed for maturation in the bottle for red wines. The flexibility of screw-cap liners (the little piece of wadding that actually seals the screw cap on the inside) and the Diam cork have varied permeability to suit the wine style. Winemakers have known for years that oxygen will enter a wine via the cork and for this reason added sulphur dioxide and chosen corks of different lengths to fit the expected ageing time of the wine.

Rising alcohol content

According to a letter published in *Wine Spectator*, citing the California Department of Food and Agriculture:

- from 1981 to 1990 Napa Valley cabernets were picked with an average of 11.9 per cent alcohol
- from 1996 to 2000, alcohol averaged 13 per cent at harvest
- 2001 to 2003, 13.4 per cent alcohol
- 2004 and 2005, the average was 13.6 per cent.

At this rate, it means that most Napa Valley cabernets coming onto the market in the next couple of years will be above 14 per cent alcohol. Their wines are getting more alcoholic and the style is softening due to less acidity and reduced age-worthiness. In their defence, some of this is due to their disturbed viticulture, thanks to phylloxera destroying the vine rootstock they best understood. They are now re-running the experiment with new rootstocks.

Just how much tannin?

A good example of the phenolic finish can be seen if you allow several cups of black tea to brew for varying times. The tea will range from pale to dark in colour, and as you taste the teas you will notice that somewhere between the palest and the darkest drop your mouth will start to dry out. The darker the tea the more astringent it is due to the increased tannin, and perhaps less drinkable. But don't start thinking that the same level of tannin in a cup of tea would be excessive in a red wine.

Really great red wines can be very tannic. You might struggle to appreciate the wine when it is young because of the drying nature of the tannin, but no doubt it will be able to rise to the occasion after a few years in the bottle. Tannins soften as they age and become barely noticeable. The most important aspect of tannin is the tannic backbone. Tannins support fruit characters along the palate and provide lingering flavours on the taste buds. I find wines with excellent tannins tend to have flavours in those tannins and the very late fruit characters of the wine can be both drying and aromatic, with sweet, ripe, red fruit characters coming through as well.

According to some very notable experts tannin cannot be smelled, however, the concentrations of some types of tannins can be detected. As my ten-year-old says of some wines from Italy, 'Smells dry, Dad', and they are as dry as his nose indicates.

The yeast world

A winemaker's relationship with yeast is another important aspect of making wine—how it is used and how it works is a remarkable tale.

Alcohol is the product of the action of yeast on grape sugar, which gives wine weight on the palate. Low-alcohol wines taste light and watery, while a high-alcohol wine can be almost sweet and quite rich with a very full mouthfeel and flavour. A good wine should never have alcohol that leaves a hot, burning sensation in your mouth on finishing a sip. The exception would be young vintage port.

Saccharomyces are a large family of sugar-loving plants from the bottom of the evolutionary tree of the vegetable family. This single-celled primitive plant is a marvel of survival and adaptation based on its ability to live in both virtually oxygen-free or oxygen-rich environments, and to metabolise sugar while secreting carbon dioxide and alcohol.

We exploit these two traits. First, it is a microscopic plant that does not need to breathe like other creatures, and second, unlike most of its microbe rivals, it likes and produces alcohol, tolerating higher concentrations than other microbes which find its effects antiseptic.

The carry-on brigade

Saccharomyces cerevisiae is a wonder bug and we are lucky to have it. But when this bug goes wrong, mainly from a lack of appropriate micronutrients, it produces stinky, rotten egg gas which, if left for too long, turns to mercaptan, the intrusive smell added to our natural gas to warn us that we have left the gas on.

Added to wine and left in an oxygen-rich environment, *S. cerevisiae* will convert alcohol back into acetaldehyde (neatly reversing the alcohol creation process), hence providing in small amounts the characteristic aroma of flor sherry and in larger quantities a nail polish remover or a vinegar-like smell.

We use wine yeast that can live on the sugar in grape juice to make wine and sometimes trap the carbon dioxide it produces as effervescence for sparkling wines. Some yeast selections in Spain, Hungary and the French Alps tolerate high alcohol and in a neat reverse use it for food in place of sugar, which in Spain produces the characteristic tang of flor and manzanilla sherry. Yeast can contribute to the aroma, texture and taste of a wine. Increasingly, different strains of yeast are available to suit different winemaking processes including some, now fallen from fashion, which produce a strong passionfruit aroma in young white wines.

In the evolutionary race for survival yeast has commandeered a part of primate and human physiology. Having learned to like alcohol from eating overripe fruit, we have been competing for the same ripe fruit sugars in a slow tango intertwined with yeast that, according to some, has been influencing our DNA.

It seems that over the aeons yeast has been selecting us as well as the other way round, thanks to its habit of producing alcohol and of Europeans drinking it. The genes of the Mediterranean and Anglo-Saxon people show a greater capacity to produce the dehydrogenase enzymes needed to remove alcohol and its primary by-product from oxidation, the toxic derivative acetaldehyde, from their systems.

Flor yeast

In southern Spain a separate family of yeast broadly described as *flor*, literally 'the flower', creates secondary flavours during the maturation phase for sherry-based wines. Once alcoholic fermentation is complete, the best wines are fortified to 15.5 per cent and stored in the coolest cellars.

Stored at cool temperatures in old barrels at Jerez and the port of San Lucar de Barrameda, a local yeast strain, *Saccharomyces beticus*, flowers during spring and autumn. It rapidly cloaks the half-filled wine barrels in its ghostly veil producing flavours derived from alcohol being converted by the yeast to acetaldehyde and another yeast family by-product called acetals.

It also draws down on the texture- and body-enhancing glycerol produced during ferment of the base wine. This enhances the texture, in this case by producing its oily roundness to a delicate, lightly textured, clean salt and nuts (almonds and walnuts), savoury-derived range of flavours.

The more evenly cool seaside of San Lucar gives the yeast a longer growing period and makes for more subtle wines with less oxidation and thickness, and a finer more aromatic walnut and almond aldehyde aroma. Both are equally delicious.

The group of people around the so-called 'cradle of civilisation' where wine first appeared (so perhaps the tag is appropriate) has two additional genes. One is linked to alcohol dehydrogenase and the other to the production of aldehyde dehydrogenase, the enzyme responsible for denaturing acetaldehyde. The gene is non-existent in up to 80 per cent of Japanese, Korean and Han Chinese people, who have a slower enzyme metabolism that slows the breakdown of acetaldehyde circulating in their bodies. Hence the resultant hot flushes and nausea that arise from drinking occurring more quickly in people from these groups. The effects are limited to the rate alcohol and its metabolites are secreted.

Incredibly, yeast possesses two ways to metabolise sugar or glucose—which gives it a way to prevent other microbes from getting near its sugar source—through air-breathing (aerobic) activity or anaerobic activity, such as occurs in a vat of must. By sacrificing an enormous amount of energy, yeast has learned to break down a glucose (sugar) molecule anaerobically using enzymes, and to convert that glucose into alcohol, thereby setting up a biological exclusion zone that is toxic to other microbes.

An impact of this process is that the alcohol contains most of the chemical energy of the original glucose molecule bound in the ethanol molecule, which means that the alcohol carries a massive seven calories per gram. Couple that with its predisposition to affect our genetic material towards tolerance—and it's watch out waistline!

Yeast has deviated from most organisms that generate energy from sugar (that includes you and me) and uses oxygen to break down the molecules into water and carbon dioxide. The energy we create along the way is stored as adenosine triphosphate (ATP), which the cells use for food. This process is known as aerobic respiration. Each glucose molecule yields about 36 molecules of ATP to us. But *S. cerevisiae* doesn't need as much oxygen and prefers to produce alcohol and only two molecules of ATP! The low ATP is the key; it's not going anywhere, as it wants to sit around in the alcohol awaiting its chance to convert the alcohol into an easier meal to digest.

So yeast, when it's safe, converts the ethanol back into acetaldehyde and gets it energy back by eating the acetaldehyde. This process is well exploited and understood by the Spanish with flor making in sherry, where they create the fino and manzanilla sherry styles. It all goes to show how involved the tango has become and how much we have learned along the way to exploit this potently flexible plant to our advantage.

Prise de mousse

Champagne's second fermentation—the *prise de mousse*—puts the sparkle in wine by capturing the carbon dioxide in the bottle. Once the yeast has done its job with the sugar it falls to the bottom of the bottle and starts breaking down, going through 'autolysis' and contributing a range of flavours and complexity, depending on the length of time the lees stay in contact with the wine. Terms associated with this additional flavour include bready to biscuity, and nutty in extreme cases.

Wildly and widely cultured

Yeast is the mother of wine—so I was told in Italy—and along with their lees (dead yeast once they have finished fermenting) is nourishment in bringing up a healthy wine. Selection of the right yeast is the key here, as yeast can be chosen for a wide variety of functions. Among the traits that it can be selected for are slow or fast ferment, or the production of aromatic compounds.

One of the winemaker's biggest jobs used to be to get the yeast culture in good order to start the vintage fermentations. The right strain, in large enough numbers and at the right time, was a challenge that needed to be met. However, packet yeasts now have taken the worry of this process away. Today, winemakers have a much greater diversity of approaches—from allowing yeasts living in the winery, often called ambient, wild or native yeast, to ferment, to using selections chosen for their performance, such as high-sugar tolerance in the making of botrytis wines. Modern winemakers have a vast array of selected powdered yeast (cultured yeast) of proven background and performance at their disposal for the rapid and safe conversion of sugar into alcohol. While standing accused by some winemakers of taking the safe path, the wine produced from them is reliable, risk free, clean, cheap and boring, but very important for affordable popular-priced table-wine winemaking.

When white wine juices have been removed from their skins, winemakers will use cultured yeast (unless barrels are involved, then they might opt to wait to see if the native yeast will start the ferment).

Increasingly, winemakers are finding ways to extend fermentation times to help to produce extra memorable fruit flavour and character. By fermenting slowly they retain aromas, thanks to a slower rate of carbon dioxide leaving the wine and reduced heat from reduced yeast activity. These winemakers see hot ferments as stripping aroma via rapid CO_2 escape, and the heat as capable of physically damaging flavour compounds.

Wild or native yeast (in reality often a mix of previously used yeast living in the winery) can contribute a distinctive memorable character to the aroma and palate of white wines, in particular chardonnay, owing to their slower onset and fermentation rates. A feature of recent years is the yeast-work with the winemaking to add a gravel dust or earthy saffron-like complexity that can hide the varietal fruit while adding textural elements to the palate.

Sur lies—dead yeast tales

Lees are principally the millions upon millions of dead yeast cells left after their fermentation has exhausted the available sugar and micronutrients. Having made the wine by the conversion of sugar to alcohol, the dead yeast lees continue to play an enormous role in building memorable wine. Use of lees divides two ways: as a potent natural antioxidant while in the cask-ageing and maturation phase of table wines, and as a contributor to flavour especially important to full-bodied white or sparkling wines.

Ageing *sur lies,* as the French express it, is the use of lees to help mature wine post-fermentation and before bottling. At its zenith in the French regions of Burgundy and Muscadet, it is most popular in Australia to enhance flavour and texture in chardonnay with more adventurous winemakers using it for sauvignon blanc and semillon.

When conditions are favourable and lees are creamy white they will lie on the bottom of the barrel, and if left undisturbed for months they will contribute texture before eventually turning sour.

Pinot noir can also benefit from lees treatment when conditions are favourable, although stirring is unlikely to help build on texture. To accentuate the effects white wine barrels are stirred in a process called 'battonage' to mix the lees with the wine to increase the creamy texture and aromas.

What's in a vat?

Fermenting techniques have greatly changed since the Victorian era when wine was fermented in open-topped square cement vats lined with wax. Cleanliness then was a challenge and temperature control was a nightmare. Men stood on top of walls and pushed the fermenting cap of skins and seeds into the wine twice a day, while small pumps meant that often only the softest tannins were extracted.

Slowly from the 1950s—with a rush in the 1970s—these vats were removed and replaced with the familiar closed stainless steel tanks, which were easier to clean and cooler. Accountants loved them as they reduced labour costs and winemakers learned enthusiastically at first to live with them.

Then a funny thing happened. The new vats increased the alcohol content of the wine and the tannins lost their soft plumpness, becoming harsh as more and firmer tannins were extracted by the increased pumping forces required to lift the juice over the top of the high stainless steel tanks to flood the skins.

Open fermentation made a limited comeback. Winemakers with a growing appreciation, somewhat reluctantly, recognised that vats are part of the process of style creation, with small batches, gentle handling and hotter ferments to help create the style. In part this was because the hand-plunging vats help extract only the softest tannins and the open top vats reduced a wine's alcohol content by 1 to 1.5 per cent through evaporation.

The vats that have survived in some of our older regions are now at the core of some of our most expensive wines with old vines and appreciative winemakers finding flavour and textural benefits mainly for red wines.

One of the biggest costs in winemaking comes from being able to cool tanks during fermentation. The use of temperature control is an important tool in developing wine character, and this marks the difference between most wine made before the 1970s and those after. Most winemakers are flexible to a few degrees concerning temperature so long as the sugar moves down evenly and steadily. If it is fermenting too fast, they will lower the temperature; too slow and they will raise it.

Modern winemaking, as part of the winemaker's individual style, has seen an increase in small-scale uncontrolled ferments, such as with barrel fermentation.

Temperature control

Most winemakers use temperature control to manage yeast fermentation activity—yeast is too cold at 10°C, and too hot and likely to die at 30°C—to carry on converting sugar.

Winemakers use different fermentation temperatures to guide the style they are seeking and to create constituents for blends, yet there are no hard and fast rules, for example:

Red wine
26°C–30°C, big soft palate with middle palate fruit
18°C–20°C, fresher fruit and lighter less tannic palate
Chardonnay fermenting in tank
18°C–20°C, lower temperature gives aromatics, simple flavours and retains freshness
20°C–25°C, gives more complexity, mouthfeel and richness, and reduces aromatic compounds
Barrel fermentation
Controlled by cooling the room the barrels are stored in, often around 14°C, but depends on the amount of wine fermenting. Aim for 18°C–20°C in barrels but will have spikes; higher depending on local conditions of 25°C–28°C to maintain aromatics and gain complexity
Aromatic whites
Start a little warm to give the yeast a chance to establish, and then drop to 12°C–16°C for most of fermentation before allowing it to rise towards the end to help the yeast complete the trickiest last few grams of sugar.

Adding the bubbles in sparkling wine

Australian sparkling wine has undergone a quality revolution with our greater understanding of the best grape varieties and places to grow them. In a development that is less than ten years old we are now making memorable white and rosé sparkling wine that can add to our fearsome century-old reputation for sparkling shiraz.

Below are some essential characteristics for producing sparkling wine.

- The right climate to produce wine just on the edge of ripeness.
- The best pressing to produce a delicate wine suitable for sparkling.
- Perfected blending to produce a wine with sufficient complexity to be sparkling.
- Use of reserve wines or grape spirit in the form of *eau-de-vie* to replace the wine lost when it is disgorged.

Science and experience has given winemakers an increasing technological flexibility. The following list shows some of the additional style determinants.

- Speed of fermentation: Slow fermenting traps aromatics, while fermenting fast removes aromas and can build extract and glycerine, but the wine holds less gas and hence goes flatter faster in the glass though it tastes fatter in the process.
- Use of old oak: This is oak that has been used many times before for fermenting in sizes from 225 litres to 1000 litres, with size influencing rates of oxygen going in and the relative ratio of the lees to wine contact.
- Malolactic fermentation: Used to reduce the zesty malic acidity to a rounder, softer and less exciting lactic acid or not, as in the Champagne Lanson style which prevents malolactic fermentation to keep the house style crispness.

The champagnisation process

Grape handling: Vintage comes early for sparkling winemakers as they seek the most pristine fruit flavours with low sugar and high acidity. The grapes are often hand-harvested into plastic stackable crates and taken to press houses. Whatever method is used, the fruit is handled carefully, although an Australian vineyard that is close to the winery may allow machine harvesting to be used.

Pressing: Grapes are gently squeezed to extract the juice. Traditionally in Champagne these presses were wide and filled shallowly with whole fruit to avoid juice draining over crushed grapes and extracting unwanted solids and tannins. The degree of solids (also described as phenolics) that are extracted once the grape skin is torn until the juice leaves the skins is dependent on the type of press used and the duration of pressing. Machine harvesting makes it possible to get the grapes off quickly to make consistently high-quality wines, in contrast to France where only hand-harvest is allowed under their wine laws.

Juice clarification: Juice is held in a tank to allow natural settling of dust and pulp. Depending on the temperature the duration of this may range from overnight to two days.

Primary fermentation: Wine is yeasted with specially selected yeast and fermenting processes commence. At this stage the sugar converts to alcohol and carbon dioxide, and as in any normal white wine, production is run at low temperatures around 15°C.

Malolactic fermentation: Some winemakers seek additional complexity from malolactic bacteria converting green-tasting malic acid into the softer, rounder lactic acid. Opinions are divided as to whether softening the wine adds to its complexity and further modifies the fruit flavours.

Blending or assemblage: Starts within three months of picking and, depending on the house style, older or reserve wines may be blended into the final wine. This is then chilled for several weeks to precipitate any potassium bitartrate crystals.

Tirage bottling: Cultured yeast and a little carefully measured sugar (the *liqueur de tirage*) are added to the blended wine. The sugar feeds the yeasts and produces wines with subtle flavours and just the right amount of carbon dioxide to sparkle the wine at the completion of fermentation. This yeasty cloudy wine is then bottled and sealed with a crown seal similar to that used to seal a bottle of beer, as the wine will have to be opened at a later stage. Some classic *cuvée de prestige* wines are sealed by corks that are held in place by agraffe clips.

Secondary fermentation: Also known as *prise de mousse*. Over the next two months the yeast in the tirage-bottled wine slowly converts the sugar to alcohol and carbon dioxide, adding about 1 per cent alcohol. During this process each yeast cell will be divided several times, producing around seven million cells per millilitre at the end of the fermentation. The carbon dioxide produced by the yeast remains trapped in the solution because this fermentation takes place in a closed bottle; however too much carbon dioxide produces too much pressure and bottles have been known to explode at this stage.

Disgorgement: Final process of clarifying the wine. The winemaker has two alternative techniques with which to do this: *transvasage* or *remuage*. *Transvasage* involves transferring the wine from its tirage bottle to a pressure tank for filtration and refilling. In the process, each bottle is emptied and transferred by machine to a pressure tank without loss of gas pressure. The wine is then filtered, sweetened and bottled.

Remuage: This clarifies the wine in the bottle in which it was fermented by the more expensive process. The bottles remain on tables while being shaken and gradually moved from horizontal to vertical positions, as the yeast slips down to the neck of the bottle. A refinement of this process is the use of gyroplates, which shake down the yeast lees into the neck of the bottle. With the neck pointed down the bottle is transferred to a chilled brine solution, which cools the wine and forms a plug of ice in the neck, trapping the yeast and a little wine. The closure is removed with the bottle upright, and the pressure of the dissolved carbon dioxide causes the ice plug to be expelled. The clean wine is topped with a wine sugar solution called the *liqueur de expedition* to adjust the final sweetness, and then the bottle is corked and wired for sale.

There is considerable variation in champagne styles. Historically it was a red wine with pinot noir primarily and meunier later dominating flavours and body. Of primary importance to modern style creation is varying the proportions of the blends of varieties. In modern wines chardonnay nearly always appears and delivers a very refined and elegant flavour (*gout de champenoise*). Crisp and clean, delicately structured, with impressive finesse and balance, it gives freshness. Pinot noir makes a bigger flavour contribution, especially in hot summers, and has more to its body which is managed by adding chardonnay.

Very few champagnes in France are still fermented entirely in oak without temperature control as would have been done traditionally. Some are cooled to retain

LAGRAIN 6.5 PRESS

fruit at approximately 8°C to prolong the fermentation time and some without cooling for quick ferments. Some may stop malolactic fermentation depending on the year and use old oak for maturation and cask-age reserve wines. The use of jeroboams and half bottles for secondary fermentation will influence the style. Their ability to influence the taste of the wine you drink is not over with the second ferment, as winemakers have to replace the wine that was lost as the frozen plug was removed with the yeast. To fill the gap they will use the same wine and sufficient sugar—when blended called expedition liqueur—to manage flavour and set the final level of sweetness. Rarely, local grape eau-de-vie will be added as well to manage the alcohol level.

There is a precision to the sparkling wine winemaker's palate that marks considerable intellectual study and experience. Tasmania leads the way in Australia as a growing region and my notes here are based on tastings conducted there. The current belief is that increasing southerly latitude is normally associated with slow ripening over long days and this gives better fruit length and suppleness. Altitude is seen to give strength of fruit or hardness but not length or suppleness. There is debate on this as some winemakers, such as John Ellis and Brown Brothers, are finding the inland high-altitude vineyards acceptable, but Ed Carr's approach says not. He finds that he gets more botrytis in the Yarra than he does on good sites in Tasmania.

In Australia the grapes that make champagne are now seen for what they can deliver in our conditions rather than for what overseas experience has shown. According to Andrew Pirie, on a visit to his then winery Pipers Brook, chardonnay is seen in the Australian context to give acidity, lightness and freshness to balance pinot noir's heaviness and aromatic qualities. Chardonnay, when grown in Tasmania, shows a flavour profile of fine acacia, hawthorn and fruity apple, lemon and pear, while age gives hazelnuts to chardonnay.

Pinot noir ripens five to ten days earlier than chardonnay and with lower acidity. In young wines it gives red fruit aromas of cassis, strawberry, raspberry and lead pencil, while age gives coffee-ish notes, and body, length and roundness. It links with yeast autolysis to give a perfect merge of the flavours known around the world as champagne yeastiness.

Its sibling variety pinot meunier has a danger of overripening in Australia and generally gives neutral wines with a family resemblance to pinot noir—strawberry, raspberry and lifted cassis, with good body, depth and density, and may show acidity. Age gives a lot of mushroom and earth character, which many associate with French fizz character. Some think meunier equals what the public think is champagne character, although meunier will peak earlier and take the yeast flavours with it to old-age character. Older Tasmanian wines have a butterscotch nuttiness and are more mouthfilling.

The winery Domain Chandon in the Yarra Valley has been working on understanding the use of solids—small cloudy particles that are created from pressing the juice to remove the skins—and whether they are a part of Australian fizz styles. Domain Chandon's current direction is seeking an Australian style. The Chandon style uses zero solids, due to the strong fruit character and high sugar levels of Australian fruit.

The winery observes the regions they are familiar with. In Australia the solids tend to be 1 per cent alcohol-riper than champagne for the same set of grape flavours, and with that extra degree of alcohol gives a degree of palate weight, body and texture. To Chandon, using solids would obscure the fruit and make the palate heavier, leading to the consistent, even and concentrated fruit being obscured.

The level of sophistication and knowledge discussed above bodes well for the ability of Australian sparkling wine to develop an authentic Australian voice; perhaps our next step could be to represent the generic champagne-like qualities of our wines in a one-word name to describe the style. Is this not too far away?

chapter 3

Varieties of wine

It's what's in the bottle not where it's from that matters
SCOTT COLLETT, WINEMAKER, *c. early 1990s*

NAMING NAMES

Grape varieties are the key to understanding wine. Most wine is bought and sold by variety and variety contributes the biggest differences in taste, and makes a strong third leg for our stool.

Surprisingly, around the world few growers are free to choose what they plant. This stems from the laws of the region for many areas of Europe. New vineyard owners are unlikely to change their varieties due to huge costs associated with removing existing grape vines to plant their preferred choice. If a grower is lucky enough to do so, their aim will be to balance the environmental and varietal factors when they plant to get the best flavour and quality from their crop to meet different levels of acceptance, thanks to historic, legal and market forces.

Over the course of centuries different varieties have been selected all over the world, and some of the history of this diaspora we know about, some we don't. For instance, the riddle of why some varieties are associated with specific regions: Did they grow there originally or was there a human or climate selection process at work? For example, the overriding German grape selections are white, acidic, low in sugar and aromatic, while the French selections are black, high in sugar, tannic and herbaceous. Traditionally, the wine drinker was not told the variety of grape just where the wine came from and the producer's name, and possibly the level of the appellation.

The traditional system of *Cru* and *appellation* worked well for the Europeans and the well educated. Many of the vineyard owners would have known every vine on their property, although the varieties were not especially important to them. Grape growing was localised and traditional, which meant that a lot of varietal names changed from parish to parish, though the variety was exactly the same. As populations grew and wine started to be sold further from its source this system of naming became problematic. Compounding the problem was the increasing quantity of wine grape vines being planted in the new world regions, leading to a huge break with regional traditions. The traditional winemaking experience of small European vignerons, handed down through generations and learned through trial and error, was under challenge. Change was slow and Alsace was the only region to label by variety until the Americans hit upon it.

American labelling by variety started in the 1950s and had the force of a revolution. The precision of varietal names came to represent a triumph of science over the art of wine and time. This is partly because the marketing of varietal wines is easier for consumers to understand, and partly because it allows producers to plan for an indefinite supply of the same variety when it's accepted, and for even larger, more efficient wineries.

Examples of the primary fruit spectrum for some varieties

Riesling:
floral · perfumed · apple · pear · citrus · lime · passionfruit · tropical fruit

Sauvignon blanc:
asparagus · capsicum · herbaceous · grassy · gooseberry · tropical fruit

Semillon:
herbaceous · straw · grassy · gooseberry · apple · quince · lemon · lime · citrus · passionfruit · tropical fruit

Chardonnay
cucumber · tobacco · grapefruit · gooseberry · melon · lime · peach · rockmelon · fruit salad · fig · tropical fruit

Pinot noir
cherry · strawberry · violets · raspberry · plum · stewed plum

Grenache
floral · boiled lolly · spice · raspberry · pepper · plum · stewed plum · prunes · liquorice

Merlot
herbaceous · leafy · fruity · perfume · violets · sappy · cherry · raspberry · plum · fruit cake · beetroot · blackcurrant

Cabernet sauvignon
herbaceous · capsicum · tomato bush · leafy · minty · eucalypt · mulberry · blackcurrant

Shiraz
herbs · spice · clove · plum · pepper · raspberry · mulberry · cola · blackberry

Early ripening stage → **Late ripening stage**

What's in a name

Following is a simple summary of the variety of naming systems used throughout the aeons (*see also* the 'Varietal pyramid' in Chapter 1, page 22).

- **The appellation system:** This is based on the European belief that when it comes to wine the vineyard's location is mightier than the variety, and that they already know the ideal variety for every location.
- **The cru system:** This was developed in Burgundy with a thousand years of experience behind it; it puts a name and a rating to parcels of hillside vineyards with different altitude, soils, aspect and subsoil.
- **Chateau system:** Bordeaux, one of the largest producers of fine wines in the world, adopts a naming system that places primary importance on the chateau's name and allows vineyards to be bought or sold without changing the chateau classification on the label.
- **Bordeaux classification or 1855:** This was created by merchants who regularly traded in Bordeaux wines and assigned a value to the properties or growths, with the highest being first and the lowest fifth.
- **Varietal:** Wine labelling according to the type of grape in the bottle.
- **Entry-level wine:** An industry term for a low-budget, low-risk product.
- **Detailed wine:** The evolution of Australian wine naming is in the detail, revealing more of the details of the variety and its region.
- **Wine show system:** In Australia there is a series of capital city wine competitions that provides winemakers with an opportunity to observe and rate wines from all over the country through blind tastings. It has been decisive in helping to build recognition of regional varietal strengths.

I should add that wine naming by region or styles wasn't just undertaken in France. In 2005 I met a delightful old vigneron in the Barossa Valley called Clarrie Kalleske, who called chenin blanc 'sherry' and semillon 'madeira', although shiraz was known as shiraz, perhaps reflecting its commercial importance. Once the varieties became paramount as labelling and marketing terms, the names Clarrie used became history.

As winegrowing expanded into the new world, varietal wines were 'created' by taking the peak of European experience and examining them in a new world light. After an early period of disorganisation, all the varieties in Australia were correctly identified by the early 1960s and a common language for describing wines, owing to the Australian wine show system, was already enshrined. This system didn't depend on the intimate knowledge of soil and vine that had determined memorable European wine up until that point. With its common language came increased scientific focus and, of course, a great degree of marketing power. It can be easily argued that the labelling of wines by varieties revolutionised the marketing of wines in general.

So the world of wine went from being described by regions without reference to variety to being described by varietal names; from where the wine came from to what is actually in the bottle; from the age-old tradition of focusing on the importance of soil and tradition to looking at the more general conditions of climate with the particularity of scientific examination. But as the saying goes, 'The more things change ...'. Nowadays, the pendulum has swung back and is sitting somewhere in the middle. We know that variety is important, and we agree that regionality is also important, and we give a big nod to the specific nature of the vineyard soil as well—terroir was back.

Battle behind the label

Varietal and regional labelling reflects two different cultures and sets of beliefs.

	Varietal	AOC* *(appellation d'origine controlée)*
Meaning	Name describes what's in the bottle	Name based on origins of the contents in the bottle
Accessibility	Easy to understand and for consumers to compare. Invokes brand values for buyer security	Hard to understand as it does not reveal the variety/varieties
Geography	The addition of geography, such as a region or a vineyard's name, is an option in the marketing	Essential knowledge of geography required to work out where it is from and what grape variety is in it
In the bottle	Quality is frequently updated by reference to wine show competitions or journalist opinions	Quality is learned through trial and error, and the result of refinement
Culture	Culture of constant improvement run by university-educated practitioners, often on large-scale holdings	Traditional culture from long-established practices and resistant-to-change small holdings

**Alsace is a notable exception having had varietal labelling since 1952*

This hybrid approach sits very well with Australian producers because grape growers are pragmatic about their endeavours—there is a long tradition of achieving success even in the face of a hostile environment. Australian farmers will use every bit of knowledge they've got in the drive to achieve a good crop.

The chaotic early importation of grape varieties to Australia have been followed by the long refinements of agricultural capitalism, producing winners and losers in the race for climatic and market acceptability. Original nineteenth century vine selections reflected the available wine varieties, and this was followed by a period of experimentation and regional refinement that saw shiraz gain the upper hand, linked to its amiable tolerance of a diversity of Australian conditions,

More recently, growing international awareness of wines successful in other market places has driven new varietal introductions in Australia where cabernet sauvignon, merlot, cabernet franc, among others have been attempted.

New selections of grapes reflect the fashion of the times—such is the current vogue for Italian varieties after the long ascendancy of the French. Understanding new varieties is a seriously complex business. Thankfully every generation dissects more understanding of the processes, delving deeper to unearth more of the mystery.

The remainder of this chapter gives a run-down of the important varieties grown in Australia and around the world.

Red wines and blends

For in the hand of the Lord there is a cup, and the wine is red
PSALMS 75:8

Red wines are different from white wines in that they rely on fermenting the juice with their grape skins to extract the colour, flavour and tannin.

The selection of varietal red wine flavours evident in different palates of European nations is a curiosity. Why are herbaceous, sweet red fruit and round tannins linked to France and a lean, less overt fruit with an extra note of dry tannin making for a chalky tannic finish associated with Italy?

Spanish varieties tend to be thicker textured and more tannic with a spicy edge. Their contrast with French and Italian reds is interesting, as some viticulture historians attribute grenache, tempranillo and mourvedre to Spain, where their tendency to survive heat gives these wines an aromatic black, brown and white spiciness, plenty of body and alcohol with soft, rounded tannins.

The ultimate source of the flavours in red wine is the skins, where anthocyans produced by the vine to protect the fruit from ultraviolet light are responsible for its dark colour. Tannins are also located there and can be found in the seeds and stalks. Sunlight intensity is strongly linked to latitude, so countries like Spain produce different amounts of polyphenols and tannins compared with the amounts associated with the more subtle light in France. Effects such as the length of day can be observed across Australia's latitudes and can influence, along with temperature, the different tannins of our regions. The ability of the vigneron through canopy management to control the amount of light results in a certain amount of anthocyans and tannins in turn impacting on the quality of the red wine produced.

Australia's climate creates some quirks in this area. One of the more profound is the increase in tannins as you move away from the coast. For example, you only need to taste traditional McLaren Vale or Langhorne Creek shiraz against a Barossa or Mudgee or Tahbilk shiraz to taste the higher 'extract' of tannins on the inlanders versus the softer coastal fruit profiles. So when referring to red varietal wines without doubt the place the vines are grown becomes important in understanding the taste of the product.

Regional character shows in other ways, such as in North American high-end winemaking where it pushes the envelope of alcohol tannin and intense fruitiness, while South America provides fresh, intense, fruity flavours and tannin that is easy on the gums. New Zealand has fresh bright fruit wrapped in medium body and intense fruit flavours. South Africa sits halfway between the new and old worlds with the medium-bodied nature of Europe and the bright fruitiness of the new world.

Palate profiles

One of the most interesting outcomes of blind tasting for me was the notion that every wine possessed a unique shape in the mouth. At one level this is blindingly obvious (forgive the pun!) though somewhat uncommented upon by generations before the 1980s, but at another level it is an additional key to accurately unlocking the characteristics of a wine. It is known as the shape of wine, and it can be mapped on a graph showing a cross-section of fruit intensity along the palate.

Example of a palate graph

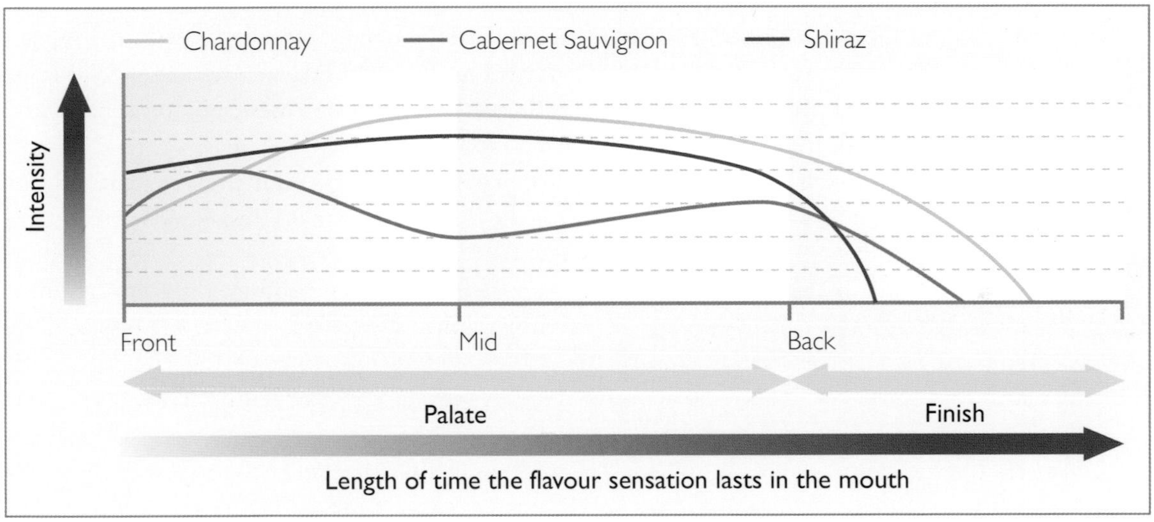

The line on the graph is the fruit profile, the way the entire length of flavour and texture unfolds on your tongue, with its characteristic shape due to variable textural elements in a wine. The length is the duration of the flavour. The finish reflects the texture and fruit at the end of the mouth, the taste you are left with after swallowing. The shape is the overall perception of line, length and finish. A similar graph is given for each main wine variety discussed in this chapter (see Chapter 4 for more information on tasting).

SHIRAZ

Shiraz has great style. It is like a great actress; able to perform on different stages in different roles and still call them all her own

ROB GIBSON, WINEMAKER

Recent DNA tests pinpointed the birth of shiraz to be around 2000 years ago in the Rhône Valley.

Shiraz is understood to be a cross between the now obscure white mondeuse blanche and the extinct dureza. It had limited planting in France, so Australia largely had the variety to itself until France reappraised it and recently planted huge volumes.

Is there any place in Australia that can't grow shiraz? Certainly there are exceptions but shiraz has shown magnificent ability to adapt to the needs of the industry and the dry, warm Australian climate to consistently produce a distinctive big burst of recognisable flavour wherever it is grown. Australian shiraz delivers like a fast bowler in their prime with line, length and finish.

The lines of shiraz are well defined with structured abundant fruit flavours, not jammy, that continue evenly along the palate. Length of flavour is critical as the trend to use softer tannins and higher alcohol has given us plump flavours that can struggle to find length and finish past the middle of the tongue. Great shiraz delivers length of fruit and tannin on finish that allows you to enjoy the wine for minutes after swallowing.

Shiraz palate graph

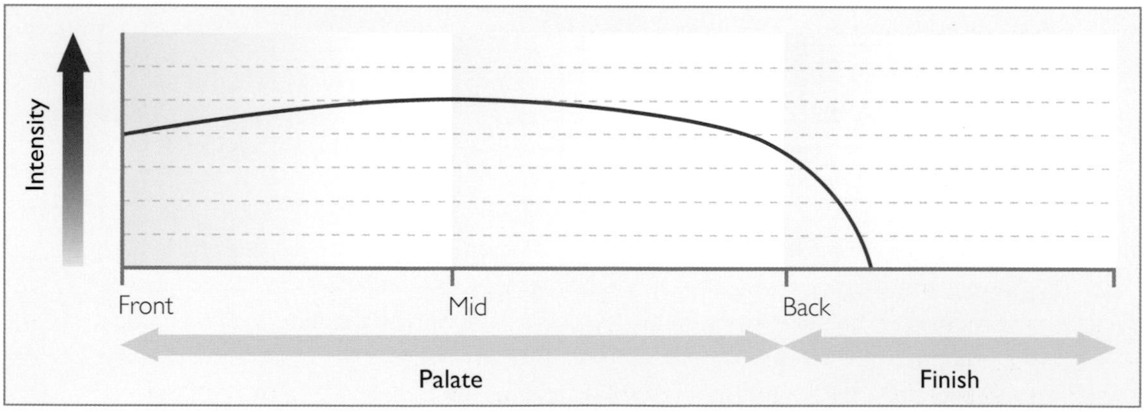

Shiraz characteristics

Scents

spices, particularly brown cinnamon, clove and nutmeg • pepper, both white and freshly ground black • mint • eucalypt • blackberry • dark cherry • chocolate, including dark • mocha and coffee notes from oak

Flavours

fruit cake • fruit cordial • blackberry • peppery • meaty • beef stock • black olive

Regions

Barossa Valley • McLaren Vale • Clare Valley • Coonawarra • Hunter Valley • Mudgee • Great Western • Yarra Valley • Heathcote • Great Southern • Margaret River • Mt Barker

Shiraz regions

Such is the sweep of shiraz that fashion has always taken a role in its identity. First it was seen as a variety for fortification but now its identity has become increasingly attached to a number of cool climate regions and old vine releases. Shiraz is being refined by new regional climatic factions, as cooler regions of Australia push for attention against the warmer climates and traditional styles. Winemakers in traditional regions are chasing the dragon of fashion with ever higher alcohol content, and oakier wines with lower than normal acidity—but such fantastic expressions of youthful exuberance results in shiraz wines that have no future in the cellar.

Shiraz has a long history and strong regional characters, making a regional tour worthwhile to explore the nuances of this great grape and its memorable wines, starting in the Clare Valley where it can offer powerful, rich and generous wines. The best shiraz avoids the heaviness and high alcohol of other South Australian regions, while having red berry freshness and finesse with a cracked pepper overlay. The angular tannins may need time to bring out their best.

Some of the scattered shiraz vineyards near the Barossa Valley are the world's oldest, dating back to 1843. These 'centurion' vineyards give room for some real 'old vine' expressions based on yields of 500 to 1000 kilograms per acre, instead of a modern 3000 to 4000 kilograms. The vines would have been generous croppers in their youth as they were planted on the richest soils with great water-holding capacity suited to the demand of the times for fortified shiraz.

Luckily, producing tiny crops of concentrated berries is now in tune with those table-wine winemakers able to source them. Local Barossa vigneron and winemaker Rob Gibson suggests quality with age is linked to old shiraz vine roots—having had time to explore pockets of deep soil—and their complex flavours are a response to the differences in mineral content of this zone.

Thankfully the culture of the Barossa is resistant to change. These people know from family stories and experience handed down from one generation to another how hard it is to plant a vineyard by horse and hand. Their respect for vine age is reflected in their respect for those who came before.

As it turns out this knowledge and respect was tested and found to be worth more to some than the cash lure of the South Australian Government vine pull scheme. The scheme, meant to reduce a grape surplus in the 1980s by pulling out vines, sadly saw many of the low-cropping old vines removed and replaced by high-cropping vineyards— the very thing it was meant to stop! Those grape growers who could not shake their sentimental respect for their family and waved aside the government dollars now own the oldest group of producing vines in Australia.

Such continuity of culture finds other expressions such as from Peter Lehmann in the 1960s. His association through Stoneyfell winery linked him to over a century of Barossa winemaking and maintaining a traditional style of blending shiraz with 7 to 40 per cent of a white variety the locals call 'tokay', which we now know as muscadelle (a Bordeaux white variety). Peter, mindful of the excesses of shiraz, was chasing and taming the richly flavoured shiraz, lifting fruit aromas and providing more suppleness to the palate. He is known for individual style and character and this wine typifies the originality and character of the man. It's a regional classic that has been revived by his company.

The 1980s saw an Australian fashion for cabernet sauvignon and 'balance' based on early picking and leaner styles that did not sit well with shiraz or the Barossa set, who had created their own distinctive approach. The Barossa theme is a classic rich-style ripe plum and chocolate fruit, a little spice with a petroleum tang (to me) and soft but abundant tannins that show considerable vintage variation. Fruit in the right wineries makes lovely long-lived wines that need not cost a fortune.

The last decade has seen improvements in viticulture and winemaking leading to discernible differences in the southern, middle and northern parts of the Barossa Valley. The wetter Williamstown in the south delivers restraint; moving to the middle the wines show a chocolaty richness. Northern Barossa around Greenock, with its red soils fading to sand in the east, old vines and family lineages, has become an important source of supple and opulently structured shiraz that is powerful with appealing liquorice and sweet fruit flavours, plus lush silky tannins. A truly great example of this region's fruit is Penfolds RWT, created during John Duval's tenure. A great wine if you were to start a collection of shiraz that you can drink from day one or age for a decade or two, it's Barossa shiraz at another level of refinement and points the way for the district.

Eden Valley is home to the wonderful Henschke story and the extraordinary Hill of Grace shiraz vineyard planted in 1860. Here, more perfume and spices enter the picture with more tightly knit raspberry, blackberry and blueberry. There are other vineyards scattered in this area, including Chris Ringland's ancient vines that produce the opposite style, extraordinary lush flavours and pushing 16 per cent alcohol to the refined Hill of Grace with its relatively gentle 13.5 per cent.

The Adelaide Hills are a variable area for shiraz. The southern Kuipto end is about three weeks later in ripening than McLaren Vale and about 2.5°C cooler and wetter, thus giving spicy flavours. The coolest areas around Lenswood are only 1°C cooler again yet they can't ripen shiraz grapes. The region's lower and warmer areas can balance the warmer textures of shiraz with the cooler red fruits and black spices with surprising regularity.

One of the most interesting places is Kangaroo Island, producing wines of great style, medium-bodied and tighter than their mainland friends. The region is light on soil and rainfall but is powerfully cooled and influenced by the Great Southern Ocean. With fledgling quality yet remarkably delicious cranberry fruit and refined flavour, it's still at kindergarten stage but learning.

McLaren Vale on the Fleurieu Peninsula south of Adelaide has a telltale streak of dark chocolate delivered with a fragrant purity of sweet soft juicy blackberry fruit, which Philip Shaw artfully used to drive the American desire for Rosemount shiraz. McLaren Vale has regional flavours within the district, with more spice and a lighter body at the eastern Blewitt Springs' end, while the western ridge-line facing the sea produces the best fruit clarity and density. Not unlike the Barossa it's the extra notes of fruit purity that distinguishes it from other Australian shiraz.

The shores of Lake Alexander offer at once an alluvial plain and a massive cooling effect that tempers the region, producing tender soft-hearted shiraz that reached its distinctive ultimate purpose in the hands of John Glaetzer at Wolf Blass. Soft and easy, young yet possessing a fruit flavour that endures 20 years, these are perhaps the slinkiest of the South Australian shiraz types. The area has over 6000 hectares under vine and it's South Australia's second largest area after the Riverland.

Padthaway is further south and can show wines so full of fruit that you wonder if you're not drinking an alcoholic cherry ripe from the most high-spirited producers. The fruit has an intensity and brightness that ages well.

More southerly again is Coonawarra with a long track record of shiraz. Leather boot polish and spiciness is a feature. Lighter than most South Australian shiraz, the structure is the key, although the palate lacks the obvious plumpness of the warmer northern neighbours. Having tasted wines back to 1949 on several occasions one can only marvel at the philosophy of the older wines: 'If it's 11 per cent then it's ripe' was the thinking; unheard of today. With no sprays they were driven by fear of rain on the thin-skinned grapes during the Coonawarra autumn. This led them to harvest at quite low alcohol levels in the vicinity of 12 per cent with remarkable acidity. Balanced with quite short maceration times on the skins, this gave them delicate savoury styles that could age well. The arrival of effective sprays started the trend towards high alcohol by allowing vignerons to push back the harvest date to create additional ripeness.

Southern Western Australia is looking interesting for shiraz, not as mouthfilling as South Australia but the wines are very approachable, raspberry and spice when young with a refreshing structure. There are more red berries and cracked pepper, which replace the savoury earthiness of South Australia. Moving north, Margaret River is the most elegant, while the Swan near Perth is capable of blockbuster intensity and chocolaty richness.

Crossing the country to the south-west of Victoria, the Grampians–Great Western is a striking region for shiraz and home to the finest sparkling shiraz in Australia. A long knowledge of the region's vineyards and a series of great winemakers created a track record. Some recent talented winemaking has brought into the limelight a floral lift in the spicy, fresh style. Enormously long-lived, these shiraz have more richness and fruit complexity, with a cool climate structure, lovely texture and a little less power than the South Australian heartlands of the Barossa and McLaren Vale.

Bendigo in central Victoria produces wine with stunning power and intense pepper and spice—a theme started in Great Western—lashed together with more powerful berry fruit concentration and a solid acidity that varies from the restrained Pyrenees to the more intense Bendigo juiciness. Sunbury near Melbourne produces shiraz with compact body and raspberry to white pepper. These wine hold sway with an elegant pepper that charms and continually persuades like the glamour of an old Hollywood actor.

Heathcote, an hour north of Melbourne, has all of us running to understand its wines at the moment, with their charismatic sumptuous early wines packed with a collection of spice and intense berry fruit, though with a high alcoholic price. A work in progress, the sites will really matter here and some vignerons are planting with east–west row orientation to avoid direct sunlight and reducing alcohol accordingly; with less sugar, ripe and more flavourful grapes are harvested.

The old timers could tell the taste of central Victoria's Goulburn Valley shiraz by its tannins. When their South Australian-tuned palates hit a little bit of firmness on the finish they would go straight to Victoria's oldest shiraz region. The fruit is more tree fruits, such as plums, and the tannins of the greatest old vine offerings need a lot of time to lose their drag on the back of your tongue.

The Yarra Valley is a patchwork of river valleys each offering their own nuances. To me the recent work done by De Bortoli syrah—syrah is the French word for shiraz—shows exceptional promise, as it contains the alcohol and ratchets up the fruit and tannin elegance, yet gives nothing away in terms of varietal charm and character. Only the warmest sites work.

The Hunter Valley's abilities with shiraz stem from a much earlier time. The northern Hunter was home to Rosemount's white wine vineyards, which did not release a shiraz from the region under their label in over 20 years. The patchwork quilt of red soil vineyards around Cessnock offered interest and excitement to those tired of the flesh and

SHIRAZ GRAPES

force of the current fashion of shiraz. Here medium-bodied, elegant style prevails with rustic flavours of cut tobacco, roasted coffee beans, soy sauce, dusty earth with dark tree-fruit flavours, rising to red berry fruit in the best years. When it's right it's sublime, and to me one of the most rewarding wines.

The Hunter region has more moods than the sea. Depth of colour is a reliable guide to red wine, but don't be deceived as these medium-bodied wines may be lighter but not less interesting. When it comes to the great years, the wine is wrapped with fruit sweetness and is a velvety medium- to full-bodied textured style of such appeal that when it's good there is little to compare it with, although too much oak is a crushing companion to such refined fruit and flavours. The idea of vintage variation is beginning to sit with the broader Australian drinker and the Hunter will benefit from this as the years do show variety.

If the Hunter is slinky then Mudgee carries itself with a lot more solid density of texture and silty tannic power, with its intense blackberry fruit sweetness and concentration. Mudgee and the Hunter Valley make a wonderful comparison as they are virtually on the same latitude. But the Hunter's cloudy afternoons combined with low altitudes reduce the amount of direct sunlight on the vines, and as a consequence reduce the amount of colour in its shiraz.

Mudgee's higher altitude location, cloudless afternoons and red soils assist in lighting, warming and reflecting heat, which results in massive extra colour and tannin in their shiraz. The drier, inland climate also means that Mudgee gets better ripeness than the Hunter, while the cooler temperatures help trap acidity as well.

Orange can produce appealing shiraz with perfume and medium-bodied supple palates. The region covers considerable variation in altitude and the higher sites create spicy shiraz that sits well with viognier, while at the lower slopes—around 600 metres—the fruit carries itself without viognier.

Canberra stands for something special where shiraz is concerned; however, the most convincing wines are blended with viognier. There is spice and a slippery texture and huge intensity of seductive red fruits on the palate. These are balanced by a little stalk tannin to make a wine that I am often surprised is not more popular or widely regarded. It's a superb 'drink now' style that can age well.

New Zealand is the most surprising region for shiraz. To date the Gimblett gravels (part of Hawkes Bay on the North Island) are showing best, but look out Australia—this variety has potential for its ability to give cracked black pepper and an earthiness from its cool climate heritage. Then it's the black cherry fruit and sumptuous silky smooth slip of the silky tannins that glide along to give length and harmony to the effusive fruit.

The future for shiraz

Australia is now so associated with shiraz in the international markets that we should be moving to make this variety our own through the education of our customers about regions, vine age and winemaking expertise.

There is a healthy diversity in shiraz styles for drinkers, owing to the variety being grown in different climates, despite some winemakers pushing the envelope on alcohol content. When the alcohol is controlled, and depending on the year, shiraz offers full-bodied, supple textures and deep flavours with forward blackberry fruit and spicy savoury characters coming in behind. The general trend in recent vintages is towards riper, rounder, juicier fruit flavours, driven in part by overseas critics.

Currently excesses in oak, alcohol and tannin are inflaming some critics but these robust, powerfully structured wines do have a proven track record, although not at the same alcohol levels as modern editions. The arrival of new oak barrels started in the 1950s with Grange, reaching a flood in the 1970s and 1980s, but has since abated.

The increase in ripeness that accompanied the use of new oak was the death knell for the gentle, older style wines. Grapes are now being picked riper and are therefore capable of being made oakier, creating more sensational flavours. While generally regarded as lifting the overall quality of our wines, oak maturation builds complexity and stability in red wines. But the price of having sufficient tannins and fruit to withstand the rigours of the process is that both build bigger wines and move the public away from these traditional styles.

Better vineyard technology, such as the use of bird nets to allow grapes to hang safely past their traditional harvest date without fear of being eaten, has played a part in the changes. A number of producers are working on making spicier, less alcoholic wines with fresher fruit, and more detail in the fruit flavour and structure.

Chasing more fruit freshness, more spice, less oak and jamminess, and avoiding the variety's alcoholic personality (keeping it 14 per cent or under) is the direction of most cutting-edge producers, who are resisting the low-acid, high-alcohol raisiny and pruney styles.

Alcohol up to 14 per cent has become more fashionable in cooler regions bringing an exotic spectrum of flavours with distinct spice. Less oak flavour and more neutral old oak for maturation will be the future.

Australian shiraz is extremely special and undervalued. Although diverse in its regions and styles this is the grape that sings the song of Australian regions' best. It seems to me, in comparing wines that will age for 20 or more years and the prices of wines from Europe with similar potential, that we are producing wines of exceptional value, interest and style.

Shiraz blends

Shiraz cabernet

Originally blends were based on plumping up the leaner and rarer cabernet with shiraz richness to give better complexity and texture. A sense of outrage permeates discussion of this style in some quarters but I defy anyone to taste 2002 St Henri and not be impressed.

The Northern Hemisphere claims that Bordeaux and Hermitage should not meet (in other words, cabernet sauvignon should not be touched by shiraz) fly in the face of Bordeaux history, where shiraz would make an appearance in lighter years to give wines suitable for the English trade.

Memorable blends and regions include:

- Penfolds St Henri
- Penfolds Bin 389
- Coriole Redstone Shiraz Cabernet
- Tyrells Hunter Shiraz and Coonawarra or Mudgee cabernet blends

Worth considering:

- De Bortoli Sacred Hill for value and consistency
- Jacobs Creek

Grenache shiraz mourvedre or mataro

This blend uses shiraz to add structure; the almost wantonly alcoholic grenache and mataro put the finish to the wine with its firm tannins making for a complete style that can be drunk on the day it's sold.

Shiraz viognier

This traditional Rhône blend has been greeted with enthusiasm by winemakers but the market place has been more muted. A classic when done well, it's been the subject of intense experimentation as the viognier vineyards mature. Viognier's abilities go beyond its ability to lift colour, aroma, flavour, texture and finish.

With the exception of cooler climate shiraz, viognier's intensity is unwarranted in many traditional regional shiraz styles. Adding more to them is almost committing a felony as they are already bursting at the seams with flavour.

You have only so many bottles in your life, never drink a bad one

LEN EVANS, PIONEER WINEMAKER (1931–2006)

MERLOT

Merlot is the most difficult variety to grow, and make.
It is unforgiving in the vineyard

PHILIP SHAW, WINEMAKER

Everybody has a responsibility to live up to their talent. Merlot is a medium-sized, casual individual who bumps into people when squeezing through a crowd; noticeably apathetic, struggling through the masses and finding it hard to find its own way, unchecked by the crowd's flow.

But to many wine people, merlot is cabernet's little sister—and the 2004 film *Sideways* didn't help. Miles' words, 'If anyone orders merlot, I am leaving. I am not drinking any fucking merlot', were no sooner uttered and US merlot sales went into a tailspin; while sales of pinot noir, following the advice of the movie, climbed furiously. Curiously, the United States is the only market where this has happened, despite the movie selling well around the world. *Sideways* leaves many of us wondering what the next cultural incursion from the media will do—boost pinot noir or a Paris pink rosé? Popularise the wines we know now or introduce more?

The infamy that can surround this great grape is rooted in the new world where it requires very careful vineyard selection. According to its habit, it tends to overcrop with big berries that do not deliver rich colours and flavours; even if the fruit is balanced in the vineyard the winemaker must still tread a wary line between tannin and overextraction.

Despite merlot being one of the truly great grape varieties, it can make a very ordinary, rather soft and featureless wine. Large merlot tastings with prices ranging from $13 to $40 can leave you utterly underwhelmed. But there are a few high-quality specimens that may induce in you a cheerful frame of mind. I do sound a note of optimism here, for several producers are making a go of the variety.

Merlot is an early drinking wine with soft tannins, which is one reason Americans prefer drinking it. This wine doesn't have to be cellared and aged like cabernet. Early merlot, when you find a good one, can be delightful with less tannin, fleshier, thanks to its soft texture, and more suppleness and brighter fruit than early cabernet. Great merlot is not deeply coloured, has a fragrance of ripe raspberry fruit with side notes of almost leather to tobacco, but is capable of juicy fruit, mouthfilling, middle-palate richness, and sometimes lusciousness, with silky velvet tannin textures lingering on the finish.

On the palate you get ripe flavours, not jammy. Texture is really important with a great merlot—it should be supple and long without abruptness, and have nice silky tannins. Merlot often end up as wines that have front *or* finish. It's unusual to have a merlot that flows from front to back and is complete the whole way through; and for this reason it sits well as a component in blending. A palate graph of fruit intensity here is purely indicative as the variety invariably has either the front or the back palate for intensity but very rarely both.

What would a good three-year-old merlot look like? You would find a bright, purple–red colour. It wouldn't be as deep a colour as shiraz, and a little bit lighter again than cabernet. So a medium depth of colour. You would hope that the bouquet would be redolent of sweet, small berry fruit—mulberry—maybe not as much fruit as cabernet and shiraz, but more than pinot noir. You would also hope that there was a trace of cabernet scent as well as an edge of the environment in which it is grown—a little bit of the cedar of Bordeaux, the olive of California, the savoury notes of the Yarra Valley, or the sweet mulberry ripe fruit of Orange. The luxury of great merlot makes it worth the search.

Merlot palate graph

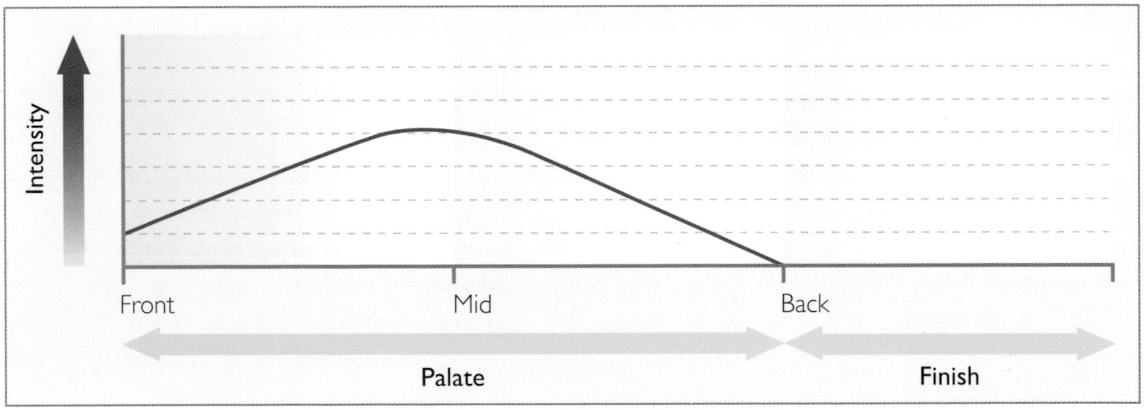

Merlot characteristics

Scents

herbaceous • aromas of ripe small red fruits • muscatels • roses • sappy • coffee • mocha

Flavours

plum • fruit cake • mulberry • blackberry • blackcurrant • rhubarb • herbal • tobacco

Regions

Canberra • Adelaide Hills • Orange • south-west Western Australia • Great Southern

Merlot regions

Merlot doesn't have a long track record in Australia. By far the greatest percentage of vines are under 20 years old and many of the best clones are only just coming into production. Merlot is both a grower and a winemaker's wine. Just like pinot noir, it needs careful handling and it is most important to identify the winemakers who can manage it for you to find memorable merlot wines.

Sensitive to water and temperature stress, merlot needs to be grown in areas where the soils via their clay content have high water-holding capacity to support its weak root system. It requires plenty of sunshine without too much heat. These are the sensitivities that make it a fickle friend to vignerons who will refine the regions where it is grown.

For terroir reasons the finest regions to date come from Bordeaux, Piedmonte, and the Tesserat region around Lake Lugarno in Switzerland. Australian vignerons will tell you that it works well in France and French vignerons will tell you that it works best in Switzerland and northern Italy, so it's not a variety that's easily transported.

In Australia, Coonawarra, Petaluma and the Hunter Valley-based Peppertree are doing worthwhile wines, while Jim Irvine is making headway in the Adelaide Hills. Two-time winemaker of the year Philip Shaw and Printhie are demonstrating that the new clones of merlot work well in Orange where the variety receives a lot of necessary sunlight but little heat. Margaret River is capable of producing serious merlot—though many of the growers prefer to blend with cabernet—and the further south you go the better merlot gets, especially around Ferngrove and the Frankland River.

Bordeaux in France uses merlot extensively from both sides of the river and the quality can range from workhorse to magnificent. Ripening earlier than cabernet in Bordeaux, it is also less tannic and requires less ageing or maturation. In Bordeaux it needs 20 per cent cabernet franc to make a complete wine except in the most blessed sites. There, merlot has an amazing ability to wrap its sweet, velvet cloak around members of the cabernet family, particularly cabernet sauvignon and franc. It ages quicker than cabernet or shiraz in the bottle at the memorable wine level.

The most extraordinary and expensive merlots come from Pommerol. Château Petrus and Le Pin in Pomerol are my most famous merlots, richly flavoured and sumptuously textured wines with silky tannins and plenty of flavour.

On the same elevated plain as Pomerol, though with different soils that host both merlot and cabernet franc blends, are Château Ausone, Château Cheval Blanc and Château Figeac which have set the world gold standard for these blends. The French have also adapted it to the soils of St Emilion to great effect, and the cool climate of south-west France through to Italy makes a happy home for the variety.

Hawkes Bay, Gisborne and Waihiki Island in New Zealand all produce merlot with class. We can expect plantings to increase there and the results to keep improving fast, as the cool island maritime autumn weather suits merlot's ripening patterns more than cabernet, although finding the right soil is tricky.

Chile produces huge amounts of merlot and it gives good affordable wines with strong upfront varietal personalities. An enormous amount of merlot is grown in California (and an enormous amount is about to be ripped up). Merlot finds a special place in California when handled with kid gloves, such as on the superstar Dominus property.

The future for merlot

Merlot's future is good on account of the new clones with exotic rose-like perfumes, which will keep the doors open for this variety. Aside from finding the right regions for it to grow in—merlot is a capricious grape to grow, but New Zealand and Orange are promising areas—the blends are where it's at.

Can it recover from its crippled reputation as a single variety thanks to *Sideways*? The answer lies in renewing its reputation with better quality wines in larger volumes, which in turn requires someone to take the risk of planting it in an appropriate climate. Not exactly an A-class investment but no doubt this silky siren will lure some growers to try as there is an international quality benchmark. While there's life there's hope, according to a grim view in the Australian industry.

Wines such as the 1990 Petaluma Coonawarra Merlot, Peppertree Coonawarra 1996, Larkhill Exaltation 2002 from Canberra, and Irvine Adelaide Hills, indicate that we can make merlot wines with potential. We have the regions that can grow it if the viticulture is precise and orderly.

It's still early days for merlot and the additional soil and climatic requirements for this variety make it a daunting task but we are getting there with a very steep hill to climb.

Merlot blends

Merlot finds a sexy partner in sangiovese grapes. This combination really hits its height in Italy although even the Hunter Valley has shown some promise in this partnership. Space availability precludes a more thorough discussion. Merlot's great partner is cabernet sauvignon for additional length and structure and cabernet franc for breadth and depth of structure and flavour. Starting in Bordeaux these blends have travelled the world.

CABERNET SAUVIGNON

You never get a headache drinking 20-year-old wine
HUGO ROSE MW, *on visiting Bordeaux*

Cabernet sauvignon is a tall, well-dressed individual squeezing through a crowd; noticeably elegant, rising above the masses and finding its own way, unchecked by the crowd's flow.

According to scientists unravelling its DNA, sauvignon blanc and cabernet franc got into bed one morning and gave birth to cabernet sauvignon, either from fertilised seeds or a spontaneous mutation. It gets its colour from the franc and the herbal edge from the sauvignon. Others hold that it is an extremely ancient vine local to Bordeaux—the Bordelaise group cabernet sauvignon, cabernet franc, petit verdot and carmeniere are in the same ancient vine family—that became better recognised as a distinct variety when viticulture improved in the seventeenth and eighteenth centuries. It must have had a lot of impact because the growers picked it up very quickly.

Given that it is the relatively recent love child of that promiscuous couple in the hallowed fields of Bordeaux, the oldest known cabernet vines in the world are, surprisingly, in the Barossa Valley, in the Penfolds' Kalimna vineyard near Greenock. This variety takes a lot to grow, make, mature and understand. It is rather more prissy than its supposed parents, it needs kissing and cuddling. It doesn't respond well to the dubious excitement of rough trade; unlike the more trusting shiraz or minxy pinot noir, cabernet sauvignon can't take any insouciance in the way in which it is treated.

Careless planting doesn't work well with cabernet sauvignon. Unlike the more robust shiraz, it is a shy and retiring type—aloof, let's say. It needs work to pull out its personality. The vine thrives on well-drained soils and grows best with a combination of warm days and cool night air, which means it is often found in proximity to the coast. Too hot and body and flavour are lost, replaced with a rich dry red wine of modest varietal personality. It hates overcropping and cannot easily be pushed to high tonnages for affordable priced wine.

Cabernet sauvignon vines produce small berries with thick skins, and seeds that contribute tannin. The challenge with a cooler climate is that cabernet definitely needs a suitable level of ripeness with fruit freshness. It needs extended warmth and can't tolerate heat spikes like shiraz. Nowadays, we know that it's not just a question of the fruit being ripe when it is picked, it's the seeds and the tannins that surround them that need to be ripe. The danger is that, with insufficient sunlight, the seeds and the tannins around them remain green and astringent. Seeds need to be brown; if they are green, then there will be problems in the way the wine tastes and matures. An early indicator of greenness is an excessive mint-leaf aroma, as it indicates a cooler year where cabernet fails to achieve full ripeness. So at harvest time, you'll see vignerons walking through these vines, pulling off grapes and inspecting the colour of the seeds and the colour of the stalk attached to the individual grapes on the bunch, as well as chewing down hard on the skins. Assessing ripeness is really important because you can't put the grapes back on the vine after you've harvested. It is almost an obsession with some vignerons to avoid any trace of greenness.

Tannins in cabernet sauvignon respond very well to cool climates, in part because of the sun's effect at lower latitudes. If you were looking at Earth from space you would see that the sun strikes the southerly and northerly latitudes at an angle that gives them much longer afternoons. These long afternoons, often characterised by warm sun and cool air, provide the heat required for the tannins in the grape seed to catch up with sugar and flavours that come with bright sunshine. Maximising on the aspect of sunlight is critical to cabernet, and the world's finest wines have come from small manicured vines on well-drained vineyard sites, with small crops, plucked and trimmed to allow light down into the vine's canopy.

Tasting young cabernet wine is a special talent; more so than other varieties given its tannin and acid structure. With food this wine will be more pleasurable than tasted on its own. Cabernet from Australia shows a crunchy, berry fruit style with a degree of fruit–acid separation, while the French show more acid–fruit integration wrapped in tannins that need time to settle.

Cabernet sauvignon can deliver a 'doughnut' texture, a hollow mid-palate. For this reason it is blended with merlot or cabernet franc, and to a lesser degree malbec and petit verdot. The resulting creation, with a seamless long palate showing silky tannins and a rounded palate with no one variety dominating, can carry substantial tannins and structure and is one of the delights of wine.

Cabernets should ideally have a fine flavour balance between berries and herbs, or leaves, with a structure that sits on the lean side of full but is even and capable of great length and compact structure, thus treading the finest line between tightness and fruit sweetness. And they should have a bit of age on them. In a nutshell, expect a mixture of berries and herbs with blackcurrants, cedar, and soft, red berry fruits lifted by a trace of something leafy and herbal. If the summer is too cool the flavours go all leafy, verging on asparagus in extreme cases.

Great cabernet sauvignon is rich in colour and aroma and has line and length and depth of flavour with an ability to take its unique set of flavours around the world and still show its personality.

Cabernet sauvignon palate graph

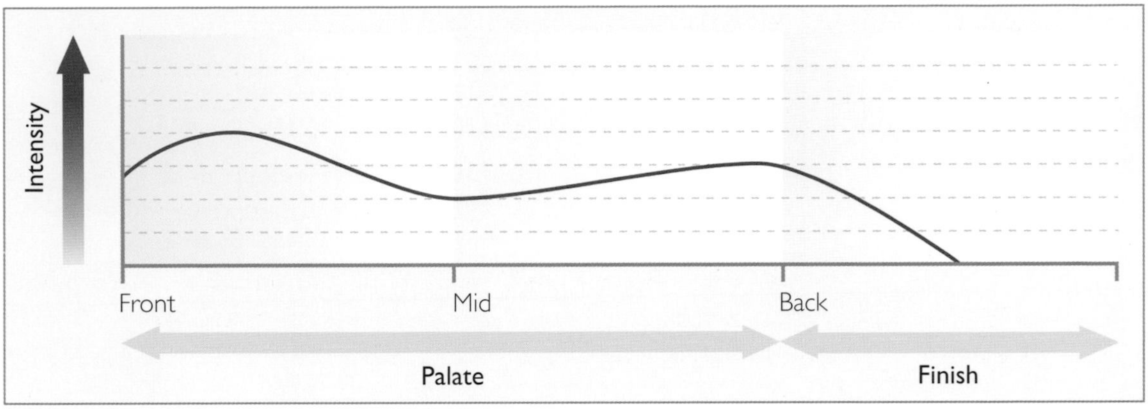

Cabernet sauvignon characteristics

Scents

redcurrants • blueberries • capsicum • mint • eucalypt • chocolate • blackberry • mulberry • tobacco • leafy • grassy

Flavours

cassis–blackcurrant • eucalypt • mint • slowly cooking blackcurrants

Regions

Coonawarra • Margaret River • McLaren Vale • Wrattonbully • Great Southern • Yarra Valley • Hunter Valley

Cabernet sauvignon regions

To understand the challenge of cabernet it is necessary to understand something of the different pressures of producing wine in a cold climate as opposed to a warm climate. Warm climates are more generous in producing flavour, reducing acid and invoking a great richness of tannins. The spectrum for acceptable winemaking is quite generous.

Cooler climate wines are more delicately balanced and reveal more about the growing and winemaking. They have a much tighter acceptable spectrum of both growing and ripening temperatures to capture the varietal expression and allow winemakers to balance flavour, acid and tannins.

Overcropping or cool summers in cool areas produce green flavours and rough textures; yet done correctly, when the fruit ripens in cool climates it gives the most regional and varietal character, as well as the best flavour, colour and silky tannins.

CVP 973

Winemaking too plays a role and Australia is moving from a period of seeking high colour and flavour, where they overlooked fruit tannins and used oak to fill out the structure. With greater recognition of the need for ripe, structured tannins the role of the vineyard has slowly turned since the late 1990s towards more precise viticulture to produce better flavoured fruit and tannins in the vineyard. Australia can produce and deal with this grape really well but currently we are in a bit of a slump. It's underperforming.

French cabernets tend to show a firmer, dry tannin structure with power and the ability to age than those from Australia's top regions, such as Coonawarra, where the cabernet can be low in tannin, struggling for structure, mulberry in youth, milk chocolaty with age and quite dark in colour (charming, nevertheless). The French wines tend to have less fruit and need a mouthful of food to bring them to their best—they are definitely best drunk with a meal—whereas softer, silkier, lightly cassis Aussie cabernets can be drunk more or less happily on their own. They age surprisingly (and for a long time if they come from Coonawarra), but many do not have the tannin complexity or length of the French.

If Coonawarra is the Australian heart of cabernet, the bush vines of block 42, planted in 1888 at Kalimna in the Barossa, hold its DNA. Cabernet had a slow start in Australia. In the 1950s, there were only four acres of cabernet in the Coonawarra, which was then the largest planting in the Southern Hemisphere.

In 1954, Wynns made their first Coonawarra Cabernet from those vines so, historically, those four acres are very important as the beginning of the longest running varietal cabernet wine in Australia. Large-scale cabernet plantings were a 1960s' introduction. Their history is a lovely story that is worth following up, and recently made glorious by the appointment of Sue Hodder as winemaker. She has lifted the overall quality of the cabernet to totally delicious.

One winemaker who has done a lot for cabernet is Brian Croser. He understands the fanatical attention to detail, the long-term dedication in the vineyard and the necessity for serious focus. He is possibly best known for his whites but his legacy with Petaluma Coonawarra is marvellous. I remember visiting him in the early 1980s when he was conducting his own early morning retasting: a long line-up of First Growth cabernet blends and probing how the French achieved their long, tannic back palates. He was applying enormous focus and concentration to do that. I was impressed.

Domaine A–Stoney Vineyard in Tasmania is another terrific producer. I remember a wine tasting in 2001 when they put their 1992 cabernet sauvignon up against a 1991 Château Latour. It held up very, very well. Only a brave vigneron would pit his wine against Château Latour.

Margaret River's ability with old vines to achieve intense flavours, fine tannins and elegant structures has elevated this region above Coonawarra in my mind. On one side the region gives more varietal character to cabernet and much finer denser tannins, requiring merlot to soften as a bottle partner to produce the most seamless and complex wines. Margaret River's intensely varietal wines need blending with merlot to achieve complexity and drinkability, and the region is capable of stern tannins and strength of cabernet character.

McLaren Vale grows cabernet and the wines are always more like a blend than a single variety, such is the warm stamp of regionality on this variety. Blending works to produce bold flavoured, looser-knit, soft reds that drink well on release but lack the finesse and varietal intensity of the cooler regions.

Wrattonbully is about 20 kilometres north of Coonawarra and benefits from the cooling effects of the Southern Ocean and shares the same red terra rossa soils over limestone. Brian Croser's Tapanapa (an Aboriginal word for 'stick to the path') wines give an indication of the greatness within, as Brian also achieved in Coonawarra thanks to his exacting standards.

Great Southern (comprising the Frankland River, Albany and Mt Barker regions) has shown that the Frankland area in particular can hit the cabernet nail on the head with ease. Blackcurrant fruit, sweet but with a tight medium-bodied structure, these wines are in their early days but show enormous potential. Malbec has also shown similar prospects there.

Yarra Valley cabernet in the hands of a few producers making very traditional styles shows great potential and there is no doubt an enormous opportunity to follow the pioneers at Mt Mary and Yarra Yerring to greatness. The question is who is there outside the old traditionalists? The heart of the Mt Mary style is a wine similar to old-fashioned Bordeaux, light- to medium-bodied, intense flavours from ripe but not overripe fruit, refined with moderate alcohol and oak. By blending low-cropping cabernet sauvignon, merlot, cabernet franc and malbec from low fertility soils, Mt Mary demonstrates the wisdom of the Bordelaise and possibly the real future for cabernet in the Yarra. More modernist interpretations compared to other Australian regions show greater fruit density, fine, dry persistent tannins and a fresh acidity.

New South Wales seems wide open for cabernet with the modern style. The strange thing is that the right vineyard and season and the Hunter Valley can do amazing things. If I had not tasted a 2005 cabernet from non-irrigated, unfertilised 35-year-old vines from the Hunter I would have overlooked this variety. Yet there it was with the full power of the varietal aromas and a rich palate, more Coonawarra on the nose and Hilltops on the palate. Hilltops produce wines with a varietal tang and I hope refinements in winemaking will deliver a more accurate calibration to the palate in time.

Making good wine is a skill; making fine wine is an art

ROBERT MONDAVI

The future for cabernet sauvignon

A continual slow trickle of exciting cabernet sauvignon will gather force as winemakers gain more knowledge and experience of their vineyards, of flavour performance, and of which characteristics directly contribute to flavour. Today, winemakers are preoccupied with avoiding green characters and the alcohol levels have risen in line. No doubt alcohols will fall as they begin to better understand the various tipping points between green and ripe. The market currently wants softness (lower acidity) in its red wines and winemakers' understanding has increased so they can now provide more supple wines with lower acidity and understand how to get better intensity and complexity with length of flavour.

In Australia, more blending and more expensive wines may be the answer, in a nutshell. The combination of cabernet merlot is showing promise, especially in wines from the west and the malbec blends from the Clare Valley (originally made under the tutelage of Max Schubert). Yarra and Orange are looking attractive as vine age and warmer vintages deliver small red fruits and cassis aromas with good length of medium-bodied texture and ripe tannins sufficient to make delicious wines without blending.

Local wines are exceptional and I sense it's a matter of the wheel of fashion turning away from the opulent high alcohol, lush oak styles to something more refreshing, no doubt influenced by the increasing international wines crowding our market place.

Overall many Australian cabernets taste more acid than their international rivals. Our top wines have a sense of elegance and restraint that does translate into current international acceptance but it may never rival shiraz as our international star. California has won some historic victories with cabernet, such as the 'Judgment of Paris', and then rubbed salt in the wounds by repeating the performance 25 years later, rewriting history. We never had that chance and our style has evolved without interference.

The increasing density, suppleness and evenness of the best Margaret River and Coonawarra wines mean we are nipping at the heels of the lush styles of the Californians. But we do not have the lean sinewy refinement of France, or the high-cost, high-profile show ponies of both California and France. At best our wines are different in a way that is not easily recognised in current times for what we see them as.

Cabernet blends

Australia does its own unique cabernet blend with shiraz, much to the outrage of some overseas traditionalists. If you take a new world view, shiraz makes an ideal bed partner. Our historical standout blend is shiraz cabernet: lovely wines like Penfolds' St Henri, a most marvellous wine that ages beautifully. Cabernet shiraz grew out of dissatisfaction with the endemic 'doughnut' cabernet structure, a term that refers to the lack of a middle palate; the addition of shiraz to fill that hole produced a much more interesting wine.

In warmer more generous regions cabernet surrenders much of its varietal character to wear the rich body of the local climate with soft tannins only keeping subtle notes of its characteristic acidity and leafiness. Blending builds layered wines with more complexity.

In cooler regions it possesses increasingly strident blackcurrant and leafy aromas, while the fruit flavour and balance show a tight core of blackcurrant sweetness against the overall dryness. Tannins grow in firmness, definition and dryness and the palate is marked by a dry, strident complexity of tannins, acidity and closed black, leafy fruit. The sense of sweetness merlot can contribute along with additional grace (or less prosaic texture!) for the front and middle palate has aided these wines, while supple lower level tannins weave a top note against the vibrating bass that is young cabernet tannin. The earlier ripening cabernet franc is the varietal insurance policy making cooler years more perfumed and building weight and width to the palate.

Western Australian cabernets surrender nothing by the use of merlot and as other varieties, such as cabernet franc and malbec, cascade in the cabernet shifts seamlessly into a mellow wine built on the bones of vibrant cabernet but within the most memorable examples.

I see a new theme developing around the introduction of malbec on both the New Zealand east coast at Hawkes Bay and in southern Western Australia where the juiciness of malbec contributes more fleshy fruit to the bones of cabernet.

PINOT NOIR

Every now and again pinot turns in a virtuoso performance that touches all the emotions, winning new hearts and leaving her devotees yearning for more

STEVE NAUGHTON, PIONEER PINOT IMPORTER

While most varieties we accept as French are relatively easy to grow pinot noir remains above all others, for variability and consistency is not part of its name in any way except for its legendary inconsistency.

Hard to grow well, difficult to make into a good wine, and variable in its response to different seasons it's a variety where a little understanding adds to its enjoyment. In terms of biological reliability pinot noir is fickle. With this variety one is actually talking about hundreds of clones. The pinot noir grape is red and a native of the Burgundy region; and as far as we can tell, it was probably planted there before 311 AD. It is not stable and has many different clones in the vineyards of the world and several viable varieties have mutated, including Italy's pinot gris (grey), Alsace's pinot blanc (white) and Champagne's pinot meunier (red).

The version that seems to be doing very well in Australia is a clone called MV6, first identified in the Hunter Valley and probably derived from a great vineyard in Burgundy. The myriad clones or subtle mutations cause a wide variation in the leaves, growing habit, berry size, colour and range of flavour in the grapes.

Even when well grown and well made by caring vignerons, pinot noir requires lots of care and attention due to its delicate and volatile nature. It can't be overcropped and so the yields are small. The extra attention and management require a small-business model to be employed, which is why not many big wine companies produce it consistently well. Two who are trying their hardest with it currently would be De Bortoli in Australia and Montana in New Zealand.

The thing about pinot noir is that it doesn't punish your mouth. I'm drinking a lot more of it as I grow older. Compared to heavily oaked Australian shiraz, pinot is an easier drink to take. You've got to ask yourself when you are drinking a bottle of shiraz whether your mouth is enjoying it, or even your stomach, because shiraz can be heavy and hard going.

Pinot noir is subtle and nuanced. It doesn't carry a lot of tannin, which means that it doesn't taste thick in the mouth. It has sensuousness because the tannins are velvety. The sensuality is also in the perfume. Pinot has a range of lovely smells, such as raspberry, cherry and plum; and something a bit like the smell of incense in an old hippie shop—hints of cinnamon and finely polished antique furniture sort of smells. It shouldn't have any greenness or leatheriness.

Under ideal climatic conditions the low-acid pinot is the richest, smoothest, most velvety variety, but it costs a small fortune. The best have a soft set of flavours, intense complexity with some berry and forest floor. The palate will have an incomparable sense of sweetness that is at the heart of its charm.

The great pinot noirs from Burgundy should be aged but pinot noir can be drunk fleshy and young when it offers a lot of pleasure. Right now the pinots we make in Australia need to be drunk within about five years. So by the time you reach a stage when pinot noir matters to you, you will have some snow on the mountains—a little bit of grey in the hair—but you will be able to fully appreciate the delectable, complex beauty of this wine. I make the prediction that pinot noir is the next favourite wine for baby boomers based on the notion that as we get older we want less alcohol and less-rich wines. The beauty of pinot is that it delivers on those requirements while still showing some leg. Many wine writers in Australia have pushed pinot noir because they prefer it over all other styles, and with this encouragement, our winemakers are paring away the fickleness of the variety to produce some impressive examples.

The touch of super-ripe fruit spice will give you the clue that this wine will be very pleasant to drink. Like chardonnay, it should have a lovely, silky texture that fills your mouth generously.

Pinot should not be warm; it should be served at a cooler temperature—10°C to 15°C—than standard for other reds (what is that?). At over 15°C, it reacts quite adversely. Too cold and the acids stand out too much. Too hot and you lose the varietal perfume. This is a particularly important point for Australian pinots because of the habitual warmth of our climate.

The best pinot I have ever had was the Paringa Estate from the freak 2002 vintage from the Mornington Peninsula. There is no doubt that they coaxed every ounce of fresh, red fruit from the grapes while maintaining a crisp, bright character.

Pinot noir palate graph

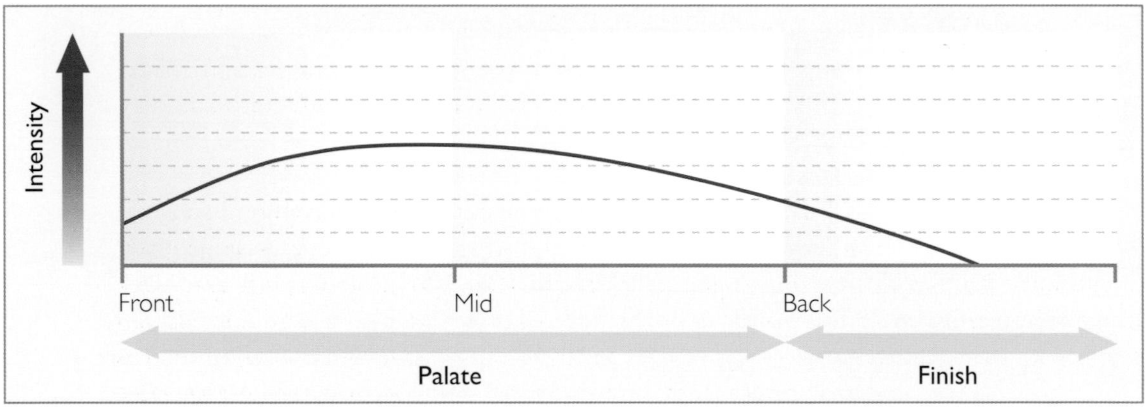

Pinot noir characteristics

Scents

herbs • spice • strawberry • red cherry • raspberry • black cherry • perfume • stewed plum • rhubarb • beetroot • generally obvious berry fruits with youth

Flavours

strawberry • red cherry • raspberry • black cherry • earthy • cow yard • gamey • mushroom • the smell of damp forest floor

Regions

Mornington Peninsula • Yarra Valley • Orange • Canberra • Central Otago (NZ) Martinborough (NZ) • Canterbury Plains (NZ) • Tasmania

Pinot noir regions

Pinot is a high-maintenance grape because it is tender and thin-skinned. Like other cold-climate grapes, it tends to show evidence of every move that the winemaker has made. So, for example, if the grapes are put into barrels that are too powerfully flavoured for a moment too long then—Bang!—you've got a problem. The wood taste just bustles through everything. So pinot grapes require very careful handling, and prefer cool climates and low crop levels. In Australia look to the Mornington Peninsula and the Yarra Valley for the best examples. As the variety develops we may see some more flashes of brilliance from Tasmania and certainly from across the pond in New Zealand, especially from the Otago region.

Steve Webber in the Yarra Valley has developed a process of handling pinot grapes which apparently replicates forms of ancient winemaking to great effect. The grapes are hand-picked and placed in little bins; the little bins are carried to the winery; the bunches are hand-sorted; and anything not good is thrown away. The berries then go into big vats after some have been de-stemmed and are fermented in these same vats, definitely not pumped around. This is an example of how much care can be taken, and allows the location of the grapes to really come through. Steve is chasing and formulating an intense expression of place that can be tasted in the wine.

New Zealand and Tasmania are both looking extremely promising. Pinot is now number three in New Zealand as the most planted variety behind sauvignon blanc and chardonnay. A number of areas shine. Martinborough with intensity, richness and power, Canterbury Plains and Central Otago on the South Island for aromatic red and black cherry flavours and enormous sweet fruit. The lesser known Waipara and Nelson, also on the South Island, have tighter and brighter fruit that appeals. Currently most pinot is coming from Marlborough, chiefly for sparkling wines but increasingly durable table wines as well. All are bright, fresh and drinkable with variable power depending on the region and vintage.

The future for pinot noir

Nothing stands still for long in the world and in particular pinot has seen considerable gains by leading producers in the past two years in Australia, and as these wines come to market there are some real treats in store for consumers.

Pinot is in a state of change driven by a new generation of producers more in touch with its thin-skinned, lightly coloured, varied, subtle perfumes and delicate mouthfeel. Most of these winemakers are no longer producing just pinot noir and most see themselves interpreting the vineyard and producing wines with a sense of 'somewhere-ness'.

The changes have come in stages but there are now a few producers with sufficient feel and understanding to seek the brighter fresher styles who have given up the Australian obsession with deep purple colour and middle-palate fullness, and replaced them with tender, more finely detailed fruit flavours and refined structures.

Replanted vineyards in the Southern Hemisphere seek the cool southern side of the hill with rows running north–south instead of east–west, and slopes are favoured as they also reduce the amount of sunlight intercepted by the vines.

Winemakers are moving to hand-harvesting and using small bins to move fruit to the winery and hand-sorting grapes on tables before de-stemming. Some producers, though, retain the stems to contribute their own textural and flavour compounds that deliver wines with more savoury texture and substance on the tongue, instead of the more mouth-coating cloak effect of oak.

Although pinot noir is a very fickle variety Australia is closing fast but then so is New Zealand. In ten years we have come from dusk to daylight with many wines up to $50 being better value and more interesting from the new world. At the highest level it is still French, but another ten years will be interesting as we resolve the strident fruit sweetness and achieve fresher, more delicately powerful styles. The Kiwis by a nose for second place for this variety.

OTHER REDS

Cabernet franc

Falling from favour for years outside its heartland in France, this varietal seems to be slowly finding a new place in the sun based on its blending ability. From regions around Chinon, Bourgueil and Saumur Champigny on the Loire and in St Emilion and Pomerol, its ability to ripen more easily than sauvignon and add less tannic, cabernet blackcurrant fruit and style has made it an important varietal.

Recent Australian blends have reduced their reliance on it but there is increased awareness of its ability to contribute something subtle and slightly softer than sauvignon, and more width to the middle palate as well. The jury is out on its role in Australia. Cabernet franc is often a lighter version of sauvignon, earthy and faster maturing and often quite an aromatic lighter touch. Exceptions are starting to appear, particularly in Hawkes Bay, New Zealand where winemakers are practising appropriate grape-growing skills.

The Loire offers the greatest range and appeal, while blending in Bordeaux also elevates this variety to greater heights than we can achieve.

Malbec

The new world is only just starting to understand this extraordinary grape. Its low acid, lush fruitiness and spice notes lift cabernet to its advantage, and it enlivens merlot, making for some exciting memories. A long-term resident of Langhorne Creek, South Australia, our best examples from Western Australia have shown that it can achieve poise and power in cooler climates. Its raspberry savouriness has been long recognised in the Clare Valley where it gives juiciness to the more austere cabernet sauvignon. Internationally it's found its feet in Argentina where some marvellous wines exist. It's a ten-year cellaring proposition from Cahors where the fruit has a particular spice note.

Malbec aromas and flavours tend towards spice, raspberry, plum and leaf. The best regions are a three-way split, with France's Cahors showing class, Argentina giving fleshy juiciness and power, and our wines with a few very notable exceptions adding juiciness and fragrance to cabernet blends.

CHAMBOURCIN *Unlike most reds this hybrid variety can survive humidity and the considerable threats of mould that render other red varieties untenable. Its toughness comes at a price and it is often described as agricultural, which means it's got heaps of colour, aroma and tannin but not much finesse. It makes a handy blender, serviceable sparkler and reaches its peak in the Shoalhaven region of New South Wales where it makes delicious rosé, ripe reds and interesting port styles.*

Petit verdot

Petit verdot's qualities are conceded even by those who can scarcely use it in Bordeaux, where its late ripening means it is rarely used except in the warmest years. In late years it adds freshness and acidity, but picked too early it is herbal and too late it gets flabby. Its decline was accelerated by modern improvements in viticulture after phylloxera.

In Bordeaux they recognise its quality and the plantings are slowly on the increase for its ability to add 'spice notes' to their wines in the manner that shiraz does in Australia. A late-ripening member of the cabernet sauvignon family with more of everything—tannin, acid, colour and flavour—yet still resembling cabernet sauvignon. When ripe petit verdot grapes are tannic, character full and may be long-lived, though they have a tendency to flabby richness if picked overripe.

Its robustness in hot climates allows petit verdot to produce intense powerful wines with fresh fruit with tight tannins and great personality. It should be better recognised by the marketplace, and its future is really in their hands. Petit verdot's quality is evident to everyone in the wine fraternity—it's the Schwarzenegger of the wine family.

Durif / Petite sirah

Most durif should come with a health warning, as this variety can hit a whopping alcohol level of 17 per cent and still taste extraordinary. An uncertain start with two names on two continents and little recognition has not blunted recent interest in this variety. Its mixed background adds fascination to this spicy character, thought to be a cross-pollination between shiraz and peloursin from a valley in the northern Rhône region.

Extended from its home in France this variety has produced interesting old-vine wines in California and especially in Rutherglen after the Morris family imported it to Australia. Old vines in the United States yield a rich, spicy red wine not unlike shiraz, while fully ripe versions retain a note of spice against massive red fruit and tannins that can age for years.

This small-berried grape gives robust dark-coloured wine short on elegance, as well as richly flavoured tannic wines, and in years gone by has been a powerful blender. This is another variety that loves heat to achieve the prerequisite high alcohols to unlock its flavours and textures. The scents and flavours are liquorice, black fruits and chocolate.

The tannins are such that in Australia they need the super ripeness of being above 15 per cent alcohol (which turns cabernet berries to raisins) to achieve the sort of soft tannic mouthfeel that counts for a ripe red. Californian examples can be less alcoholic and show tighter-grained structures with hard tannic finishes.

Renewed interest by Australia and the United States, and increased interest in spicy red wines, has given this variety a small boost. Its ability to thrive in hotter vineyard sites might offer a bigger future than it currently enjoys.

Try the Morris of Rutherglen editions as they were the first family to recognise the variety's abilities and bring it to Australia. Good examples are Morris Sparkling Durif, All Saints, Gapstead and Cofield. It is an interesting challenge as spicy varietals are coming back and the Californians know how to deal with this variety. Australia has the value-for-money category sewn up, while at the high end the Californians are doing well with more spicy complexity.

Grenache

The Billy Bunter fat fella of the grape varieties of southern Europe, grenache is a variety that likes it hot and arid. The Moors—who didn't drink—were responsible apparently for bringing it up from its native homeland in Spain to the Rhône in southern France, where it also flourished. The Rhône is a big place with 40 000 hectares of vines—though Australia has 48 000 hectares—and allows for blending with shiraz, mourvedre, cinsault and carignan to name but a few of the 24 varieties that they use. Incredibly interesting wines and history.

Rich, softly tannic, warm and sometimes too alcoholic, grenache needs its mates shiraz and mataro in Australia. Grown on low-yielding bush vines it is traditionally blended with other varieties for extraordinary examples.

A quirky sideline is the rancio style in Spain. To make this wine, the grenache grapes are picked as late and as ripe as possible. This gives an alcohol level of up to 17 per cent after fermentation, with some sugar left in it. It is then decanted into half-filled, four-litre glass jars and buried out in the paddocks and left for a summer. This treatment produces a tawny, oxidised character—it's a little like burnt orange rinds with a bit of chocolate.

Grenache is a component of Rioja along the banks of the River Ebro in northern Spain and reaches its pinnacle in Priorato, where very old vines in tough dry conditions give something special. Generally, it is not a grape variety given to self-control or self-restraint and many drinkers of the style have probably been given to similar losses of same, because the damn thing is so alcoholic that you can wind up flying on it. At its biggest, it has no finish; like Billy Bunter, it is completely round and fat and over the top. When it gets old, the crop level goes down but the vine still produces big berries.

Grenache with shiraz is a good mix. Chubby Checker in thongs meets the Big Guy in a suit. Another good mix is grenache with mataro or mourvedre—thongs with black T-shirt guys. By and large it is a variety that needs to be blended although there are some Australian producers that do a grenache on its own. Australian regions that do grenache best are the Barossa (spice and earth); McLaren Vale, which has weight, texture and elegance (cherry fruit and bright); and the Clare Valley, which has sweetly fragrant and sweet fruit. You'd find some tannin in certain years, but you would be lucky and it wouldn't come every year. This is why shiraz is so useful to balance it out.

Currently in Australia the GSM or grenache shiraz mataro/mourvedre blend is looking like a winner. There's no tangle with your tonsils but there's that bit of tannin wildness to liven it up. These are the greatest wines to take camping.

The French learned long ago that grenache needed blending to give it structure. At Châteauneuf-du-Pape they did this very well using other varieties, giving it succour, strength, spine and sensitivity from other grapes such as shiraz, mourvedre and carignan.

Mataro / Mourvedre

At home in warm dry autumns we can glimpse the power of this varietal as it's seen in southern France in Bandol, where it contributes nearly 50 per cent of the blend to produce one of France's great dry reds and rosés. While it has suffered a decline in France, this is a ballsy, big brother wine with loads of everything: spice and game flavours, alcohol in particular, and tannin that can produce more refined powerful wines that many Australian producers appreciate. A long-serving but not a widely available variety in Australia, it offers meat and strength in a somewhat one-dimensional flavour and some stern tannins.

Its renaissance has come from old vineyards and new winemaking where it is wholesome, fleshy, with game aromas overlaying the typical concentrated blackberry and firm tannins. It has an overriding earthiness with licks of blackberry, cloves, cinnamon and spicy black pepper with a very rustic gravelly tannin finish.

Aside from a handful of remarkable single-vineyard, old-vine bottlings, this varietal is consigned to blending with the less substantial grenache and the more balanced shiraz. Grant Burge, Charlie Melton and Rosemount are evident in the GSM version. Spain has the edge with mataro and increasingly the technology to make the most of their old vineyards. Our scattered vineyard survivors show what old vines can do here, while overall these days our blends lack a perfume and jam that exist in Châteauneuf-du-Pape .

TANNAT *Originally from the mountains between Spain and France around Madiran, tannat has a legendary reputation for toughness and producing wines of longevity and dense tannins. It's travelled as far as Uruguay and has yielded some delicious wines. Tiny amounts grown by Robin Tedder MW in the Hunter on Glenguin and by Peppertree Wines in Coonawarra suggest this variety has a place in Australia. Tannat aromas and flavours deliver rich tannins and a gentle spice with a cranberry-lifted red fruit.*

Beaujolais (Gamay)

This very pretty region and its wines are worth discovering. The vivid, zesty, unpretentious wines deliver quality on a vineyard-by-vineyard level. The Beaujolais (hence the wine's name) region's village quality distinctions are great value, and gamay grape can age.

Made famous by a unique mix of a single variety and a single soil type, this vine has failed to perform anywhere else to date. Granite soils and the red gamay grape make Beaujolais unique, with the top-end wines part of the Burgundy mindset and the nouveau wine a great marketing idea that has run off the rails.

Condemned in the court of public opinion thanks to some uninspiring wines and marketing at the bottom nouveau end, this delightful drink will probably languish in relative obscurity while its Burgundy neighbours, chardonnay and pinot noir, run rampant around the world.

It is a white-wine drinker's red, with a vivid cherry fruitiness. It is best as a great drinking wine that suits a whole variety of fatty French-style cooking. Top Beaujolais has vibrant, well-defined fruit flavours and is far from lightweight.

The district has the usual mix of fine family estates, co-ops and many more than usual very strong merchants, yet somehow they have lost their way, and quality in some areas has slipped horribly. Look to Beaujolais villages for an introduction.

Sangiovese

Sangiovese is one of the most outstanding (and most important) Italian varietals. Literally translated as 'blood of Jupiter', this variety produces some of Italy's noblest wines. Sangiovese is associated with Chianti and Brunello di Montalcino, as well as Vino Nobile di Montepulciano and many other super Tuscan styles (a blend of French and Italian grape varieties). It has always needed a little help and it's surprising what a few per cent of another French variety can do to lift it.

Sangiovese has a stronghold in the King Valley, Mudgee and increasingly in McLaren Vale. Lots of Australian winemakers are interested in it and seek to tame the acidity and tannin dryness to give something more friendly and comforting. There are parallels with shiraz in terms of volume of flavour but the structure is utterly different, with very different chalky versus silky tannins at best.

It ripens about the same time as shiraz in Australia, which means that it likes a good slab of sunshine in order to work. In Italy, it is most successfully grown in the mild central regions, such as Tuscany and Umbria and around Rome. When grown in cooler regions, the grape tends to show really high levels of acid and tannin. In Italy, sangiovese is traditionally blended with other varieties including one called canaiolo, which frankly has nothing much to recommend it. In Australia, the variety is successfully blended with cabernet sauvignon and merlot, which can boost the colour and flesh out the palate; the blending can particularly give a bit of sweetness to the front palate which really helps to fill out the wine.

We have seen some interesting unblended wines coming out of McLaren Vale and also one made by Peter Gago at Penfolds. Other features of sangiovese include quite intense fruit, a high degree of savouriness with earthy tannins; it can be lip-smacking in its dryness (which is why the blending works well for many drinkers). And like all good Italians, it really complements food—in fact, it demands food in order to get the best out of it. Drink it with any meats, especially osso bucco, and meats that have richness and sweetness would be complemented.

With a serious sangiovese you don't get softness. You certainly don't get slushy fruit flavours. There is a tighter-bodied strawberry and cherry but with a nice, articulate cut of acidity and then an articulate cut of tannin. They are quite intellectual wines in their own way; the antithesis of fat; and in that sense they can be just lovely. In Australia we can grow and make sangiovese into great wines with a defiant sense of their variety and our own richness and structure. Exciting stuff.

PINOTAGE *This variety is a cross between pinot noir and cinsault created in 1925. It is at the heart of South African grape growing where its rustic fruity strength is appreciated.*

Barbera

More stable than sangiovese (which shows a propensity to vintage quality swings), barbera is grown at a higher altitude in Italy. It is typically a late-ripening, high-acid grape that tends to produce light, fresh red wines that are pretty easy to drink due to their low tannin, and can taste pretty good. It does hold onto its acid in warmer climates, which makes it quite a useful little traveller with juicy red, softly textured wines.

Barbera suffers from a bad image in some quarters, but it is found in abundant quantity in the high hills of northern Italy (Barbera d'Asti and Barbera d'Alba), and it is probably the most popular wine of that region. At its best, it has a nice, mouthfilling character with some earthy tones and plum flavours. It can be quite like shiraz without the sweetness, but with a big slash of acidity to finish off.

In Australia, sangiovese offers a bit more slender suppleness. Barbera is a bit more blocky and blunt; if they were body types, you'd say that barbera was short and stocky, while sangiovese is of a taller, thinner variety.

Interesting examples of this variety in Australia come from McLaren Vale, Orange and Mudgee, in particular, Coriole, Angullong and Montrose. Vitello tonnato would be the dish to eat with it.

Nebbiolo

Native to the part of north-western Italy where there are snow-capped mountains in the near background, some growers are nevertheless valiantly growing nebbiolo in parts of Australia that have nothing to do with snow at all. Until the beginning of the nineteenth century, nebbiolo was traditionally made into a sweet, sparkling red wine. While travelling through this part of Italy in the 1780s, Thomas Jefferson commented that there wasn't a dry wine to be had. But some time in the early 1800s vignerons of the region decided to make dry wine, so there's about 200 years of tradition of producing dry red out of nebbiolo.

Nebbiolo is subject to considerable clonal variation, which is the same as saying there are lots of regional dialects of a language. In grapes, the variety produces differences in berry weight, size, colour and tannin. The colour is typically a medium-deep red in Italy and a dark red in Australia. When the wine is young it really can give the taster an attack of the killer tannins and acidity, but these do soften over extended ageing to give wine of distinct character. When made well, nebbiolo shows a more generous range of aromas and the taste is dry but not sandpapery in its effect. Nebbiolo aromas and flavours are fennel, mushroom, perfumed tar and truffles, violets, roses, raspberry, plum, fruitcake, liquorice and savoury. It will perhaps remain the Mt Everest of red wines to make. Decanting is standard procedure in our house.

SANGIOVESE GRAPES

Dolcetto

Literally translated as 'little sweet one', dolcetto grapes make a soft, light-to-medium-weight red that is good to drink early. A grape from north-west Italy with a saturated colour, vivid cherry fruit, and finishes quite dry and savoury. The colour can be deep and massive and they are fleshy wines, but short-lived, being very short on acidity.

The best is Great Western, which probably has the oldest dolcetto vines in Australia and they make a yummy, scrummy, rippy little wine. Dolcetto is traditionally well known in Italy in the same regions as barbera. It makes a great picnic wine, or a wine at a big event when you know you are going to drink more than one glass and where other glasses will be of different varieties.

CORVINA *This is the most important of the traditional varieties of Valpolicella and its Amorone wines where its thick skins contribute fruit flavour and tannins. Superior to its blend brothers in the bottle, molinara and rondinella, corvina is the star and we are seeing some of this planted, albeit in tiny quantities, by Brian Freeman in his Hilltops vineyard in New South Wales.*

Primativo (Zinfandel)

The Vesuvius of red wines in terms of its effect on the world wine trade is primativo, or zinfandel as it is called in the United States where it is increasingly popular. Much of the southern Italian grape-growing area is given over to this exuberant and prolific vine in the heel of the boot (Puglia) on Italy's south-eastern coast. It appears to have arrived there from Croatia. Italians loved its ripe flavour that could be drunk as a nouveau at around 10 per cent alcohol, or aged, making it a great variety for home winemaking.

Italian farmers in the United States took to primativo with alacrity because it is a generous cropping grape variety. Thick-skinned, it can show enormous variation in its large berries; even within one bunch there can be black, fully ripened fruit, medium-level ripened fruit, and green fruit—all at the same time.

This tendency to uneven ripening explains why it is fashionable to pick primativo when it's very, very ripe, which makes for high alcohol and quite jammy wines. It is thicker, juicier and jammier than shiraz, with its own berry-like fruit always coming through. Primativo is a good little guzzler. It can produce bargain basement rosé (pink zinfandel and zinfandel blush wines from the United States) through to very expensive wines. There are a handful of cult zinfandel producers in the United States which make complex explanations as they are often from small blocks of old vines scattered across the Napa Valley, Sonoma, Russian River and other sites.

The styles can vary from the sweet and fruity to the dry and savoury, even among the most expensive wines. A unique set of flavours features rich aromas with berry, pepper and chocolate, and treads a fine line between over- and under-ripeness on the palate with savoury Italian tannins to finish the palate. Drink it at a barbecue. It's a big, powerful wine that needs a big, strong steak.

From its initial start in Margaret River (blackberry and leafy) and McLaren Vale (juicy fruit and spice), it has moved to the Barossa Valley and the Adelaide Hills. It works in the west for Cape Mentelle and Watershed, while in South Australia, Kangarilla Road, Nepenthe and Darryl Groom's are on fire. In California, Ravenswood, Cline and Ridge all walk the talk at the big end of town.

The Californians are also shining models in the white and sweet pink styles that have turned a few generations onto wine. Though no comparison in the white and pink area, our wines are full of interest and not given to the excesses of many Americans. The United States wins for vine age and sheer weight of quality wines. Given its varietal flexibility and our climate, could our versions of this variety create some waves in the United States?

LAGREIN *An obscure variety that is making headway well out of the native climate from which it grows in northern Italy, with deep colour and rich cherry fruit, finishing dry and savoury. The Victorian edition from Cobaw Ridge was voted best red at the Australian Alternative Varieties competition at Mildura for two years running. Such acidity in our hot climate stands for something exciting.*

Touriga

This is the most famous grape of vintage port production for its masses of fruit balanced by richness and tannins. Capable of great longevity and complexity, it has been grown in the Riverland in Australia for 40 years. Originally top makers of vintage port, Seppelt, used it to bring a sense of dryness, almost dried currants and extra complexity similar to Portuguese port.

Grown at Wagga and promoted by the winemaking college as a table wine, touriga is a robust hearty red, which runs a steak to the plate and mouth pretty well. Its spicy fragrance suits dry reds here, notably in blends such as Sevenhill's reliably vibrant and delicious STM (a blend of shiraz, touriga and malbec). St Hallett, as well as using the variety in the GST blend and others, makes a straight touriga. Check around at wineries, as it's often part of a cellar-door-only special offer. It's such a friendly fruity wine with a distinctive personality that I had to include it.

Tempranillo

Known in Portugal by its alias tinta roriz, tempranillo is Spain's premier variety and the backbone of a great, long-lived, dry red wine tradition in both Rioja and the Ribera del Duero.

Capable of incredible intensity, character and acidity, as well as surviving long-barrel ageing, it is a tough early ripener that often smells of leather and blackberries and can age with finesse to achieve appealing complexities.

Spain has an interesting style called joven, standing for unoaked. Early releases give delightful rosé styles that we will see more of in this country, while in Portugal it does a mighty job in adding fruit and intensity to vintage ports. The variety seems to love our climate as long as the viticulture is spot on. Cascabel in McLaren Vale at Gapstead and Ross Estate have it under control.

Flavours vary but expect strawberry and raspberry in a rich pinot noir way, as its silky tannins and body also mirror pinot. Luckily, tempranillo is low in oxidative enzymes, so it is capable of long cask ageing.

White wines and blends

Before leaving home to serve a one-year jail sentence,
a white-collar criminal was quoted as saying,
'I'm not worried about the reds; they'll keep OK.
But I am worried about the whites'

ANONYMOUS

White wines deliver on a different level to red. Equally memorable yet delivering a distilled version without skin colour and tannin to mask texture and fruit structure, allowing for brightness and varietal fruit expression and unmasked acidity to reveal origins and grape variety.

CHARDONNAY

How does one describe chardonnay, a wine that has been so important to the education of the Australian palate in both quantity and quality? Let's start with a visual metaphor.

If you could see a wine in terms of a country landscape, what would you see? If it was riesling, you'd see crisp mountains; if it was shiraz, hot hills rolling away in the distance; if it was chardonnay it would be a vast, treeless, featureless plain, skyscrapers and towns always in the distance, because this wine depends so much on what is done to it and who is doing the doing. You see, the fruit is quite subtle on its own, but brilliant in the right hands.

Chardonnay's easy-going charm is its ability to produce serviceable wines in a very wide range of climates; it is something like the charm possessed by Bill Clinton, in which many different personas can be harnessed out of one variety. It can be an elegant and fine sparkling wine (blanc de blancs), a table wine or possibly a dessert wine, depending on how it is treated. Its social acceptability in the wine-drinking community has led to a certain laziness by winemakers, and nowadays a glass of chardonnay anywhere in the world is almost guaranteed to be nearly dry, mellow in flavour and reasonably full-bodied.

Chardonnay is friendly to grape growers in a range of climates owing to its tolerance of a range of temperatures. But not all chardonnay grapes are equal and different clones will have a strong influence on quality and style. The mendoza clone, for example, is well regarded for its smaller than average golden bunches and is one of the most flavoursome in the group. The treatment of its vines and the making of the wine have moved with the times and this influences the final product.

Years ago there were a number of characteristic styles with enormously divergent personalities. In Burgundy they fenced their vineyards but in Australia we gave chardonnay a wooden coffin and nearly buried it with too much oak.

As chardonnay can grow anywhere and virtually taste of anything, it has been subject to the vagaries of fashion. It was fashionable for ages to work it really hard—lots of malolactic, oak and plenty of barrel stirring. That led to the 1980s and 1990s style of pronounced oak, which wasn't very friendly to the mouth and was hard to match with food. This full-flavoured style was encouraged by wine shows, which awarded medals to obvious oak flavour: 'No wood, no good' was the cry from one prominent winemaker of the period, directed at reds but equally true of chardonnay. Winemakers were wrestling with the notion of how to give chardonnay a bit more length and oak seemed to do the trick, but it was overbearing in taste.

It was also widely believed that chardonnay had to be aged in new, not old, oak barrels. There was a funny story (perhaps apocryphal) about this dictum: many Burgundian cellars required a lot of new oak barrels as crop levels increased in the 1960s and the chardonnay-mad world that was banging on the doors at the time assumed new oak had a more important role. Under new oak, chardonnay felt thick, the fruit smothered, heavy and intense by comparison with present preferences.

Planting of chardonnay in the expanding cooler climate regions (for example, there are 3000 acres of chardonnay in the Adelaide Hills today) helped the evolution to a more interesting and complex style. We still like intensity, but that's more focused on an intense silkiness which chardonnay can display at its best. A really well-made chardonnay flows across the palate with a lovely soft, sweet fruit and texture. This texture needs to be balanced by cunning winemaking to really sing. All of the techniques and tricks that were used in the 1980s and 1990s are still current but in a less heavy-handed and more virtuous way.

Wherever it is grown, chardonnay can produce a reliable, early-ripening crop of relatively neutral-flavoured fruit and therefore, wine. It requires someone to do something to it to make it a creature of appeal, unlike riesling where purity of fruit is its appeal and protection the aim. If any one grape really aspires to diamond status, it's chardonnay. It should show both controlled fruit richness and detail from the winemaker. It should flicker, multi-faceted, with artful little licks of flavour and winemaker complexity.

The lavish high-alcohol chardonnays of the early 1990s, with their broad expression of individual sites' flavours, have increasingly been tamed thanks to changing attitudes of winemakers and different harvest times. Broadly speaking, there are three types of chardonnay today. The first is the fresh, affordable, unoaked accessible style; the second is the fruity, warm climate, big, peachy Dolly Parton style; and the third is the smart, complex, detailed wine that is gaining favour today. These modern detailed styles, based on the increased richness that vine age gives and encouraging trends to do more in the vineyard and produce less oak from the cellar, are continually refined at the top end and move closer to a more ideal chardonnay personality of subtle power with complexity and seamless fruit hinting at richness.

Better viticulture plays a role in selecting cooler climate sites, restraining crop levels, refining canopy management, and a changing appreciation of what constitutes ripeness. At the same time as turning down the volume on flavour ripeness winemakers are turning up the contrast by increasing the use of techniques that blur the purity of fruit, and adding savoury complexity and contrast by fermenting with solids or sediment in the must and native yeast.

The level of sediment in juice contributes both savoury flavour and its own blurring of the fruit picture—as the level of cloudiness increases there is a decrease in the level of fruit brightness. Almost like chilli in food, though, too much sediment kills the character, while in balance it lifts and carries the wine's personality.

In terms of winemaking difficulty my gut feel is that chardonnay is probably more difficult than pinot noir at the highest level. It is quite interesting to speculate on the importance of extracting the right tannins and leaving the unpleasant ones with their skins, as these may be responsible for the good mercaptans, minerality and texture of truly great chardonnay. The type of extraction also explains why so many of the world's great chardonnays are made with some fairly rudimentary equipment.

STEVE WEBBER, CHIEF WINEMAKER, DE BORTOLI, YARRA VALLEY

Yeast choice makes a difference to the wine's style, and increasingly natural ferment with a mix of yeast adds a potpourri effect. The addition of wild yeast in its truly feral state contributes a malt-like character and greater texture, which is seen as part of the jigsaw puzzle of great chardonnay. The restrained use of malolactic fermentation adds subtle dairy flavours, again a part of the jigsaw to piece together.

Oak gives chardonnay an extra depth and character, influencing the palate from front to back by increasing texture and flavour. Today's attitude to oak maturation is a contrast to previous belief in an overcoat of 100 per cent new oak shrouding the fruit, to a more cardigan-like mix of old and a little new oak to help the fruit show through while providing extra roundness and supporting the oak. An increasing number of producers are making unoaked styles to increase the balancing act, as it is not the natural personality of chardonnay to impress solo unless the fruit is exceptionally flavoursome.

Chardonnay palate graph

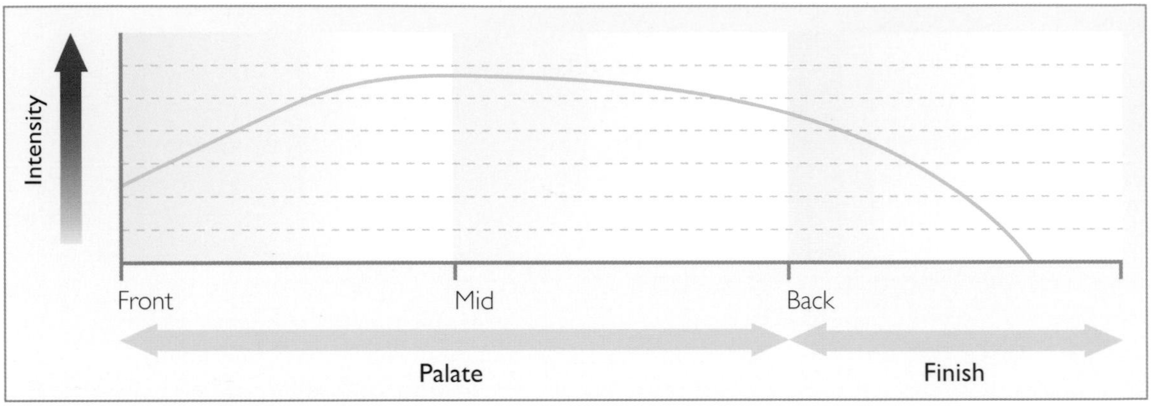

Chardonnay characteristics

Scents

saffron • damp earth • struck match • cucumber • apple • grapefruit • rockmelon • pineapple • nectarine • peach • fig • tropical fruit • fruit salad • toast • honey • fig • nuts • almond • cashew

Flavours

nectarine • peach • fig • cashew

Regions

Orange • Hunter Valley • Tumbarumba • Beechworth • Mornington Peninsula • Yarra Valley • Adelaide Hills • Margaret River • Frankland River

Chardonnay regions

The ancestral home of chardonnay in Australia is really New South Wales. It was first grown in Mudgee (where, legend tells, it was made into cream sherry by Alf Kurtz), and then renowned winemaker Murray Tyrrell moved it into the Hunter Valley. Rosemount was quick off the ranks, thanks to Alf's grafting ability, and developed vineyards there, and the grape expanded across Australia to different regional areas.

The South Australians, except for Seppelt, thought riesling would be the next white trend and largely ignored chardonnay. Today, it is a star in many regions including the Adelaide Hills where 50 per cent of the region is planted to chardonnay with a variety of producers pushing the region forward. Its faintly pink grapefruit aromas and citrus flavours with fine acidity offer finely textured wines.

The Yarra is a series of different microclimates based on river valleys with the warmer ones delivering rich nectarine generosity, great texture and structure, but still showing finesse and controlled richness, while the cooler areas go to sparkling wine such as Domaine Chandon.

Mornington Peninsula produces wines with detailed fruit showing rich citrus and stone fruit, packed in a medium body in the best years, with a distinct delicate structure underpinned by good acidity that make them deceptively light in the first few years.

The cool mountainsides around Tumbarumba are turning out increasingly classy examples that are looking more assured every year with their strong nectarine fruit.

Orange, with less flesh and better length than Tumbarumba, is producing outstanding chardonnay and has several wines with lovely purity and line of flavour and elegance.

The Hunter is enjoying a renaissance where old vines and a better sense of the style is giving up some tightly structured, complex and forceful examples on one side, and an increasing search for lighter more long-lived wines is producing wines with age-worthiness. Overall, quite sweet-fruited and early maturing. The Southern Highlands has produced wines with potential where the higher slopes can avoid the rain, and careful site selection is helping produce medium-bodied wines with length and a sense of quality.

Tasmania is contributing chardonnay to sparkling wines for most of the big companies and makes up a component of some high-quality regional blends. Local wines from Freycinet appeal where they couple ripe fruit (tropical to nectarine) with a piercing acidity.

In Margaret River, the chardonnay vine flowers at about the same time as the winds pick up from the sea. Now, any vineyard manager will tell you that, ideally, flowering should occur in the days of mild, not strong wind. Strong wind blows a lot of the pollen away. So with Margaret River chardonnay, we get an incomplete flowering and resulting small crop. However, the small crop combined with the lovely coolness of the climate ends up producing wines that are just magnificently elegant yet with intense powerful fruit. It would be hard to go past the diverse styles of a Leeuwin Estate, Pierro or Cullen's chardonnay.

New Zealand is offering some of the most vital high-quality chardonnay, in particular the Brajkovich family near Auckland where the Mate's vineyard continues to scale the heights of finesse. Gisborne has more grunt with pineapple and peach flavours in a full body, while the South Island especially around Waipara or Canterbury gives strong citrus grapefruit flavours.

The future for chardonnay

Despite the ABC (anything but chardonnay) movement, nearly 50 per cent of Australia's white plantings are chardonnay and people are returning to buy the top examples of this variety. We can see the next great white trend from the United States where the sales of pinot grigio will soon replace chardonnay as the most popular variety.

Drinking chardonnay? It's great as a sparkling aperitif, and Croser has got to be the epitome of a sparkling chardonnay, with a lot of zip and freshness. The Kiwis have us with finesse and fruit; the French with mineral and longevity; and pockets of very determined resistance suggest that Australia might get there in our children's lifetime. Our top wines still have a hint of the exuberance that came before, but we have a group of wines with tightness and tang that augurs well for the future.

Chardonnay blends

The 'great white hope' or the 'great hopeless white'. The vast majority of chardonnay and semillon blends achieve their purpose in being sound reliable wines at a good price. Pockets of resistance to this bleak view of the blend have existed with both Tyrrell's and Geoff Merrill appreciating the inherent tightness of semillon suiting its lush chardonnay cousin but as they say, 'winemakers provide, markets decide'.

VERDELHO

Originating on the Portuguese island of Madeira in the Atlantic, verdelho reached an early point of distinction in the seventeenth and eighteenth centuries.

Here, it was brandied in casks and loaded onto sailing vessels that sailed out to explore the world and trade with America. Madeira was well loved and often took the name of the ships in which it was transported. Presumably, the combination of good grapes, fortification with spirit, and cooking in the crucible of creaking wooden vessels gave each load its distinctive flavour. But this marvellously romantic early history is only the beginning of the verdelho story—one grape that has made the jump from fortified to fermented wine.

Cuttings of verdelho made their way to South Africa and from there to Australia, where it became the most widely planted variety in Victoria in 1900. As a wine, it was hugely popular. However, a combination of susceptibility to new fungal diseases and volatility in ripeness made it increasingly unpopular with vignerons. It's a variety that has a highly sensitive tipping point—one day there are no fungi to be seen, the next it's gone powdery all over; one day it's not ripe and the next it's overripe.

Verdelho is not a tractable grape. Actually, it can be a prat of a variety! However, it has persisted in certain areas where its body and longevity saw it held in good regard. The result is a full, rich taste that does very well over a range of foods and preferences.

Verdelho palate graph

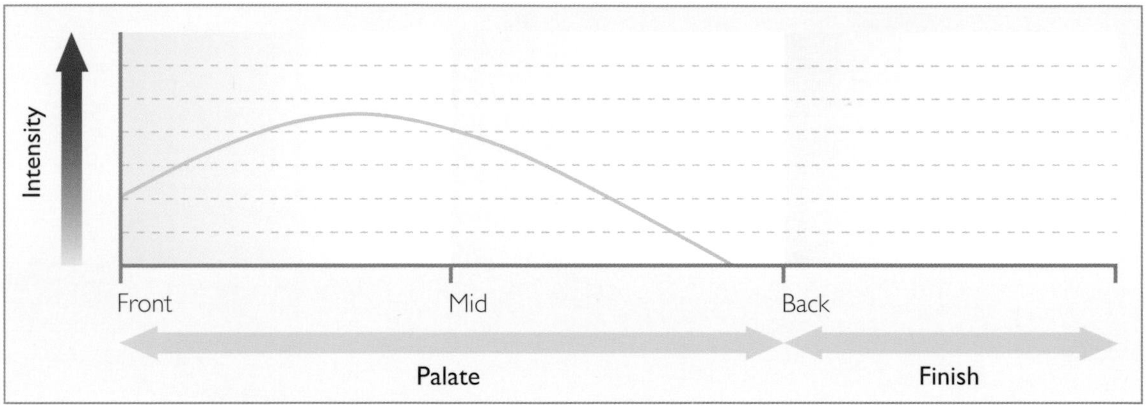

Verdelho characteristics

Scents

fruit character goes from green melon through to tropical fruit • short structure with moderate alcohol • good acidity

Flavours

herbaceous • spicy • grassy • melon • pineapple • guava • honeysuckle • tropical fruit • fruit salad

Regions

Hunter Valley • Swan Valley

Verdelho regions

The Swan Valley and much of Western Australia makes a good verdelho. The hot, dry climate combined with increased rather than decreased planting (by Houghton Wines for their white burgundy) led to some serious understanding of how to manage the grape.

In the Hunter Valley it is picked early, which leads to a finer, sensitive and delicate wine that is great for an aperitif or an al fresco lunch. This is an interesting contrast with the Swan Vally because, in fact, wines from these two regions usually tend in exactly the opposite direction—fine and delicate from the dry Swan Valley, big and fruity from the humid Hunter; but not verdelho, which is a singular grape.

The Potts family in Langhorne Creek in South Australia produces a fortified verdelho, which is made from vines that were planted before the age of steam engines, pre-1860. It's a relic, but it's interesting to taste and more so to visit.

The future for verdelho

The industry has cast verdelho rightly as a niche grape due to its challenges and it looks set to stay a minority player against its more talented and popular cousins. Why would anyone want to compete? Value for money, regional styles and a different flavour range make the verdelho world our own.

SAUVIGNON BLANC

That's sauvignon blanc, green one year, under-ripe the next and unpleasant most of the time

LEN EVANS

It was a winemaker from Sancerre in the Loire Valley, France, who claimed the sauvignon blanc grape was taken by the Romans (from the banks of the upper Loire on the way through) to Bordeaux.

Others claim the reverse: 'It's from Bordeaux!' I guess there aren't any Romans left to ask. Having said that, sauvignon blanc is not really a traveller; it's more at home in a limited number of either cool but sunny regions, or cool humid environments. Its green grassiness can shine in hot climates where it can still add a dash of acidity when picked early, but its real zesty aromas are reduced to an almost chardonnay level of aromaticity.

Sauvignon blanc is a multi-faceted variety within its climatic origins with quite different flavours and structures to the wine. In the Loire, we have styles with a gooseberry fruit flavour, which can be modified by a producer's use of old barrels to give a house style. The flavours that follow from the soils on Pouilly Fume are more flinty, smoky and hessian-like, and are exploited as a local flavour profile. Other French examples of note come from Quincy and Sauvignon St Bris in Burgundy. Closer to home, seldom can one wine and place be so associated with a variety as the David Hohen-led Cloudy Bay in New Zealand is for the world's sauvignon blanc drinkers.

Cool climate sauvignon blanc is herbaceous, meaning it has traces of salad greens and green capsicum smells and taste. Driven by methoxypyrazine (MOP), a natural deterrent for animals and insects seeking to eat it, the pungent green flavour at low levels can deliver rhubarb and gooseberry flavours. Sometimes with riper picking it's almost tropical with hints of blackcurrant leaf—sounds weird but it's the same chemical family. Fermentation can modify this character giving a more measured aroma and flavour.

MOP is so pungent that the Kiwis claim, and I have no reason to doubt it, a thimbleful will give you a sauvignon blanc-flavoured swimming pool. The human nose can certainly smell it at approximately one part per trillion. Sauvignon blanc is absolutely the wrong partner for new oak, which takes away its purity, destroys the vibrancy of the fruit and removes the delicacy. Ideally, it should be a gorgeous, crisp, crunchy dry white. Sauvignon blanc rarely ages gracefully, so drinking early is recommended except when blended with semillon in Bordeaux.

Sauvignon blanc palate graph

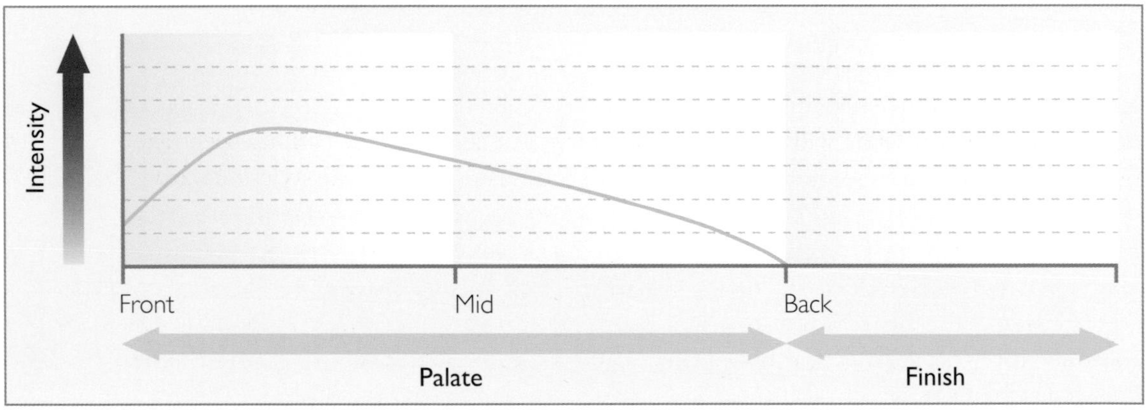

Sauvignon blanc characteristics

Scents

vegetal • green apple • asparagus • salad greens • green bean • peas • capsicum • tomato bush • lantana • herbaceous • freshly cut grass

Flavours

grassy • lemongrass • gooseberry • honeydew melon • passionfruit • tropical fruit

Regions

Tasmania • Adelaide Hills • south-west Western Australia • Margaret River • Marlbourough, New Zealand

Sauvignon blanc regions

The warmer Margaret River provides stunning examples, giving yellow to pink grapefruit or lemongrass flavours in the best of them. The wonderful acid in these flavours adds a certain raciness and freshness. So the combination with the softer semillon is a blend made in heaven. Our most interesting sauvignons are grown in the Adelaide Hills and Orange.

Tasmania is a halfway house in terms of style, with a delicate fragrance. It appears that only small blocks on scattered sites are capable of suiting this very fussy variety.

Marlborough in New Zealand is the ideal mix of soil and site and the world stands glass-in-waiting as they continually refine their style from a cut-grass herbaceous to a more rounded, almost tropical fruit drop. There, the style has undergone a change from the lean and herbal, cut grass, tomato bush, green bean and gooseberry, towards more passionfruit and tropical characters that show sweet fruit without sugar thanks to better winemaking and vine age. Winemaking for these styles has undergone a revolution with the use of natural ferment, possibly in older barrels, followed by lees age. Minimal oak is giving these wines more aromatics and layers of complexity, while retaining freshness and ponderability.

The future for sauvignon blanc

This is a variety with a lot of potential, though in the current commercial climate with New Zealand selling strongly it will take a determined company to challenge this dominance. Perhaps Chile will be the next big thing, but certainly the ball has been taken out of court in the mass market leaving the small producers to bring the styles forward.

A lot more blending to create a point of difference and to overcome its acid-edged personality in Australia will see the semillon blends in their dry variants continue to climb, as they represent life after sauvignon blanc. Nicer things are definitely coming.

From a tiny, tiny base our new Yarra Valley textural mineral styles are stepping nose to nose with Sancerre, but the Kiwis have us in a herbal headlock and just won't let go. This is one for the Kiwis.

Sauvignon blanc blends

A key phrase to remember when we are working with white wines, particularly sauvignon blanc, is the notion that when you blend grape varieties together they shouldn't fight with each other. Varieties when blended together need to have a little bit of fruit electricity between them; they need to open up the tastebuds to food, and they need to encourage drinking. This is why you find semillon often requires only a bit of sauvignon blanc to lift it, whereas a 50/50 blend is a totally different style and the best of both varieties.

SEMILLON

The world looks to Australia to set the standard for semillon
GERALD BOYD, WINE WRITER, SAN FRANCISCO CHRONICLE

One year before Max Schubert made Grange, Maurice O'Shea made the first semillon at the Lovedale vineyard he had planted in 1946.

Why the man with an Irish surname and a French first name chose such a sandy, flat and uninteresting site is part of the paradox of this wine. The semillon grape is big-berried and thin-skinned, and seems to be a native of Bordeaux. It was traditionally known as the green grape. It is so fragile that it doesn't suit being machine harvested. It's not a very acid grape when picked fully ripe and can be overcome easily by botrytis. This variety has done well out of modern wine technology as it requires protection from oxygen at all stages of the winemaking process and temperature-controlled fermentation. Technology has aided the retention of all of the rather scarce fruit characters. Having hit its technological pace in the 1960s, semillon has been running a literal marathon to widespread critical acclaim ever since.

Early picking and being fermented and bottled quickly works beautifully for semillon. It shows lemon-edged acidity and lemongrass flavours at its delicious heart. The wine ages marvellously—10, 15, even 20 years—showing smooth, honeyed, toasty flavours and gaining remarkable richness of texture. Most five-year-old Hunter semillons have not left the puppy phase, thus making it easily, along with Eden Valley riesling, the longest living of white wines.

Semillon breaks all the rules. It starts life pale and insipid, faintly vegetal flavours with a chalky drying acid. The shy subtleness means many people would overlook it without guidance. The wines are low in alcohol and the best vintages in the Hunter come from the relatively colder and distinctly wetter years. But time makes this wine sing and gives it a complexity of flavour and richness of texture that makes semillon one of the great wines of the world.

This is a subtle variety that sits in the middle of the spectrum with savoury acid, citrus grapefruit-like characters and great intensity. Some examples leave you chewing your mouth as the flavour unfolds through its strong acids and fruit intensity. At its worst it's simple and grassy. Winemakers are challenged by this variety and its subtleness needs structure, but it is so tender that if it's been tricked up it shows. Ageing is really the only answer, although a subtle touch of oak ageing can do wonders for early drinking styles.

Semillon is one of the great white wines of Australia, especially when drunk as an accompaniment to fish and seafood. Drink it on a night out because it's low in alcohol and high in taste. But mind, inferior semillon will leave you with a furry, dry tongue. If you can, drink the older rather than younger vintage. Young semillon is delicate and crisp and goes well with oysters; older semillon is toasty and feels richer in body, so it goes well with richer flavoured foods.

Semillon palate graph

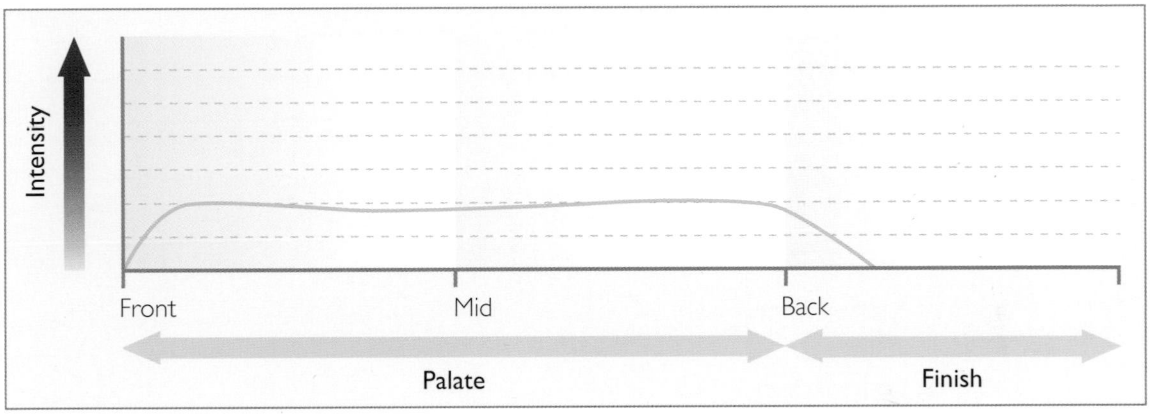

Semillon characteristics

Scents

pea pod • parsley • thyme • straw • lemon • dusty • lemon sherbet • citrus blossom • lanolin

Flavours

citrus • lemon • lemongrass • wheat husk • toast

Regions

Hunter Valley to Granite Belt • Margaret River • Barossa Valley

Semillon regions

Great Australian semillon is paradoxical on so many levels: How can a delicate white wine come from a hot climate such as the Hunter? But the best do come from New South Wales, particularly the Hunter Valley style, which is crisp, tangy, low in alcohol and unwooded. It also thrives on the rainy eastern coastline, from Nowra south of Sydney, to the Queensland border around Tenterfield and Richfield, and onto the Granite Belt.

Semillon conforms well to the particular pressures of the Hunter Valley climate. It likes the coast and it doesn't mind the wet. You can also pick it early and even though it lowers the alcohol content, Hunter semillon still has enough flavour development for this not to matter. The humidity of the Hunter, especially towards harvest time, is also a great friend to this grape. It allows the vine to set down flavour instead of concentrating its energies on sucking up water from the roots to keep its leaves turgid.

Most Hunter semillon is drunk in Sydney, which shows that once people understand the style they will support it. This wine is remarkable as it is totally at odds with the overall Australian wine market for full, soft, round whites, which has led some producers, such as Margan and Brokenwood, to pick riper grapes and temper the variety's inherent austerity without losing the distinctive regional flavours.

Margaret River can deliver some good examples, but the green notes are far too common in all except the very best. Semillon is a long-term resident of the Barossa Valley where it continues to perform from dry (try Peter Lehmann's editions) to sweeties from the same producer. The Clare Valley can also do semillon well with Tim Adams leading the way. But generally, it's probably true to say that while South Australia is superb for other vinous achievements, you can't really trust them to make semillon that well. Leave that to the east coasters.

The future for semillon

Semillon lovers are a secret sect of wine drinkers worshipping a dry herbal variety in a world dominated by carefully sweetened sauvignon blanc. It seems that on a global scale, semillon will play second fiddle to sauvignon blanc outside the Hunter Valley and a few selected regions on the east coast of Australia. The variety is destined to enter most mouths as part of a delicious blend that should conquer all markets in time. It is just a little too orthodox for everyone on its own.

New South Wales has the largest semillon plantings, and the Hunter Valley and eastern coastline has the most consistent varietal character in the world, while Western Australian blending with sauvignon blanc makes totally delicious wines on a level not available anywhere else. Washington State has plantings but it is sold in the United States as budget white wine, dragging the image of the variety down.

Semillon blends

More often than not semillon is blended. In Bordeaux, where the grape originated, it is almost always blended with sauvignon blanc. The two come together extraordinarily well in cooler climates, drawing on each other's strengths to achieve great heights. Traditionally in Australia semillon was combined with chenin blanc in the Barossa Valley; more chenin blanc and less semillon it was white burgundy, more semillon and less chenin blanc it was chablis.

Semillon chardonnay

A love child of an early promiscuous period when chardonnay was in short supply, this is a viable style in terms of flavour and longevity but not sales. The reputation has been dragged down by a tidal wave of same-name cheap wines. Some Hunter Valley chardonnay carries small (legally allowed up to 15 per cent) amounts of semillon, which is a winemaker's choice to be welcomed for adding restraint to the force of the style.

Semillon sauvignon blanc

Not accustomed to travelling far from its ancestral home in Bordeaux, this blend has become closely associated with Margaret River in Australia. The synergy here is at the pinnacle of wine experience and only surpassed with the cabernet blends for the racy aromatic way sauvignon blanc can lift the stolid, round-structured semillon to such gulpable heights.

When blended with lemongrassy, gooseberry, herbal sauvignon blanc in the Margaret River region it draws on the palate weight (from picking at 13.5 per cent alcohol) of the more butter and peach semillon. The two blend quite harmoniously and the style really has nothing to do with the green methoxypyrazine flavours of the cooler climates. These enticing, freshly aromatic wines are moderate in alcohol and acid with even fruit definition, and deliciously cover the summer hay and grass fruit spectrum yet carry juicy fruit flavours. Basic examples are little more than herbal.

In Australia, dry wines are a major work in progress. As the evolution of soils, sites and the climate of southern Western Australia unfold I sense a world beater at the highest levels and lots of pleasure for everyone. Memorable wines are widely available from this region. Look to the regional leaders Cullens and Mosswood for the best.

New Zealand is waking up to the style, so expect to see more of this blend on its march to replace sauvignon blanc, chardonnay and pinot grigio as the world's drink.

Most memorable wines from the extraordinary Domaine de Chevalier, where even one of the lesser vintages of the last few decades, and more widely known Haut-Brion Blanc and Laville Haut-Brion Blanc will bust your bank account if you need to see the ultimate in this coupling.

Semillon botrytis

Darren De Bortoli recognised that Griffith semillon was affected by botrytis in 1982 and has built on the style. Since then semillon grapes are cultivated in a deliberate fashion to create botrytis. At home in Sauternes and Barsac, under the king hit of botrytis this variety delivers again with a level of complexity and refinement that puts it in a league of its own. The blend varies from 80 per cent semillon and 20 per cent sauvignon blanc to the reverse, with the exception of Château Climens at 98 per cent semillon.

RIESLING

Riesling translates terroir in a profound way like no other variety

ANDREW CAILLARD MW

If ever a grape variety has suffered the perils of purgatory for a combination of political, social and cultural reasons that bear no relationship to its essential quality, it's riesling.

In the middle ages it was called Rhenish, a catch-all phrase that included Alsace, Mosel and Rhine under one term. Germany still has 29 per cent of the world's riesling. One of the curious things about riesling in the old world is the decision by the Germans to show when it's ripe not by its 'ripeness', but by the amount of sugars that have not fermented! Tastes were different then. Most people preferred a much more acid, dry riesling than they do today, although the Scandinavians still like very acid wines such as Mosel Trocken.

Riesling is a late ripener and therefore fussy with soil. It prefers acid soil which is commonly found in much of Australia, where it is often backward and restrained when young, and easily masked by shoddy winemaking. Canopy management matters for this variety because the sun makes the juice phenolic if it turns the skins sunburned brown; this will lead to thickening and can show in the wines as it did in 2001.

The contribution of schist soils, including slate and shale, is open to interpretation. They are seen as giving gunflint in whites; and from Douro to Banyuls and into middle France a rich spiciness; and a minerally aroma in Nahe and Mosel. Limestone seems to contribute a fuller floral aroma.

Perhaps it was because riesling was generally seen around the world as a sweet, slushy, confusing wine, shockingly ordinary, yet occasionally great—but for whatever reason, this great grape has long been on its knees, its head bowed, and there's been every reason to think that someone would come and put it out of its misery. Yet the famous riesling vintages of the late 1880s and 1890s saw the wine being sold for as high a price as fine Bordeaux, a fact that astounded me when I first discovered it.

The reasons for the collapse are myriad. Filtration, grower expectations and plant breeding all have a role. Today filtration (removing solid debris or yeast from wine) is a mainstay of modern winemaking, but its single-minded application to produce value-for-money sweet wines in post-war Germany took the riesling industry for a dive. Paradoxically, the German curse on vinous Europe was the genesis of the modern Australian wine industry.

The effect this double-edged discovery had on bringing affordable sweet wine to market speedily and cheaply was extraordinary. But the downside was that riesling and liebfrauwein became corrupted, broadened, fat-bellied and bloated, turned into cheap wines with lots of sugar and grown on great big, cheap vineyards.

The Germans have made a huge contribution in Australia, from the first vine dressers, who came out at the behest of the Macarthurs at Camden, who brought riesling vines with them. A Mr Mengler, who travelled with Colonel William Light to look through the regions of South Australia, was a German with wine knowledge who helped propagate riesling in South Australia. The Germans had a strong influence on winemaking in general in this country, especially in the Barossa Valley and Watervale regions.

Later, Leo Buring—a wonderful thinker and doer and businessman of wine—was very successful in the Barossa. On the back of that success he organised to plant a vineyard in Watervale in the Clare Valley, mainly because he had German cousins there and he felt among family and friends. Leo Buring's riesling from Watervale was a classic wine of the post-war era. The Knappsteins also planted and made riesling in the same area. The variety became legendary under the auspices of the Stanley Wine Company and riesling is still the largest-selling white wine in South Australia. Tim Adams is the modern inheritor of much of this wisdom.

So how does one describe this variety? It is high acid, late-ripening, with a piercing floral aroma and a considerable ability to age. It is a gorgeous grape with a relatively high malic acid level so you can get some brisk crispness to it; the best are subtle, long, lean, not very textural and very refreshing.

Riesling is at its best when young, for me ideally around its first birthday when it shows off its liveliness and acidity. Often around four years it shows a pleasing fatness—great wines will age for ten years and many can go to 15 years if you can wait and they are great value for a cellar wine if you like the aged flavours. Riesling accompanies any foods that have an inherent sweetness in them such as seafood or ripe vegetable salads.

Riesling characteristics

Scents

floral • fragrant • perfumed • citrus • lime • pineapple • quince • cold tea • passionfruit • toast and honey • kerosene • tropical fruit • fruit salad • cumquat • apricot • dried apricot • honey • toffee • caramel • golden syrup • treacle

Flavours

green apple • pear • lemon • citrus • lime • grapefruit • pineapple • fruity • peach

Regions

Clare Valley • Watervale • Auburn • Eden Valley • Frankland River • Porongurup region, Great Southern • central Victoria • Tasmania

Riesling palate graph

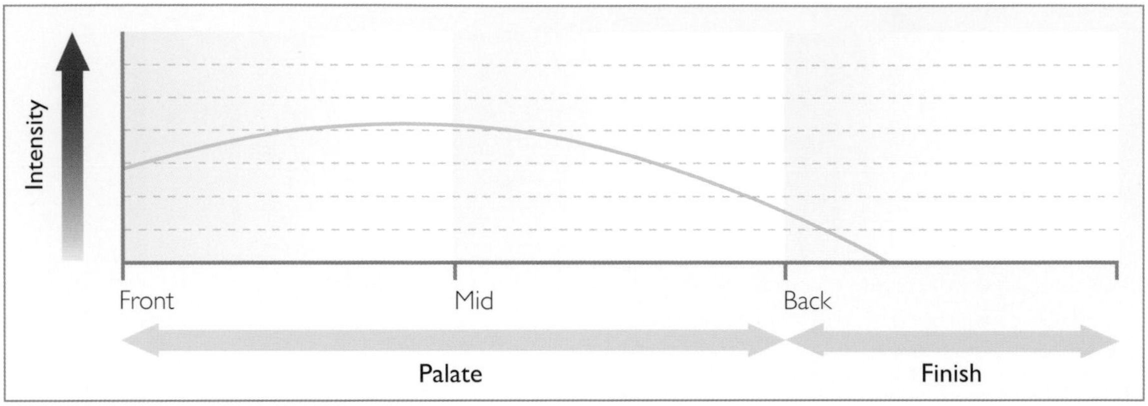

Riesling regions

Of the places in the world where riesling does well, Australia has a large number of them, if ageing is part of the criteria for greatness. Great Australian rieslings can age well, especially from the Clare and Eden Valleys in South Australia, and central Victoria. Western Australia, in particular Frankland River, Mt Barker and the Great Southern region, produce long-lived wines of note. Finer flavours are found in Western Australia where the cooler southern regions can give a marvellous fruit juice character almost like Juicy Fruit chewing gum. No doubt they will age well too. Sub-regionality, perhaps based on soils, is in its early days with some regions such as the Clare Valley offering insights as different soils and aspects carry varying amounts of water and hence the grape tolerates dry summers in different ways to give a delightful spectrum of flavours year in and year out.

Watervale is on softer limestone and terra rossa-based Jurassic soils only 133 to 195 million years old (limey and according to the locals like their famous local lime juice cordial Bickfords). Clare Valley, Lodge Hill rieslings on 500-million-year-old Cambrian hard slate (show brown lime) may also have a hint of clove deepening the citrus and floral characters that define a good riesling. Locals point to sub-regional flavours in Sevenhill (blossom and perfume); the Skilly Valley (almost roses and musk); and the tighter, minerally more elegant Polish Hill River's weathered soils.

The Polish Hill River character also comes from the vineyard being limited in its biologically effective sunshine by shading from surrounding hills. The vineyard doesn't warm up until 11 am and is in shade by 2 pm. It is three weeks later in ripening than Watervale. Watervale's richer soils give a fuller flavour and more rich fruit and fullness. Watervale and Clare Valley rieslings, are more forward and generous in style to those of Eden Valley, which are tighter and leaner, limey and lemony but with a strong structure and finish.

The Adelaide Hills is entering the fray with more melon to grape fruit flavours (think of almost sauvignon blanc), while the Western Australian style is more mineral and tighter fruit but equally delicious at its best, and there seems to be a wide area where riesling performs well across the Great Southern regopm, from Frankland River to Porongurup.

Victoria (lime, citrus blossom) shows similar character to Eden Valley but with a surprising delicacy, while Drumborg (grapefruit rind pith) is our most Germanic region in terms of style, as well as the most delicate and piercing, and will age exceptionally well. Tasmania has a fresh liveliness and water-white colour with perfume, while Canberra shows greater strength of fruit and is equally appealing in a fuller way. New Zealand is a dab hand as well on both the North and South Islands but in particular Marlborough, with the Stoneleigh wines from Montana and their botrytis lushness.

To me the heart of riesling lies within the German river systems where poor soils, steep slopes and small growers coax the variety to its greatest heights. In a comparative sense, here we find less alcohol and greater minerality, especially where the Mosel style climbs the walls with searing acidity balanced with residual sugar and enough flavour and low alcohol to provide generous refreshment. Richer dry styles and fashions are prevailing and the move to trocken wines holds hope of the variety climbing back onto the perch of international public acceptability.

In Europe, riesling does very well in Alsace as it does also across Germany and then into Austria. As white or Johannesburg riesling in California the medium-sweet edition is of little interest, while it is a safe bet from main regions in Canada. Oregon and Washington State are a cut above but buying Australian makes more sense.

The future for riesling

All the indicators suggest a surprisingly good future as demand in the United States is growing very rapidly for dry riesling, which suggests that the baby boomers will go on influencing the wine market for some years to come. Expect growth in area under vine.

Australia's crisp, clean, pure affordable lines of flavour give us a strong position against the sweeter German styles. Alsace styles are expensive at many price points, which is in our favour. Strong competition from Austria for dry wines is less clear-cut with their spicy lingering flavours offering something we can't.

Mosel remains unchallenged for low-alcohol delicacy, although it will be interesting to see what the next few years provide. Our sweet wines while exceptional are not in the same league or price!

OTHER WHITES

Never trust anyone who asks for white wine, they are posing
BETTE DAVIS, ACTRESS

Colombard

Allied to semillon in a general way for its freshness and acidity and loved by winemakers for it, colombard has a nice dry edge to it when well made. It's not a favourite of wine connoisseurs but it can be elevated beyond its normal station. One vigneron who knows how to do this and has made a specialty of it is Joe Grilli, the one-time dux winemaker of renowned Roseworthy College in South Australia. He has planted the grape on the Virginia Plains north of Adelaide and makes a carefully marketed, carefully controlled colombard of some interest and appeal.

Where does the grape come from? There's a lot of it, called generically *Vin de payes des Cotes de Gascogne,* made from vines grown just outside of Bordeaux region. This wine was originally used for the distillation of cognac and has never really made it to a higher status of table wine in Europe, though in Australia we have managed to do something exciting with it.

The aromas and flavours of colombard are herbaceous, grassy, apple, citrus, lime, melon, passionfruit, tropical fruit and honeysuckle. Joe Grilli has turned an obscure cognac grape into an art form that nothing from overseas can match.

Viognier

This white grape variety comes from the Rhône Valley and it's spreading across the world because of the aromatic, almost 'Southern Comfort', heady apricot, peach-stone fragrance. A very mouthfilling, almost oily, slimy variety, it carries significant tannin which is unusual for a white variety. The real beauty of this grape is how well it dresses up shiraz. It is shiraz's new hairdo and perfume—the beautiful woman on the arm of the old man.

By tradition, a small amount of viognier is blended with shiraz grown on the Côte-Rôtie slopes—literally the 'roasted slopes'—of sunny southern France. They already grow the most beautiful shiraz and the addition of the viognier has an uplifting effect that provides additional aromas. It also seems to give the palate a little bit more subtlety, and a smooth, slippery texture as it comes into your mouth. In Australia quite a bit of viognier is planted in warm regions and blended with shiraz. But I think this grape makes a great contribution when the wines are grown in a cooler climate. It makes a huge difference to wines grown in the Canberra and Yarra Valley regions.

The sort of words that great viognier attracts include: exotic, creamy, spicy perfumed, peachy, apricot, luscious, deliciously complex, heady, mouthfilling and fleshy. In short a big, buxom babe; a good sort.

Viognier is an uneven cropping, low-yielding variety, and was nearly extinct due to local indifference. It was discovered by new world vignerons eager to spice up shiraz. Château Grillet within Condrieu makes a more reserved wine from its four-hectare apellation. I chose to include it because it is definitely the drink to use when you are trying to seduce someone. The decadent, opulent, nectarous richness is so obvious that it's the most flirtatious wine you'll ever drink. It's designed to give joy. It is a variety that boasts generous alcohol—a good one is going to be more than 14 per cent. It is this alcohol that puts the flesh on the viognier. With its naturally low acid, the high-alcohol sweetness and fat fruit taste are allowed to shine.

If we imagine riesling as a delicate sheet of finely milled paper, and a thick, textured cardboard for pinot gris, then viognier is the thickness of a Saturday newspaper. Viognier is very textural. It can be oily or it can be light, but it must have a bit of gritty or powdery tannin as well. The tannin in white wines is quite important, especially for viognier, or indeed chardonnay (which is why oak is often used with the latter); the tannin can build on the 'front' flavours of the wine, such as the alcohol and sweet fruit, and provide them with something to finish on.

Despite its promise and great potential, it's easy to be critical of viognier in Australia because presently there aren't too many good ones. Viognier seems to challenge Australian winemakers because we train our winemakers to be able to finely balance acid and sugar. But viognier just wants to go fat, generous and juicy, and it really is at its best when it is young. I don't think any wine aficionado in the world wants to see an aged viognier unless it's the 2 to 3 per cent stuck away in a good shiraz–viognier blend.

South Australian vignerons have planted a lot of viognier, which is used mainly to lift shiraz. Often, it's arguable whether warm climate shiraz actually needs the viognier—it's definitely the cooler climate shiraz that benefits from the extra kick. Yalumba have led with this grape with benchmark styles under the guidance of winemaker Louisa Rose. The wines from Canberra are also showing fantastic form.

The other difficulty about viognier is that it really should be very ripe on the vine before being picked. The grapes should be almost starting to shrivel, just the slightest dimpling on the berry, and the smallest deflation of those otherwise turgid, pouting grapes.

Unlike chardonnay, which usually starts off neutral and then tends to be forceful with the help of winemaking engineering, viognier is a pushy personality from the beginning. In its purest form, viognier is chardonnay on steroids or amphetamines. Many devotees of chardonnay may struggle to finish their bottles of viognier because of its high alcohol and richness. Great examples are from Yalumba, Kangarilla Road and Clonakilla.

Viognier aromas and flavours include floral, peach, apricot, viscous, musk stick and toffee apple. Eden Valley is a happy home for this variety and our wines are consistently interesting and a lot more affordable than France. There seems to be much more opportunity for this wine to expand but it is hard to pronounce and often to finish the bottle.

VERMENTINO *Under the Murray–Darling label vermentino's high acid teamed with the hot climate of the Murray River seems to hold hope for the next generation of wines. Australians are adapting high-acidity European varieties to the acid-depleting climate of inland Australia and thus producing a richly textured wine with personality.*

Marsanne

Marsanne has a longer history in Australia than is generally recognised. On its own this often overcropped variety makes boring wine—it's the dumpy librarian or comb-over bachelor of white wines. In its home in the Rhône Valley it takes third place behind viognier and roussanne. It should always be happily engaged in conjugal relations with roussanne to render it fuller and more interesting, or succulently rampaging with viognier.

Grown with care marsanne can produce a golden, citrus-blossom flavoured white that gains resin and honeysuckle with age. It needs time in the cellar (or library, so to speak!). Tahbilk in Victoria has made a continuous rendition of this variety, in fact it is the world's oldest planting of marsanne in existence. Made with a nod to both riesling and semillon by picking early to avoid its inherent low acidity, not messing with it in the winery, early bottling, then bed in the cellar—wait five to 15 years and you get a lemony yet rich delight.

Marsanne used to be very popular with the Swiss winemakers of the Yarra Valley and Geelong regions and owes its early fame to their support. Today it is heroically supported by Tahbilk. But it is an Australian fancy to produce marsanne unpartnered. Other good supporters are Yerinberg and d'Arenberg.

If you were a French winemaker you would not think of planting marsanne without rousanne. This is a later ripening, golden-coloured grape, which gives a thinner, more blunt-edged wine. Great examples come from Giaconda, Yerinberg and Tahbilk. The smart French winemakers blend the two. Marsanne is grown in France around Hermitage or Saint Joseph or in Crozes Hermitage; and some southern climates around Châteauneuf-du-Pape.

Blends are featuring more as this tough vigorous variety can tolerate heat, and in my view there is potential for a very steamy ménage à trois between marsanne, rousanne and viognier: marsanne for structure and steel backbone; rousanne for flesh and the party frock; viognier for the shape, the perfume and the sex appeal. Check out the Mitchelton Airstrip blend or Siromet's edition.

Marsanne aromas and flavours are lemon, peach, honey and honeysuckle. Victoria has several iconic producers but the blending of marsanne and roussanne together leaves us in the dust of Hermitage.

Pinot gris (Pinot grigio)/Pinot blanc

The pinot family is a fickle bunch, given to excesses on one side of the family and mute sulkiness on the other. Pinot noir gets all the colour and rarely makes up its mind to perform; pinot gris missed out on colour but gets an outgoing personality; and pinot blanc drew a blank on both. A fourth member, pinot meunier, technically a periclinal chimera of pinot noir, literally jumped out of its skin to take on a new form with hairy leaves while maintaining the typical family traits best inside a sparkling wine.

Named for its grey skin, pinot gris (in French) and pinot grigio (in Italian) will display a spectrum of colours even in one bunch of grapes—ranging from a rose pink to distinctly grey to blue—but lacks colour enough to make anything other than a white wine; although some winemakers will allow very subtle pink tones to show through. Its close cousin pinot blanc is a truly white grape, but being relatively neutral it is easily overlooked as dull if solid textural fare. Pinot gris delivers more taste (and oomph!) without overpowering the picnic fare.

Pinot gris can be grown across a wide range of climates. It's a good traveller and has a well-stamped passport because of its ability to come up with interesting flavours no matter where it roams, although its acid does drop very quickly upon ripening.

There is a lot of confusion about the name and styles both here and overseas which reflects the chameleon quality of the variety. It can be softly perfumed through to quite powerful when picked ripe, where it can look like a kindred spirit of gewürztraminer and will most likely appear in the gris format with more than 13.5 per cent alcohol.

Because of its low acid content pinot gris retains a soft, fleshy texture when nurtured in cool climates. In Italy, it is grown prolifically in cooler parts of the country where it takes on an almost neutral, faint mineral and herb fruit character, and a savoury mouthfeel makes it an ultra-friendly food wine. At its best, Alsace pinot gris varies from quite sweet to delicious, spicy fruit and texture, and generous alcohol thanks to late harvesting.

Pinot gris should be fresh, lively and pretty simple, and lower in alcohol from early picking. It could be mistaken for unoaked chardonnay with similar freshness, texture and alcohol although the finish should be brisk. It's a syrupy, slurpy, smooth-on-the palate, sensual white wine with a lick of minerals and the best that you can happily glug away at. You are not going to be taxed when drinking a glass of pinot gris; unlike a glass of Hunter semillon with bracing acidity when you will have to think a little.

Compared to semillon or chardonnay it is not a great ageing wine, getting fat and oily easily unless made with real talent. Grown in warmer regions it achieves a nashi pear to pineapple fruit spectrum. In Australia, it's grown in the cool climate regions of Orange and in the Adelaide Hills where Hardy's have planted 400 acres of it in one hit. The production of pinot gris seems to be doubling annually in Australia.

In the United States, where nearly all the pinot grigio drunk is Italian in origin, the variety is probably going to overtake chardonnay as the wine most consumed by Americans. One ACNielsen report dated June 2005 indicated that pinot grigio grew by 46 per cent in dollar volume in the previous year, making it the fastest-growing white wine in America. New Zealand also have some great wines made from this variety.

As for pinot blanc, it's a homely little wine not unlike a shy chardonnay with less obvious flavour but with a sweetly curling lick of creaminess that makes it very moreish. Its attractive creaminess and very subtle white nuts such as hazel or brazil nut-like fruit character make it an ideal picnic wine.

Aromas and flavours of pinot gris are hay, perfume, cut pear, fresh apricot, pineapple, stone fruit kernel, savoury, mineral, nutty, honeysuckle and honey. Great wines from this variety are available from Miceli, Brown Brothers and Stefano Lubiana.

There seems to be little unity of style and taste in the overseas offerings. The dry Australian wines are as interesting as those from overseas, but go to the top levels of Alsace *vendange tardive* and we have nothing equivalent to offer. From a small base we are doing incredibly well, and at this time look to boutique producers because the rush to catch a share of the market will influence quality. The Kiwis are ahead of us in style.

ALBARINHO *This variety has caught the imagination of most who taste it for its somewhat 'richer than riesling' personality and texture. Unoaked it is a fleshy wine with a striking exotic feijoa/peach character that appeals and is not easily forgotten.*

Muscat

The most well-established Italian wine in Australia would be moscato, otherwise known as frontignac. Under its French title as muscat à petit grains it is used for sweet wines that have been strengthened with spirit and sold as *vin doux naturel*. It was the Italians who tamed the variety in its friendly table wine version over 100 years ago, as a low-alcohol, lightly fizzy sparkling. The variety and style has had a huge boost from the farseeing Brown family, and their delightful moscato with low alcohol, peachy freshness, zippy acidity and well-balanced sweetness gives a faithful rendition of the Italian classic.

Fosters under their Yellowglen jersey have also entered the fray, albeit with a lower-key edition aimed at a less sophisticated market. The wine is a delight with fruit salad or fresh peaches. Primary fruit characters include floral, perfume, scented, aromatic, spicy, rose and blossom.

Another muscat sweet wine that has made its dent on the vinous psyche of Australians is spaetlese lexia. Lexia is the shortened version of Alexandria and refers to the ancient roots of this grape variety, which is muscat of Alexandria.

Gewürztraminer

Gewürztraminer is a fusion of two German words—*gewurz*, meaning spicy; and *tramin*, referring to the Italian region from where it originated. Though this doesn't mean that this 'spicy' wine always goes well with spicy foods. Rather, think of it as the perfect accompaniment to foods with a complex flavour and a rich texture, such as quiche Lorraine, mild green Thai curry (not red curry), a Thai-style salad, or fish with a coconut-based sauce.

Aromas and flavours found in gewürztraminer are floral, spicy, perfume, rose, lime, scented rose petal and fresh green apple blossom, with treats of passionfruit, lychee and lavender. Alsace has a strength of experience and range of styles that gives them a head start but we do have shining, if occasional, dry examples.

Other wine varieties

SWEET WINES

Sweet wines have been made in enormous quantities all around the Mediterranean basin since the dawn of agriculture.

The Romans wrote about falernian, which was a sweet wine aged for ten to 20 years until it became the colour of amber. It was good enough that some vintages were being talked about 200 years after they had been made. Originally, they seem to have been made simply from late-picked sundried grapes that were high in alcohol and sugar, which was a great preservative especially against some fairly rough winemaking skills.

There has always been a strong market in Australia for sweet wines. Penfolds pioneered consumer recognition of the table wines with their Trameah wine after the Second World War and we have been refining it ever since. From the early 1970s many have appeared with gewürztraminer (or traminer as they called it) as part of the blend, answering the call for something sweet and easy to sip, as they were generally a moderate 12 per cent in alcohol. The roll call of sweet wines that have been before includes both local and imported wines such as Muroomba, good old Ben Ean, Black Tower, Liebfrauwein and Blue Nun.

Launching these wines in the 1970s, particularly in association with the food and wine experience, meant that many of them were originally introduced to people in Chinese restaurants when they were the only national network of oriental cuisine in Australia. The arrival of more diverse Asian cuisines, notably Thai, has broken the stranglehold of Chinese restaurants, yet these wines go on being drunk in significant quantities. Wines like Penfolds Bin 202 Traminer Riesling, Wyndham TR2, and Rosemount Estate Traminer Riesling have all been big sellers in their day.

Today's growth is driven by a new generation of young sweet-wine drinkers who are moving on from RTDs or Coke to something more interesting and food friendly—wine! Based on recent sales figures we now have a new generation of sweet-wine drinkers who are not afraid to go past the more traditional dry styles in pursuit of a wine that they are comfortable with. The continuing success of Brown Brothers' Crouchen Riesling #8 positioned as a top-selling white is testimony to this. In layman's terms at least one out of every 72 cases of white wine sold is sweet. TR2 currently sits at number ten and has some 1.3 per cent market share.

Traminer riesling

Sweet as two-sugar tea, tasting like a fresh apple and smelling with the grainy spice of passionfruit, banana and musk

PHILIP WHITE, ADELAIDE ADVERTISER

Now put up your hands those of you who have drunk a bottle of traminer riesling and enjoyed it? There must be plenty of closet traminer drinkers out there who have underpinned the fortunes of many Hunter Valley winemakers. This popular fruity, sweetish, low-alcohol blend covers ground that no other wine does in Australia. However, the more memorable moscato styles will fragment this market further.

Traminer riesling is the Australian version of gewürztraminer, which hails from Alsace. At home in Alsace, gewürztraminer can be a rich and unctuous wine with characteristics of high alcohol, extraordinary fleshiness and a generous amount of residual sugar. In Australia, the variety is usually blended with riesling which produces a medium-sweet style. This Australian hybrid generally has an alcohol content of around 10 to 11 per cent, with a pleasantly sweet, grapey taste that is perfect for drinking chilled with just about anything, especially on a hot day. It's sometimes been sneered at as a bit of a McDonald's wine (and some bad examples can smell like old-fashioned hair oils in the style of California Poppy), but it can be much more delicate than that.

Apart from certain vineyards in the Hunter, the Eden Valley in South Australia has produced some decent traminers. Normally the grape is grown in cool climates. It is a bit eccentric to take such a delicate variety and grow it in a baking hot climate but it works. The variety has enough power to hold on, although the differences in climate will bring out different personality traits. For example, a thick-set rugby player of a wine will come out of the Hunter Valley, but it's definitely more AFL when coming out of the Eden Valley or central Victoria.

Botrytis wines

Botrytis has its own terroir based on those regions with the right mix of damp, misty mornings that slip into bright, warm sunny days in late autumn after the crop of white grapes is ripe. The grapes turn an unsightly brown and shrivel often to yields of only a glass of finished wine per vine. These locations are generally near rivers with the city of Griffith being a notable exception. Australia's sun-drenched vineyards produce super-ripe grapes that have been made into a number of traditional fortified styles which, more recently, include lexia and the porphyry of Lindemans with the occasional outbreak of botrytis in the 1950s creating an interest.

Global knowledge of botrytis is much older and diverse with Hungary and Germany both vying for the earliest examples. The Czars kept a cavalry unit in Hungary in the nineteenth century specifically for the transport of their Tokay Aszú Eszencia (botrytis-infected local grapes) *furmint, hárslevelı* (yellow muscatel and oremus grapes), grown close to the Bodrog and Tisza Rivers. Made from the juice that seeped from unpressed berries and fermented for years in old oak before bottling as *essencia,* it was the most concentrated and possibly long-lived of all wines.

Nearby in Bürgenland in Austria they have a similarly long tradition with welschriesling, while the Germans recall that the failure of the Bishop's outrider to arrive in the 1740s and tell the locals to start harvest, led to the harvesting of late-picked, mouldy riesling grapes which, despite the peasants' hesitation, produced a delightful wine.

In Bordeaux the origins were linked to supplying the needs of the Dutch wine trade in the 1780s for sweet wine to trade with their colder northern neighbours—the mix of semillon, sauvignon blanc and muscadelle is the most sublime.

A glass of sweet wine can be a great joy, but it is all too often taken at the end of a meal. This is, I think, unfortunate, because sweet wine plus sweet dessert can equal gastric distress, dehydration, taste confusion and an overall loss of respect for what these potentially gorgeous wines represent. Try this as an alternative. Sit down with a bottle of German spaetlese riesling with about 8 per cent alcohol at around three in the afternoon on a lovely sunny day. It will be completely delicious. It's not alcohol, it's not water and it's certainly not a cup of coffee but it is a lovely drink that has an almost health-giving pleasure for the mouth.

Knowledge of microbiology and international styles increased understanding of botrytis and since the late 1970s there has been an explosion of styles following in the heels of Darren De Bortoli's Griffith successes. This infection is called noble rot when it sets onto ripened fruit. It's called grey rot if it appears while the fruit is still ripening and will destroy the crop. In red wines it produces laccase, which creates cloudy juice and hastens oxidation and the destruction of colour. Other moulds found in the vineyard include aspergillus, necessary for making soy sauce but a disaster in wine.

Under these conditions the arrival of botrytis is welcomed, and while feeding on the ripe grape it introduces its distinctive flavour to the juice, making the result far more interesting and complex than merely alcoholic raisin grape juice. Botrytis is a mould that feeds on the water and sugar in the grape, which results in a concentration of flavours including the sugar by evaporation of water. This concentration can see a 75 per cent reduction in crop weight and a tiny 1 or 2 per cent of juice.

At the same time it consumes some of the acid, converts sugar to glycerol and produces gluconic acid which alters the aroma, flavour and body of the wine. In dehydrating the berries of ripe grapes, botrytis changes the flavour of the grape, replacing the primary fruit with an almost apricot to tropical lusciousness, with honeyed citrus and candy characters, or pineapple and mango when the mould is extreme.

The best of these wines are expensive as they come from repeated pickings (up to four is common) and sometimes down to individual berries, as at Château d' Yquem in Sauternes. Botrytis-affected wines have been continually improving. The earlier examples combined incredible sweetness with huge oak and volatility (vinegar smells), but the more recent wines are finer, less oaky and less volatile.

Some strong Australian contenders in botrytis wine production include Darren De Bortoli's Noble One Botrytis Semillon, Tamar Ridge for its riesling, and Morilla Estate for its botrytis sauvignon blanc.

There is more sweet power in the Australian style with 200 plus grams of sugar putting them ahead in blind tastings. The French style of around 120 grams of sugar is more a sweet wine with a dry finish that puts them ahead at the table with food.

Ice wine

Canada's greatest contribution to the world of wine to date is some of the most incredibly sweet wines ever made. Ice wine was originally a German invention but global warming is reducing their frequency there. Grapes are left on the vine in the Niagara region as late as January, when the big freezes come regularly, and can fall to –8°C or even as low as –12°C.

While most of Canada is too cold for wine grapes Niagara has natural assets, aside from the cold winters, that allow vines to grow there. This is due to the moderating effects of the Great Lakes and the sloping vineyards along the Niagara River moving the cold on in the growing season.

The statistics are scary. These wines are expensive, requiring six times as many grapes for a bottle as table wine. This is owed to the production style of pressing only frozen grapes and removing the ice that constitutes 90 per cent of the water to retain the concentrated sugar and acid for fermentation. The result is an incredibly rich and luscious finished wine with over 200 grams of residual sugar per litre. To put this in context, this is more sugar than many table wines have at harvest.

The acidity at 13.3 grams per litre is twice as much as white table wines and saves the wine from being cloying and sickly. The Canadians have surpassed the old world winemakers in perfecting this style. However, international rivals are using the 'ice wine' name for freezing the juice of normally harvested grapes in the cellar to concentrate them, and are producing wines that seem to be impossible to pick from the originals. The Canadians are crying foul, as these impostors are not using the same frozen-on-the-vine techniques.

There are a number of these ice wines made with skill in Australia, particularly the Wellington Ice Wine from Tasmania. But one has to ask, is it better? The catch with leaving grapes late in the season without botrytis to modify the acidity is wines with extraordinary acidity and sugar. Canada makes them from riesling, cabernet franc, pinot noir and the hybrid variety vidal, while the best are riesling from the Niagara Falls region. Having judged a class of 35 of these wines in London I am all too aware of the effects of high-level acidity on your teeth, gums and stomach and find them a marvel definitely to be shared. The Australian styles have more balanced acidity and sweetness with fresher fruit. The ice wines of Germany and Austria are expensive and hard to find, but well worth the effort.

ROSÉ WINES

Rosé is a pink wine that at its best combines the dryness and body of a red wine with the freshness of a white wine.

There was a time when you had to add 'just kidding!' if you said you drank rosé in Australia. The leading Australian rosé 25 years ago was made by Kaiser Stuhl. It was cheap, made like a white wine, had a very high acid content and was very, very pink!

The history of rosé in Australia has been clouded by these shocking pink wines, which only goes to show how the industry here picked up the plot and went off on a completely different, and not very successful, tangent. The tangent stems from the wine industry's way of dealing with a high-alcohol grenache. The grapes' acid had fallen so they balanced it with an acid addition; in the process of tidying up the acid they needed to add some sugar in order for the acid addition to be palatable. Away they went. An Australian wine book in the 1930s suggested that rosé should have the body of a red but the refreshment of a white. We ended up with the body of a cheap white wine and the refreshment of a semi-sweet white wine but it was pink. We completely missed the mark. These wines have nothing to do with the ideal of rosé and nothing to do with the rosé that is drunk in France.

To me, real rosé is the kind that the French have been making and drinking for aeons. Up until about 25 years ago, the French drank hardly any white wine; less than 10 per cent of their consumption was white and of the 90 per cent red wine they drank much of it was rosé. The old guys playing boules under the plane trees in Parisian parks are often sipping on it. But it's not the shocking pink variety, rather it's the colour of super petrol or bruised red rose petals. Dark pink.

In the mid-noughties, 2005/06/07, many winemakers in Australia sought to make a good rosé as an alternative to full-strength reds. The key has been moving the goal posts from sweet to dry and the play from white to red. As I write, the modern Australian rosé style is coming of age and the techniques employed could not be more different from the traditional Australian style. Modern rosés are made with specific fruit (generally pinot, shiraz, grenache or cabernet sauvignon), often machine-harvested, but after that it's a very French approach.

They avoid over-handling, and de-stem the fruit straight into a press; then press it all to ferment, no pressings cut; the fruit is left to roughly settle overnight and then racked to old French casks for both natural yeast and natural malolactic fermentation. The wines are sulphured on lees in cask after malo and racked out in July and prepared for bottling with no lees stirring. The traditional acid addition is being restricted and the wines usually end up with a high pH of 3.9 and low total acids, much lower than whites.

Their colour is quite pale and looks quite European, not the galah pink–purple that most Australian rosés now have. The wines are bone dry and the higher pH and lower acidity gives them terrific if un-Australian natural texture.

Rosé works well as a warm weather wine and that is the direction in which we are going. It also goes well with Thai food, which is very popular, as well as medium-bodied fish such as tuna and anything Spanish or southern Mediterranean.

Nowadays, some producers are moving right away from the word 'rosé'. You will see the word 'saigné' from time to time—this wine is rosé, but the new word refers to the process of bleeding a bit of juice off the skins—and it's also the French word for blood.

Rosé palate graph

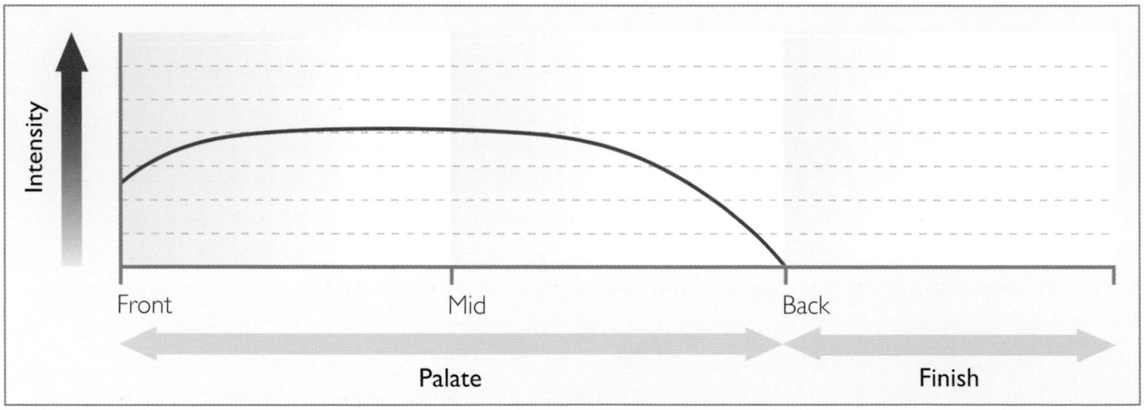

Rosé characteristics

Scents

fresh red fruits • raspberry • blueberry • strawberry • cherry

Flavours

delicate • thirst-quenching • smoothly tannin free • soft acidity • supple in the mouth

Regions

a versatile style that can be from many regions • pinot from Yarra Valley and Mornington Peninsula • Barossa Valley shiraz and grenache are among the best

Rosé regions

To get a good one, go for the Barossa or Yarra Valley makers. Other than that general advice, there are some specific standouts: Charlie Melton's Rose of Virginia, a pun on the region from which the fruit comes and his wife's name; Yerring Station; Miceli; and Turkey Flat. There is one totally iconic little rosé that has been plugging away honourably at the market and that's Rockford's Alicante Bouchet. Three international regional benchmarks are Tavel and Bandol for marvellous wines while Château de Sours makes Bordeaux's most popular rosé from merlot.

The future for rosé

Globally, rosé is on fire. In the United States it is called 'blush', made from zinfandel grapes, and is credited with launching a whole generation onto the slippery-dip of wine. But zinfandel blush is really very sweet—again, more white wine than red and now in decline in the United States as consumers move on to pinot gris among others. In the United Kingdom, the increase in wine consumption by young women (two or even three times more) has seen rosé as one of the fastest growth wines in popularity.

Rosé is primarily about a more flexible lifestyle, fun, easy to drink, unpretentious, enjoy with friends or on social occasions, and yet dry enough to carry on drinking during the meal. Many of the sweeter rosés are too sweet, do not go well with food and will fade from the scene having done their job of introducing a new generation to wine.

Less will be made from cabernet sauvignon or franc over time, as these varieties do not suit the style's need for less tannic varieties, such as pinot noir will gain. You can eat pretty much anything with rosé. And as the baby boomers mature, they are going to need something that is lighter on the stomach. Just like the old guys under the plane trees in the south of France.

Australia's production of rosé is getting there in a rush with the latest crop of high-quality rosés using more traditional methods. Currently there is more quality dry rosé from France though Australia is closing the gap.

CHAMPAGNE

Before the champenois vignerons perfected their craft, most champagne would have been pink because most sparkling wine is in fact made from red grapes. In the time of Dom Perignon vignerons perfected the pressing method to obtain white juice out of red grapes, and improved the finesse and subtlety of their wines by adding chardonnay to the blending process.

Too much of anything is bad,
but too much champagne is just right

F. SCOTT FITZGERALD

One of those quirky little moments in history: it was the English who invented champagne.

It seems that in 1662, when French winegrowers reported that they had produced their first bottle of sparkling wine, the Royal Society in London was describing methods used by the English to make brisk and sparkling wines by adding large quantities of sugar and molasses to stimulate the second fermentation of finished wines that creates the bubbles. According to champagne historian Tom Stevenson, it made the English wine not just lively but unequivocally sparkling.

Every second around the world seven bottles of champagne are uncorked. There is no doubt that this is a wine of celebration. It is used to launch ships, mark marriages, celebrate races that are won or examinations that are finished. It is as uniquely elegant as it is uniquely joyous.

Dom Perignon, according to some sources, is supposed to have exclaimed on his first taste, 'Come quickly, I am tasting stars'; appropriate for a blind man although many heard the story as 'Come quickly, I have discovered the stars'. And, either way, surely he's right. When you hold a glass of champagne up to the light it is possible to spot tiny bubbles forming right at the bottom near the stem, and then watch them rocketing upwards like a basketball to the hoop.

To me champagne will never be anything but French. But Australian sparkling wines, with their characters derived from their diverse climatic backgrounds and near champagne-like appearance, are making a definite splash. Champagne and sparkling wines are best drunk when they are young, because once they get old they start to lose some of their bubbles. After about five years they start to go downhill as their flavours broaden and their effervescence declines. Old champagne is not for everyone unless it is

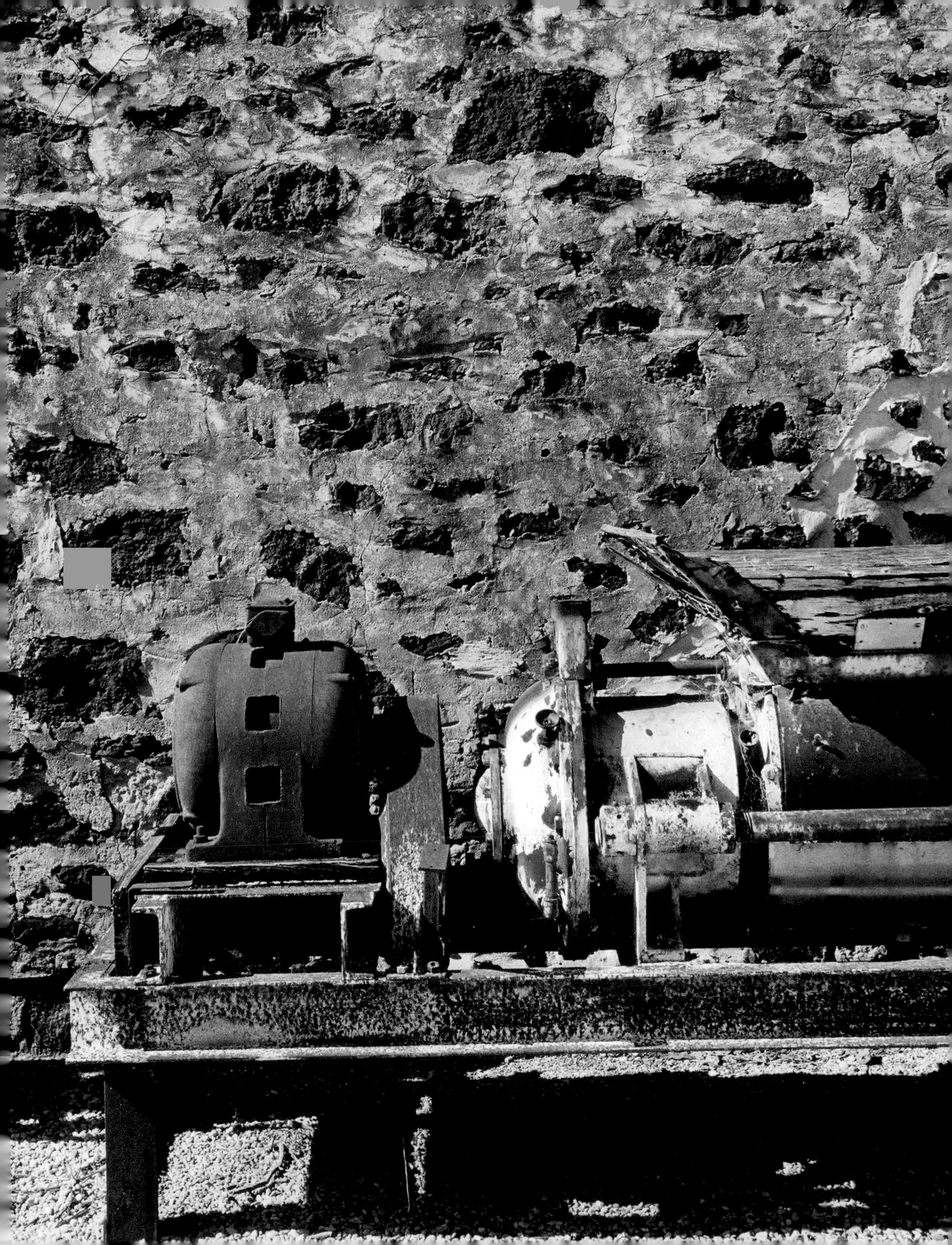

from good producers; then it tends to develop flavours of French patisserie almond, vanilla, caramel and toffee.

It is accepted wisdom that champagne must be blended and that no one variety or place can deliver a great quality wine consistently, or is it? It is curious in France that their typical focus on single vintages and individual terroir wines has been discarded to focus on blending, which coincidentally suits making large quantities of quality wines. Whether in large or small production, the skill and sensitivity of the local palates and the deep insights the French have concerning style, varieties and region elevate their wines to a pinnacle of the winemaker's art. Champagne is unique in the French wine world for its continual sales strength over many years and its image of quality, luxury and association with celebrations.

Australia's premium sparkling wines are made from the grapes of chardonnay, pinot noir and pinot meunier, all sourced increasingly from the cooler southern regions of the country. Properly grown in these cool climates the grapes have high natural acidities, and the characteristic tight, varietal fruit characters respond very well to the magnifying-glass effect created by million of bubbles lifting their flavours to the nose and palate. Besides, the effervescence's pleasure and acceptability lies in the balance of sugar and acid.

Naturally high acidic (almost makes you squint) grapes from cooler climates with their meagre, lower alcoholic structure rely on sugar to balance the acidity, and make these sparkling wines seem more fruity, full and pleasant tasting. Many French non-vintage types of champagne carry quite high acidities (ten to 11 grams, twice the level of many red wines). They get away with this as fruit flavours kick in at quite low ripeness (around 9.5 per cent alcohol), balanced by high sugar (11 to 15 grams) to create the style. These wines gain another 2 per cent alcohol with their final ferment, which creates the effervescence and the alcoholic strength you read on the bottle.

The challenge remains for sparkling wines to be fine and delicate on the front palate so that you can taste what happens on the back palate. Too big on the start of your tongue and the rest of the palate gets lost in the flood. The softer, less acidic Australian wines carry less sugar (9 grams) to balance the acidity and a touch more alcohol (around 10.5 to 11 per cent). This gives a more mouthfilling structure that challenges winemakers to retain delicacy along the length of the palate; finding the elusive balance between the elements keeps winemakers in both countries on their toes.

The mass market Australian wines under $15 are about increasing drinkability by balancing the acceptability of sugar with lasting length of flavour that is not heavy, broad or flat and that is free from obvious acidity. In the premium or luxury market, winemakers seek greater finesse of body and subtle refined flavours with an even delicacy of fruit across the palate.

SPARKLING WHITE WINE

Australian sparkling wines were struggling for many years because early picking led to green, hollow flavours, but vine age and better growing regions and viticulture have boosted local fruit quality.

Today, great Australian sparkling wines exist with tight fruit styles with front-palate lift derived from chardonnay and pinot noir to carry the flavour through to the back palate.

Many Australian and overseas wines don't show well due to either lack of fruit or excessive sugar on the front palate, which overwhelm your chances of finding anything on the back palate but short and tart or sweet. The fruitiness of Australian wines can create front-palate fullness so that they lose the perception of fruit on the finish.

The challenge for Australian winemakers is to produce more elegance on the front palate to show off the finish. For some winemakers this has been remedied by choosing fruit from lower latitude vineyards, such as Tasmania, where the fruit's inherent quality has better length of flavour and the suppleness needed to make great wine.

Sparkling white regions

Most of the finest wines in this style come from Champagne in France, but they have just about reached their maximum production and opportunities for further vineyard growth are controversial.

The regions below Champagne along the river Loire, such as Saumur, historically contributed to the *champenoise* when frost or war reduced the capacity in Champagne to supply. There are a number of very affordable wines from that region, some based on chenin blanc or from Alsace with pinot gris in them.

The mantle for sheer volume of sparkling white wine production goes to Spain with their Cava, which ranges from the everyday to remarkable wines of breadth and depth. Locally we look to Tasmania for finesse; the Mornington Peninsula for more weighty complex wines; the Adelaide Hills for delicious aperitif styles; and the Macedon Ranges with more intensity.

The future for sparkling white

This style of wine requires specialised skills, production facilities and lots of capital to finance the maturing stock in bottles; it will be the terrain of the big, well-capitalised businesses and small producers with a passion for the style. As with many of the classical historical regional styles the joker in the pack is global warming and riper, less acidic styles.

Australia is able to produce some of the flavours of champagne but we still need to build more length, complexity and depth into our top wines and they will always be slightly bigger. Buy locally for value with confidence, but top French champagne is sublime.

Sparkling white palate graph

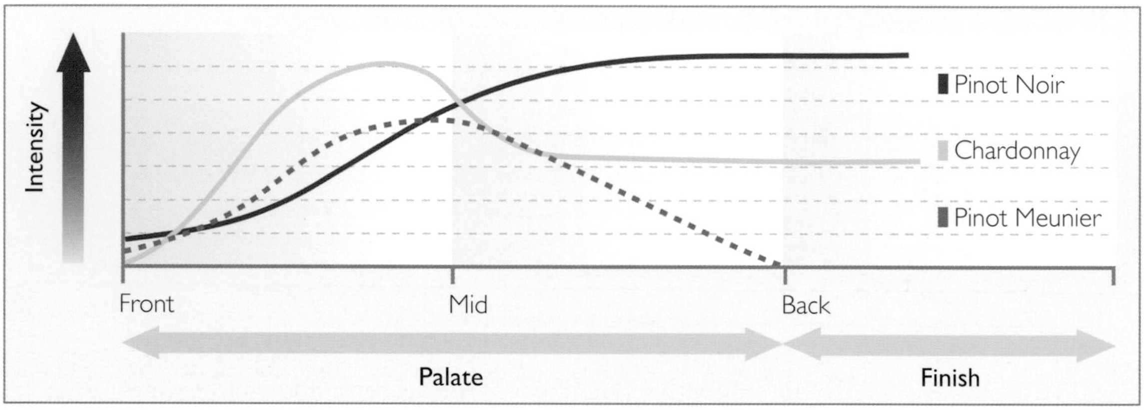

Sparkling white characteristics

Scents

lemon • citrus • grapefruit • green apple • red apple • nectarine • green melon • rockmelon • strawberry and confectionery • yeast • fresh bread • vitamin B • cashew • honey • brioche • vanilla • hazelnut • roast nuts • mushroom

Flavours

intense subtle flavours: fresh apple and nectarine to cashew, mushroom and toast, depending on style of wine and its age

Regions

Tasmania • Mornington Peninsula • Adelaide Hills • Macedon Ranges • New Zealand • Champagne • Saumur • Cava

In victory, you deserve champagne. In defeat, you need it

NAPOLEON

SPARKLING ROSÉ

It is a frippery, dippery little drink.
Some love and some hate sparkling rosé or rosé champagne.

It is a bit all over the shop in terms of variations in style, price and quality, and some people confuse it with a kir royale, which is champagne with a dash of *crème de cassis* to give the colour and sweetness. But when it's right ...

Colour has been everything with these wines since Veuve Clicquot produced its first edition in 1777. 'Staining' an already finished sparkling white creates most of these wines—there are a couple of methods that can be applied. The simplest is to use pinot noir, which solves the colour issue but gives a rather robust style that few producers consider acceptable. It is, however, the most widely used method for non-vintage wines, with 10 to 15 per cent pinot noir added to the blend before the second fermentation. The second method is to soak pinot noir skins in the assembled base wine blend (generally chardonnay and pinot meunier) until the desired colour is achieved. This is laborious and time-consuming as it requires great skill to match the colour across each blend and each year. No wonder many of the most expensive champagnes are rosés.

The consumer can end up with a delicate, pale-pink drop or something that is big-flavoured and nudges a red burgundy with serious colour. The deeper-coloured rosé wines have a different range of flavours and textures to champagne and make great food wines. The flavours are crisp for aperitif styles, and rounder and more generous for accompanying food, while at the end of the spectrum you can see strawberry and raspberry flavours (from the pinot noir) but not sugar sweetness. A rule of thumb here is, the more money you spend on the sparkling rosé the more interesting and exciting the wine is likely to be.

Sparkling rosé characteristics

Scents

combination of bread-like yeast or toasty aged-yeast characters with fruits of the forest jam spread very thin • fruit in the mould of strawberry, cranberry, raspberry

Flavours

immediate berry fruit flavours should lead with strawberry, raspberry, and then build to a complexity of yeast and toast and finish dry

Regions

Mornington Peninsula • New Zealand • Tasmania

The future for sparkling rosé

This style has a long way to go in terms of matching consumers' expectations, with sparkling rosé wine showing many different styles. The challenge is to get stable colour and the type of flavours that suit the different groups attached to this style.

SPARKLING SHIRAZ

This appeared as a wine style in South Australia in the 1870s, courtesy of early winemaker Edmund Mazur. The style was transported to Great Western and it became very much identified with that area due to two historical factors.

First, Great Western was to become predominant as a sparkling-wine-producing region in Australia. Second, Seppelts decided to concentrate all their production there in 1874, which meant that there was a huge investment of intellectual capital in the district upon which those winemakers could draw.

Despite the fact that sparkling burgundy and shiraz rose to great heights in Australia, there has been a lot said against them. When I started in the wine industry in the mid-1980s the style was on its knees. Because I was working in wine education in South Australia, I had access to vast quantities of Seppelts sparkling everything, including burgundy, and I used it for student tastings at every teaching session on sparkling wines. Nearly everybody could grasp the style on first taste. I'll never forget that one of those students sent a letter to the Wine Information Bureau complaining that nobody drank sparkling burgundy unless they were a down-and-out hobo. At which the manager laughed, heartily!

Sparkling shiraz started to take off in the early 1990s thanks to a concerted effort by local wine writers to inform and persuade Australians that this was a valid style. Fashion swung, sparkling shiraz as it was now called came rapidly into fashion.

Going to a barbecue on a freezing cold day in Adelaide some ten years after my disgruntled student's letter was written, it was a surprise to find that, of the 22 guests, 17 people had brought sparkling shiraz. We had a very memorable day tasting them all. Today, it is a wine style that is in better health in terms of profile. It has an enormous ability to age well in the bottle and develop real style. Winemakers in the Swan Valley, Coonawarra and the Barossa are trying it out, but it is quite expensive to make and needs good technology, which is why it's still not widely produced.

While any red variety of grape can be used—including durif, merlot and pinot noir—cabernet shiraz is best for the traditional style as it has soft tannins and potent spicy fruit, while pinot noir makes a more refined wine. Once a staple of Christmas Day, you can expect from this wine a big personality and an explosion of sweetness followed by a riot in a fruit salad bowl of small and large red fruit, followed by a calming dry finish. The best examples show a finely tuned finish with acid and tannin in balance. And there's no need to chill heavily.

Sparkling shiraz and burgundy characteristics

Scents

intense blackberry • plum • spicy plum

Flavours

sweet, ripe red berry fruits

Regions

Great Western • Barossa Valley • McLaren Vale • Swan Valley • Coonawarra • Clare Valley

The future for sparkling shiraz and burgundy

This variety will remain a homeside favourite playing on its own turf. Sparkling shiraz is so Australian that it defeats the purpose to consider the rest of the world's offerings at this time.

FRIZZANTE

The frizzante wines of Italy are lambrusco, muscato d'Asti, or good old Asti spumante—fermented in tanks for a short period of time to create a low alcohol level and a light sparkle.

This is usually 5 to 6 per cent, compared with the 12 per cent of other sparkling wines. Top wines made under the spumante method involve multiple fermentations and must exhaust the yeast food, chiefly micronutrients like nitrogen, in the grape juice so that after several tries there are no trace elements left to feed the yeast in order for it to restart the ferment.

The feature is the appeal of muscat as the only grape to produce wine with the same flavour as the grape itself. A celebration of fruit with citrus, peach, orange and floral fruit freshness, and the best are briskly fresh to the finish thanks to the protection given to fruit through sparkling-wine winemaking.

The best muscatos come from northern Italy, specifically Piedmont around the town of Asti. Taking its name in part from the variety muscat blanc (blanco in Italian), a petite grains blanc. It is naturally fermented and a good muscato is light, refreshing and low-fizz or semi-fizzy (frizzante) with a lovely spicy fruit flavour, which is reminiscent of Turkish delight, frangipani flowers, rose petals and maybe even honey. The combination of these flavours, low alcohol and the light fizz gives a sweet and tingling sensation. Muscato can be very moreish. I think of it as a fantastic Christmas Day finish—just a glass —or a great finish with a simple dessert after a big and complex meal. It is also a great match to a lovely warm day in the back garden with a piece of sweet fruit.

The best of the imported wines is moscato d'Asti, it is expensive and highly complex with refined, subtle, complex fruit flavours with a range of citrus blossoms flowering in the glass. As the price goes down into the styles of Asti spumante the wines become thicker, sweeter, less distinguished, better known and widely available.

Italy has multiple appellations for these wines and Asti spumante is the most readily available. But I caution you to first try either Brown Brothers' local version or the more expensive imported moscato d'Asti. They are not about alcohol but invoke sweet, fresh fruit such as passionfruit and lychee with the scents of orange blossom and rose water wrapped in low alcohol that's gentle on the tummy and kind to the intelligence.

Brown Brothers was the first company to make a serious Italian-style muscato in Australia. It is a fantastic wine made from muscato Alexandria Gordo grapes grown mainly in the Sunraysia region of the Riverland. Brown Brothers report that sales of this wine are limited only by its availability, which in turn is limited by the amount of grapes they can get to make it. So there is still an enormous capacity for uptake with the Australian muscato.

This wine is best served as a post-lunch refresher, mid afternoon with fruit, a pre-dinner drink on a hot day, or with fresh fruit with cheese as a dessert.

Frizzante characteristics

Scents

some of nature's most alluring smells: vivid and juicy as roses • jasmine • peach • citrus • apricot

Flavours

sweet with bright fresh flavours and clean fruit attack

Regions

varietal style and requires cool climate for fruit to produce fine aromas and palate

The future for frizzante

I predict that this wine has a fantastic future because of its low alcohol content (6 to 8 per cent) and high pleasure attributes. For Australians, it suits our love of all things Italian, as well as our climate and lifestyle. It is probably one of those rare sweet wines that are popular with punters and critics alike.

There are no bad examples yet from a fast-evolving Australian category that could see a shortage of quality grapes in the near future. Rest assured that you can buy locally with confidence.

FORTIFIED WINES

As a genus, these wines have been in decline due to the current fashion for avoiding high alcohol in heavy or sweet wines.

This is a shame, as there are some superb styles that are well worth exploring. Fortified wines keep well after opening, giving you additional reason to return to them over a couple of days or a week or so, with the exception of tawny port which can last a lot longer. The production of fortified wine is arcane, traditional and a minefield of details. Broadly speaking, fortification means the addition of alcohol to protect the wine and to slow down the destructive process of oxidation. This was absolutely essential to transport wines from one location to another and became an important aspect of trade after the 1700s.

There has always been a hefty exchange in sweet Mediterranean wine to the cold northern climates. The rise of European sea power started to change the way in which wine was made. We see the Dutch, for example, great seafarers and wine consumers, pressuring French vignerons to pick their grapes later and thus leading, over a generation, to the creation of the wines we call sauternes and barsac. The English traded their cotton goods for wine with Portugal and port was developed. Port emerged over time as a wine that was very much in the preferred style of the era—fiery, red and strongly alcoholic.

Fortified wines tell a story of the glorious combination of history and politics, and trade and money exchange, and wealth. But for practicality I am going to talk about the characteristics of each style of fortified wine rather than how they are made, in order for you to have some idea how to use them. Of course, there is always the opportunity to have the vicar round for a glass of sherry, but these days most of us don't see the vicar very often so we don't see the sherry pulled out regularly either. Anyway, the vicar is more likely to be a guru or a pilates instructor, both of whom would probably refuse this archetypal aperitif and have a glass of muscato.

The production of fortified wines tends to take place in warm, generous liberal climates for grapes, and with vignerons who have the capacity and profitability to age them sufficiently. For this reason, they can be hard for small companies to make.

If penicillin can cure those that are ill,
Spanish sherry can bring the dead back to life

SIR ALEXANDER FLEMING

Sherry

A fabulous history, sophisticated styles and declining sales make for one of the wine world's tragedies as table wines take over from the leisured times of pre- and post-dinner drinking. The future looks bleak for this wine as both local sales and imports are declining.

Great dry sherry is a lightly fortified dry white wine with an alcohol content of 15 per cent that has been subject to additional ageing. Dry sherry is a great aperitif and an admirable substitute for sparkling wine with a dry and nutty twist to the finish. As we experiment widely with varietal styles all over the world, it appears that sherry is a product associated with a bygone age.

True sherry is from the province of Andalucia—the sherry triangle between the cities of Jerez de la Frontera, Puerto de Santa Maria and San Lucar de Barrameda. It is made from three grapes in total—palomino, pedro ximenez and muscat—but it is really only the palomino that matters.

Australian sherry making is following the market into decline and is not an art that comes easily to our winemakers. Angoves and Mildara have for years carried the lantern. We once made sherry by simply leaving barrels of half-filled white wine out in the sun to oxidise. The great innovation was the addition of the flor yeast that was smuggled into a winery in the Clare Valley in the pockets of a thoughtful winemaker. One of Australia's great sherry brands, Grand Fiesta, rose and prospered. One day the flor yeast mutated and that was the end of it and Grand Fiesta sherry, too.

Fino and manzanilla

There are nine sherry styles of which the greatest to me are the two driest: fino, and her lighter and eminently racier younger sister manzanilla. Both are quite white in colour, and both feature the effects of the growth of a film yeast, one that grows on top of the wine, not in it like most fermentation yeasts. It is called flor yeast and it flourishes in a humid climate and temperate ocean air. The yeast literally flowers over the partially filled barrels; it metabolises some of the acids and feeds off bits of alcohol, some of the nutrients as well as the air. The effect looks like a dense, white mat.

In a process not dissimilar to the human metabolic system denaturing alcohol to acetaldehyde before excreting it, yeast metabolise alcohol to release the energy by creating acetaldehyde, and thereby create their food and the typical flor sherry aroma. Flor yeast allow these sherries to develop a characteristic aldehyde 'tang', which is at the same time salty and nutty (almond and cashew) with soft acidity. The most intense effect of flor is evident in manzanilla, which comes from San Lucar de Barrameda (Christopher Columbus's home town) on the seaboard. You can smell the tang of the sea in it.

Fino traditionally comes from further inland, a more continental climate, from around Jerez. It is more golden, with an oilier body and more texture because the flor can't live over the top of the wine for as many months of the year, so the wine has a bit more development from the air. It has a different balance to manzanilla. Fino is the most wonderful restorative, but it's much more huntin'-and-fishin' in style.

Both fino and manzanilla are the most gorgeous drinks and are imbibed routinely in Spain in half bottles with little whitebaits and salty dishes. My ultimate sherry experience is sitting on the quay at San Lucar with some seafood and two chilled half bottles—one of manzanilla and one of fino—and bottoms up (if you can't get there, serve on a really hot evening before you serve seafood. It sets everything up beautifully).

Today, we make flor fino but our base wines tend to be a bit heavier and the style overall has a bit more weight. For delicious local examples try Seppelt Show Fino DP 117, Peter Lehmann, Angove's, Sevenhill, and Chambers Dry. A reduced Australian market makes getting fresh wines from retailers difficult. Nothing approaches manzanilla, while local finos can match their overseas counterparts.

Amontillado

Amontillado sherry is an aged version of fino showing more complex, nutty flavours and alcohol. Ageing happens through oxidation which occurs after the protective veil of flor yeast has fallen away. Oxidation allows the wine to grow further in richness which emphasises a walnut character to the taste—the almond and cashew recede.

There's something quite Edgar Allan Poe about amontillado; it is heavier, more dramatic and still a great drink on its own. All of these associations mean that it is really a drink for the beginning of a meal, albeit a bit excessive. Somehow, it needs to be contained with all these sorts of food as a separate feast on its own.

Amontillado is still quite dry; although when made in Australia can display sweetness. Seppelt DP 116 Show Amontillado is a bargain, while others come from Morris Old Premium and Yalumba.

25

Oloroso

Oloroso is a rich, heavy wine that is made from the later pickings of palomino grape and can quite often be blended with some flor-based wine before maturing. Many Australian oloroso are lightly sweet while the majority of Spanish are dry. They are fortified quite early so that they don't show any flor yeast qualities, and present a delicious amber colour.

'Oloroso' means fragrant and I think they have fragrance and a fabulous voice—with a great timbre and base note to them, a ballsy power. Oloroso is a voice in full flight; full-bodied and velvety and at the same time powerful but finishing dry. Characterised by a distinct nutty taste that is a bit oily, a bit sweet and very ripe, syrupy and rich, oloroso should be drunk with French onion soup, tapas mouthfuls based on eggs, anchovy, meats and strong cheeses.

Seppelt DP 38 Show Oloroso is the greatest, a bargain. Excellent wines come from Yalumba and Chambers. The richer sherries classically suit a rich and thick French onion soup, with lots of cheesy croutons—and splash a bit of what you are drinking into it!

Cream sherry

Cream sherry was originally produced for the British market by blending Spanish oloroso with pedro ximenez. It led to wines with a very strong aroma, velvety palate and full body. It's called cream sherry because of the creamy palate. Bristol cream sherry is a development of this original style, using clarified grape juice to make the wine clear.

In Australia, we understand and make sweet sherries quite well, especially cream sherries which are very sweet with an often muscaty edge, are clear and white and ready to drink straight away. They should go well with chilled grapes or other fruit; however the style has fallen in the past 50 years and is now very ordinary.

Pedro ximenez viejo

This is the Spanish wine to rival an Australian liqueur muscat or tokay. It is darkly sweet, the colour of old mahogany, with a smooth, sweet palate. There is also a touch of alcohol and tannin for depth. It is claimed that this wine is made by using sundried grapes; they are harvested, brought into the courtyard and laid on racks to dry out the berries. While this tradition runs the length of the Mediterranean coast as well as up into Switzerland and northern Italy, it's not clear whether in fact the Spanish still use this method.

Unlike other fortifieds, pedro can be drunk over a period of time. It can be put away to savour again and again although I warn you that they are very moreish in their sweetness.

Two local producers still making these as varietal fortifieds are the Settlement Wine Company in McLaren Vale and Turkey Flat in the Barossa Valley. It is one of the few wines to partner chocolates, and brandied figs with mascarpone.

Cammaradaria

It is eccentric to include this wine but its very existence is a miracle and it's probably as good a taste as you are going to get of the sort of sweet wines that were prevalent in Shakespeare's era. It was part of a sweet-wine group like canary and sack from sherry.

This Cypriot wine is made by a technique common to the Mediterranean, using sundried grapes, which after harvest are brought into the winery courtyard and laid on racks to dry out the berries and increase the sugar. The increased sugar ensures that the wines finish fermentation while still carrying a fair degree of sugar.

It is still done in exactly the same way. The grapes are left lying around in the courtyard for two or three weeks until they raisin up excessively, then pressed to get the skins away from the juice, and then fermented without adding any more alcohol.

The natural alcohol content of this wine tends to be around 15 per cent, carrying a mother lode of sugar, redolent with summery spices, honey and traces of wood and wax and maybe toast. It is a generous, luxuriously sweet wine without the whack of alcohol that is added to Australian equivalents.

The original is very different to our wines, thanks to higher alcohol and better fruit freshness and richness, but then that's what cammaradaria is. No comparison.

Madeira

Madeira (Portuguese for wood) is a tiny island 850 kilometres off the south-west coast of Portugal; it has been a stopping point for water, fresh food and wine for sailing ships since its discovery in the 1400s. The wines were rustic, often helped with cane sugar and often sweetened with grape must. They were then drunk over the rest of the voyage and increasingly sold as people realised that the rocking and rolling of sailing ships matured the wines into a new kind of taste.

The style was refined in the eighteenth century when sailing vessels would take on wine in barrels and it was found the style was improved by long journeys through tropical regions. It is one of the few wines that is quite capable of outliving its cork, owing to the use of the *estufagem* or heated rooms at around 50°C for lower-quality wines to replicate what happened on the sailing ships.

For many years under honourable managers the wines were blended to style, yet named after a combination of the boats they sailed in and the grape varieties that gave them distinctiveness. After suffering a loss of fashion the island's largest winery is back in good hands and the wines are regaining their rightful place as distinctive fortifieds with strong citrus notes and a distinctive style of their own.

Madeira has entered the wine world on a number of levels. It's in the term madeirised when you encounter an oxidised dry wine, and it's a style of fortified wine similar to port and sherry from the island that comes in aged and now varietal styles.

A venerable style with much improved production under the Blandy family of late, this style while out of favour is nevertheless improving in quality and consistency. A matter of tradition for this long-aged wine is to store it standing up so that the cork does not touch the wine as the risk of oxidation is of little concern. All fortified wines with a stopper cork should be stored this way.

SEPPELTSFIELD *The greatest shrine to traditional Australian wine is Seppeltsfield in the Barossa Valley. This spectacular and venerated place is inhabited, fittingly, by a man who is notable for his tall, monkish and rather acerbic demeanour—James Godfrey. He is the guardian of one of the world's oldest continuous collections of fortified liqueur ports, dating from 1878 to the present day. According to instructions from the Seppelt family, these are only to be bottled when they hit 100 years old, which means that Seppelt's current owners, Fosters, are able to release a continuous annual stream of the world's oldest wine on regular release.*

Port

Port, dark chocolate and coffee should finish any major meal! While sherry is made from white grapes, fortified when it has finished ferment as a dry wine, port is made from red grapes with the alcohol added to stop the ferment and keep the wine sweet. There are three main classes of port: ruby, tawny and vintage.

Ruby port

As its name suggests, ruby port is very bright red with strong, fruity aromas, mildly tannic with no oak. If you leave a good ruby in a barrel and forget about it for a while it will start to turn into tawny; it will begin to oxidise and go brown, the wine will evaporate and the sugar levels will go up.

We use the term 'rancio' to describe the mocha, coffee, chocolate colour and flavours of these older fortifieds. The finish on a good tawny is long—20 to 30 seconds worth of taste.

Ruby port is fruity, fiery and sweet. Once opened it needs to be drunk quickly to enjoy its red fruit freshness.

Tawny port

A classic tawny port has a dry edge because it has been aged in barrels and the barrel tannins tend to impart some flavour to the finish. On the level of flavour alone, it makes a great drink, especially in winter. It's great with a coffee or after a meal.

Our tawny ports are sweeter than Portuguese port sand have great age although a declining market is seeing ports with less freshness. The richness of Australian tawny is unique: try Seppelts Para Port for a shining example. The top tawnies are Seppelt DP90 Tawny, 21-year-old vintage-dated Para, Morris Premium and Yalumba 25 and 50 year olds.

DANGER
KEEP HANDS CLEAR

Vintage port

The market for vintage port is in a state of sad decline at present. The term 'vintage' may be confusing. Vintage port is port made and bottled in the same year. The term vintage (indicating the year of its production) can only be applied to tawny if it comes from one year when it goes into the barrel for maturation until bottling—hence tawny vintage port. Penfolds did this for quite a while. There is a perception that the older vintages are quite rare, but this hasn't been reflected in market price. Vintage port should show intense berry flavours with an almost liquorice trace, and lots of tannin and noticeable brandy spirit. Late-bottled vintage port or LBV is a lighter version of the real thing but it has its place.

Vintage port is a Portuguese specialty and the dryer finesse of these ports put them in a unique position. Our sweeter styles are interesting but hard to finish the bottle. The great Australian vintage-dated ports are most importantly Hardy's, Chateau Reynella and Seppelt. For an elegant, fiery, aromatic lighter style try one from Portugal, such as Taylors, Dows, Warres, Fonseca, Ramos Pintos or Grahams.

White port

Unique to Portugal is a wine called white port, made in two styles. The first is just fortified white wine, which is sweeter; the second is a drier style, which doesn't make for a bad drink at the start of a meal on a hot day. When I was in Portugal, we'd start our midday meal on a hot day with a glass of well-chilled white port, and finish the evening meal with a decent bottle of vintage port. Shared among all of us, of course! Tintilla in the Hunter Valley is keeping the white port style alive.

FORTIFIEDS

Australian winemakers have made a special contribution to the array of fortifieds with two wines—muscat and what used to be called tokay, which is now called correctly after the variety it is made from, muscadelle.

Liqueur tokay, now muscadelle, is an Australian idiosyncrasy. The muscadelle grape variety that is used in tiny amounts in the Bordeaux region has morphed into a delicious, viscous sweet wine with rich fruit in the district of Rutherglen in Victoria. You have to have at least one good bottle of it once in your life.

Liqueur tokay

Tokay is a style native to Hungary where it is a botrytised dessert wine. It is made by adding buckets of botrytised grapes to already fermented, quite sweet wine. The addition really boosts the sugar levels. The Australian wines are basically fortified grape juices so there is no comparison really. However, I was once privy to a bottle of Hungarian tokay essencia made illegally under the communists in the 1950s, bottled in the 1980s and then smuggled to Australia. There was a workmanlike similarity between their black, treacly, sweet and oily style and ours, which gave me an insight into how the wines came to share the name.

Australian tokay is unique and good for its dark-barrel-aged, pure fruit sweetness and luscious style, while Hungarian tokay is a golden complex botrytis reminiscent of sauternes but with more richness and generosity, showing the tropical fruit and candied fruit spectrum. These modern wines are well worth seeking out.

Liqueur muscadelle can be put with food but then you may suffer calorific overload and you may ruin the purity and fabulousness of the taste. You should drink it on its own, in small glasses, riotously and decadently with good jokes.

Liqueur muscat

The other Australian idiosyncrasy is an extraordinary liqueur muscat from Rutherglen. The particularly deep, nourishing soil of the region gives the muscat vines a cracker chance at developing their berries. The richness that the little brown muscat achieves in Rutherglen is absolutely out of this world for its concentration and balance of sweetness and lusciousness. Griffith also gets muscat right, with McWilliam's and the De Bortoli family winning vast clutches of medals with this style.

The very pure grapiness of these wines has to be smelt and tasted to be believed—floral, luscious and ripe with a classic rich, nose of dried muscat fruits, raisins and oranges. I feel bad about saying too much about it because currently there isn't enough to go round. With the good ones hitting $50 a bottle it's a worrying thought where prices will end.

Muscats can be good with desserts. Put it in the fridge for a couple of days before opening so that it chills to a thick slurry. Serve it with a bitter, dark chocolaty dish, which will work well with the sweet darkness of it all.

A regional side note is the Swan Valley liqueur verdelho, which is a regional treat. In this case, it is their very old vines and featuring the grape variety in a format that owes more than a passing nod to madeira.

Muscat age quality

The following categories explain muscat age quality and rarity; these also exist in a similar form for liqueur muscadelle (tokay).

Rutherglen muscat: A youthful style exhibiting fresh raisined-fruit flavour and a luscious balanced palate. Would expect to have an average age of two to five years.

Classic Rutherglen muscat: A maturing style exhibiting raisined-fruit flavour, cask-aged flavour and the beginnings of rancio character. The palate shows balanced lusciousness, richness on the mid-palate from cask ageing and some concentrated characters. Would expect to have an average age of five to 12 years.

Grand Rutherglen muscat: A mature style exhibiting aged-fruit flavour and rich cask-aged character. The palate shows balanced lusciousness, rich mid-palate from cask ageing, concentrated flavours from ageing and rancio flavours. Would expect to have an average age of 13 to 20 years.

Rare Rutherglen muscat: A rancio style showing all the flavours of prolonged cask ageing: lusciousness, extreme rancio concentration. Would expect an average age in excess of 20 years.

PERSONAL FAVOURITES *These wines are as unique and excellent as the kangaroo for getting around a wide brown land. Remember that you get what you pay for in these wines, so only select from the best examples of: All Saints, Morris, Chambers, Bullers, Stanton & Killeen and Seppelt. Non-Rutherglen beauties also come from McWilliam's and De Bortoli.*

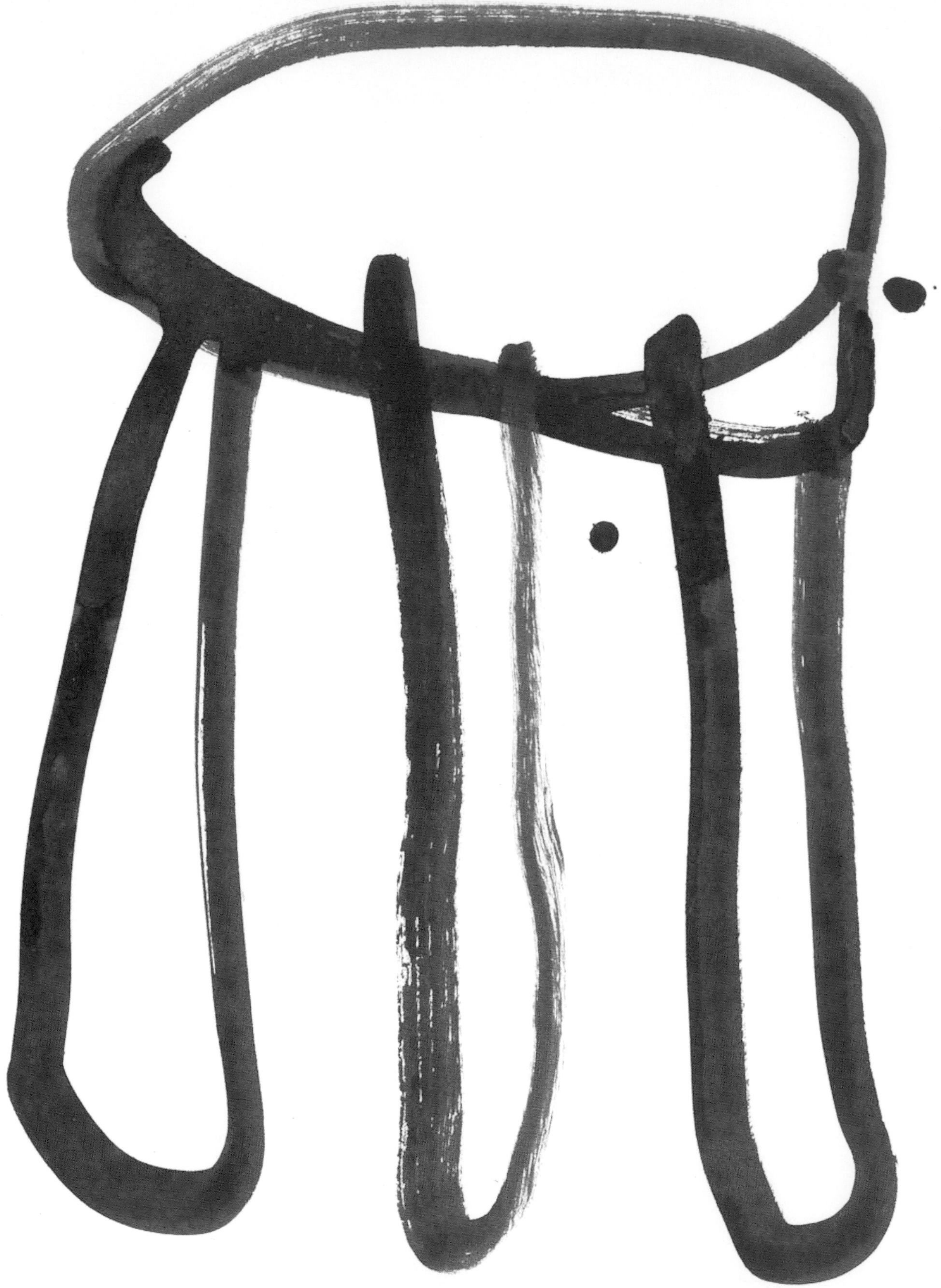

part two

On top of the stool: You

Ernest Hemingway commented many years ago that **wine drinkers never had it so good**, as wine was one crop that was cultivated to the greatest perfection.

If only he was alive today to see the explosion in wine flavours and value, thanks to new regions, new approaches to varieties, and refinements in winemaking styles. Sitting on the stool of modern wine puts you in a position to enjoy the pleasures of this three-legged industry, which is improving every year. And with a little knowledge it allows you to make the most of your precious dollars.

Too often good money is wasted on wine we just don't like. This part of the book offers you the chance to soak in the aroma, taste the hard work of the grape growers and winemakers, match the right food with the right wine, and indulge in the tipple of your informed choice. I want to give you the tools to make choices that suit you.

Your view from the top of the stool divides into significant cultural divisions between the old world in Europe and the new world where vines had not been traditionally planted. European winemakers use what they are given by nature and have cultivated traditions for growing grapes and making wine within their regions. They provide us with a deep and detailed insight into man's relationship with the vine on unchanging specific locations. Some of these sites have been under cultivation for up to 500 years affording them ample opportunity to work things out.

Leading the vines' migration from Europe and into North and South America has been an exciting trip. Free from legislative constraints on what can be planted where and how the wines have to be made has seen an enthusiastic explosion in the wine world of new perspectives, flavours and definitions of flavour—all of which are pushing the envelope in a lusty burst of exploration. Often with large tracts of land at their disposal for expansion, quality wine bursts from warmer vineyards with increasing flavour, exuberance and concentration. As Master of Wine Andrew Caillard observes, 'Australian fine wine is not for the masses but it is for everyone'.

The Australian industry's approach to wines at affordable prices is to continually improve winemaking to provide the most pleasing wines, as winemakers learn new approaches to their varieties and regions, and better understand consumers. Each year consumers can expect the quality of these wines to improve or at least remain the same subject to vintage vagaries. Historically you are paying less for better wines.

The wine industry is composed of many parts. What follows is your personal odyssey into understanding the world of wine tasting and to buying and owning wines with the pleasure that increased knowledge and understanding brings.

chapter 4

Wine on the nose and tongue

Elegance is for tailors
ALBERT EINSTEIN

FINDING YOUR LEGS

This is the fun part of wine—the tasting. The more you drink the more you will understand the wines you consume; could there be a better excuse?

I will be talking mostly about aromas, because smell is integral to the tasting experience. I'll also discuss palate, bouquet and other terms and ideas behind the experience, so that you can unlock more of the details and pleasures that make a wine memorable to you.

The Sphinx who guarded the gates of Thebes allowed no-one to enter or leave the city without answering a riddle: What walks on four legs in the morning, two legs at noon, and three legs in the evening? No-one who tried was able to answer (losing their lives in the attempt) until Oedipus solved the puzzle, answering: man crawls on all fours in infancy, walks upright on two legs in adulthood, and uses a cane as a third leg in old age. There is something in this answer, especially when discussing our taste evolution over the course of our lives.

Without doubt as babies, with a plethora of tastebuds but a fairly narrow diet, we tend to develop a notion of what foods we regard as safe and make highly emotional connections to certain foods. We find it quite hard to appreciate other flavours—we crawl.

As an emerging adolescent or adult we start to change our preferences as this is a time when we try lots of new things. Yet within some cultures there are people who never ever move into this stage and we make reference to it when we talk about comfort food, such as mashed potatoes, pasta and bananas, which are considered texturally satisfying but narrowly flavoured 'baby food'. So during the second stage when we may run on two legs,

DO ALL MY
STUNTS

providing we make that leap, we become culturally challenged and explore drinking and eating by trying new flavours. In the third stage we become three-legged people, needing our canes (of knowledge and experience) to guide us.

Unfortunately, age tends to commit a great crime against taste and we lose our accuracy, which is compensated for by our increased experience. Despite the fact that our receptor cells, which detect flavour, are constantly being replaced, our ability to perceive taste just seems to slow down. Age also influences our change in preferences. The baby's preference on four legs is for sweetness, and the adult's on two legs is for sour flavours, but we tend to return to sweetness again when we're on three legs. I think many people on their journey through life will find this to be true. So what is this thing called 'taste' or 'flavour'?

Flavour is the combination of smell and taste. Taste contains five primary sensations: sweet, salt, sour (acid), bitter and broth or umami (a Japanese word for savoury or meaty glutamate-like flavours). How do we perceive taste and make sense of it?

Yes, taste is on the tongue: the interaction of the item in our mouth and on our tastebuds. But it's not just that. Taste is a very complex sense that also involves our sense of smell. Our nose and sense of smell are highly sophisticated tools. The human genome contains 347 olfactory genes—fully 1 per cent of our total gene count. So I guess, in a way, the best place to start is the nose.

THE IMPORTANCE OF SMELL

In his novel, *Remembrance of Things Past*, legendary French writer Marcel Proust described memories brought to mind by the smell of a morsel of a small cake (madeleine) dipped into a cup of tea. The entire town of his childhood sprang into life from that simple combination of scent and taste.

Mammals rely on their sense of smell to interpret their environment to a degree that humans have lost. Why did we lose it? One reason is that around two million years ago, the amount of our brain devoted to vision, particularly in the development of colour vision, started to overtake our sense of smell. Another contributing factor was the improvement of our analytical functions, which meant that we didn't have to smell as acutely any more. But despite the fact that our sense of smell diminished, it remains a primary, if under-appreciated, tool. Smell is a primitive and powerful dance between flavour and emotion. It has a direct effect on our memories and taste sensations.

The biological changes in our genes have left us with some interesting side effects, such as the ability to remember many of the smells of our childhood but not many of the tastes. Challenge someone by getting them to smell baby powder without seeing what they are sniffing, and asking them in what time of their life the aroma reminds them of. Smell is certainly evocative.

THE SMELL LOWDOWN *We have five million scent receptors and the average person identifies 4000 smells. With training, this total rises to as many as 10 000 smells. A bloodhound has 200 million scent receptors; with so much keener a nose than a human they have been known to follow two-day old scent trails.*

Smelling is not just sniffing

Basic smelling is inhaling. For liquid, the shape of a glass helps create a plume of vapour and directs it up to your nose. A single intake through the nose is regarded as the truest delivery of an odour and the best chance your brain has to make an informed decision. Then thanks to biting, chewing and swallowing the same smells arrive a second time via the retro-nasal passage of your nose. This is a different experience to inhaling. Thus with wine the aromas are rarely identical to the first sniff because the whole sensory system is brought into play when your tongue contributes its taste perceptions of sweet, salt, acid, bitter and umami. Your tongue also warms the contents to give you a physical experience of flavour.

Aroma sources

For you to smell any compound it needs to be volatile to allow the gases to be detected with your nose. There are a multitude of odorants in wine and it's still early days in our understanding of all of the processes and interactions involved in what we smell and why. For example, the smell of ripe fruit entices us by its appealing scent, yet grapes synthesise large amounts of volatile compounds called precursors that we cannot smell or taste as they are bound with glucose. Only 5 per cent of the aroma compounds produced in grapes become liberated from their amino acids and contribute to the characteristic aroma of wine. Not much in the grand scheme of things, but certainly enough to create a complicated (and often flawed) system to describe what we do know.

There are different classes of fruit aromas in wine and some are readily aromatic and can be smelt in ripening vineyards just before harvest. Others are released only by fermentation to give us the characteristic aromas of the varietals. The 95 per cent of fruit precursors untouched by yeast represent a huge amount of potential aroma compounds that remain locked in the wine. Research into how we can make yeast release more amino acids is underway in Adelaide and may in time give us the opportunity to experience more aromatic wines.

What does that mean?

Consumers who are not connoisseurs often complain about the jargon, the descriptions, used in wine tasting and smelling. True, some wine connoisseurs use this jargon to overly complicate matters, a form of talking down to people. If we rework that idea in the positive, though, we can say that wine tasting and smelling has its own rich language.

The oral traditions of wine shouldn't make your eyes glaze over or turn you off. The way into the language is to start at the beginning and to actually experience the process of decoding a wine's scent and taste. Let's look at aroma and bouquet for instance, two essential definitions that are used constantly in 'wine speak'. Aroma is the smell of young wine; and bouquet means the scent that develops after time in the bottle, the smell of older wines.

The aromas winemakers and wine writers describe really exist although sometimes the language used for them is not accurate. For instance, describing a wine as spicy is quite different in chemical origins to the terms peppery or spicy as used to describe food; there is also no relationship between the wine's flavours and those of the spices we typically associate with the smells. For a good guide to the aroma descriptions used, take a look at the aroma chart on the next page.

If you are having trouble identifying either the aroma or bouquet, then try this old trick used by botanists to identify the smell of flowers. Place a small amount of wine in a clean, dry jar with a tight lid; leave it in a warm place (such as a sunny windowsill) for a while then open the jar and inhale. You will be surprised at the intensity and definition of the smells that emanate, but beware that your nose may get a shock as the alcohol will also be more noticeable.

Aroma chart

We all inhabit different taste worlds thanks to our DNA and the cultural environment in which we live, so an aroma chart is to some extent subjective. You may disagree with some things in the chart but as an analytic device it is immensely valuable.

Note that under the character of pungent are both hot and cool (see 'Aroma chart' next page). Hot is alcohol as a mouthfeel and sensation; cool is menthol, which is again an aroma and a taste. That's what happens, as there are two sides to the debate.

I am sure many tasters might feel anxious if they are unable to detect the aromas that other tasters are able to describe in the same bottle of wine—is it one-up-manship or superior olfactory sensitivity?

The potential for different aroma descriptions to the chart has definitely increased alongside the growing complexity of aroma and flavour details in wines. That said though, the aroma chart is the best tool for organising your thoughts when starting out in wine tasting.

Aroma chart

General		Specific	
Fruity	citruso	grapefruit	lemon
	berry	blackberry	raspberry
		strawberry	blackcurrant (cassis)
	(tree) fruit	cherry	apricot
		peach	apple
	(tropical) fruit	pineapple	melon
		banana	
	(dried) fruit	strawberry jam	raisin
		prune	fig
	other	artificial fruit	methyl anthranilate
Vegetative	fresh	stemmy	grass cut green
		capsicum (pepper)	eucalyptus
		mint	
	canned/cooked	green beans	asparagus
		green olive	black olive
		artichoke	
	dried	hay/straw	tea
		tobacco	
Nutty	nutty	walnut	hazelnut
		almond	
Caramelised	caramelized	honey	butterscotch
		diacetyl (butter)	soy sauce
		chocolate	molasses
Woody	phenolic	phenolic	vanilla
	resinous	cedar	oak
	burned	smoky	burnt toast/charred
		coffee	

General → Specific

Earthy	earthy	dusty	mushroom
	mouldy	musty (mildew)	mouldy cork
Chemical	petroleum	tar	plastic
		kerosene	diesel
	sulfur	rubbery	hydrogen sulfide
		mercaptan	garlic
		skunk	cooked cabbage
		burnt match	sulfur dioxide
		wet wool	wet dog
	papery	filter pad	wet cardboard
	pungent	ethyl acetate	acetic acid
		ethanol	sulfur dioxide
	other	fishy	soapy
		sorbate	fuel alcohol
Pungent	hot	alcohol	
	cool	menthol	
Oxidised	oxidised	acetaldehyde	
Microbiological	yeasty	flor yeast	leesy
	lactic	sauerkraut	butyric acid
		sweaty	lactic acid
	other	horsey	mousey
Floral	floral	linalool	orange blossom
		rose	violet
		geranium	
Spicy	spicy	cloves	black pepper
		licquorice/anise	

On the nose

Part of the magic of wine is in the scent of it, which holds out promises for the tongue. Drinking wine can be one of the highest levels of sensual experiences, the zenith of experience to which good winemakers aspire. Newly baked bread, fresh coffee or hot soup send pretty strong aromas through a house and strong messages to the brain. Your nose detects the smell and your brain processes the data, particularly if you are hungry.

Our sense of smell works on a molecular scale—an aroma molecule meets minute aroma receptor sites. Our olfactory system can pick up the smell of decay in meat within a millisecond and the sensory nerves in our nose can quickly detect noxious substances as well as the foods and drinks that appeal to us. Current theory suggests that the olfactory region of the nose contains a wide variety of receptors. Each receptor is responsible for identifying a particular type of molecule, which come in many shapes and sizes. Aroma receptors are very sensitive; it is believed that the aroma receptor cell carries a charge, which locks onto a particular molecule and checks it for confirmation. If it receives the right message the cell will change its ionic balance and trigger a nerve message to the brain.

That's one side of the argument; another suggests we should not be able to smell at all, as some molecules with identical shapes can smell widely different, while other molecules with the same vibrational frequency but different shapes can produce similar smells.

As most frustrated wine drinkers know, an odour does not always create an immediate reaction or connection. Our return thought upon sniffing is tinged with an emotional response. We easily access verbal descriptions for vision and hearing but smells do not enjoy the same easy recognition. People smell the same things but perceive them differently. Odour memory at a primitive level (such as rotting meat) bypasses language thanks to the part of the brain that does the interpreting. You can observe an odour, even if you don't have a name for it. This works neatly when teaching novice wine tasters. Give them a smell and then name it, they will then match that name and smell forever … well, nearly always.

Don't feel pressure if you don't smell what an expert smells. Your DNA, life experiences and personal preferences need to be considered here. But aroma is influential because our bodies use it to seek the most nutritious and desirable substances. Studies have even found that the pleasantness of an odour in a shop can increase the time people linger in the store. Another found that odour produces memories with a greater intensity of emotions than any of the other senses. This may well be why so many people in the wine industry are so passionate about wine; it's a passion that can be reignited with a single sniff.

The way you taste it

It is true that some people are unable to smell very well. Of the 347 genes that affect smell receptors many are inert. Researchers have found that about 50 of the active genes are optional and in some people they work and in others they don't. This means that each individual has their own unique pattern of receptors that influences their perception of aromas and flavours. This pattern holds true for taste receptors as well.

There is a big difference in the number of taste receptors on the tongue that can influence a person's approach to diet and therefore their susceptibility to certain diseases. For example, some people are classified as 'super tasters'. They live in a world where flavours are about three times as intense as for most other people. For this reason they tend to avoid very sweet or very fatty foods (which consequently can lower their risk of heart disease); but they also find that vegetables taste very bitter and will tend to avoid them (which could lead to a higher risk of cancer).

To gauge the strength of your response to taste, swab a little bit of blue food dye onto your tongue. The pink bumps you can see standing out against the blue are your fungiform papillae which house your tastebuds. Now take a small, round plastic ring used to reinforce punched holes on paper; place it over the centre of your tongue and count the bumps inside the hole. Researchers have used this method to investigate our personal taste experiences. The average number of bumps is around 20; 50 or more and you are considered a 'super-taster' who experiences certain tastes up to three times as intensely as 'non-tasters' (people with just five bumps). Add this to your individual experiences of smell, mouthfeel and consistency and you end up with your own personal flavour sensation.

NEW SCIENTIST, 19 AUGUST 2006

Tongue wagging

The structures in the mouth associated with the sense of taste are much simpler in structure and programming than the sense of smell. In fact you can lose your sense of smell much easier and more permanently than your sense of taste. People rarely lose their sense of taste.

Your tongue carries about 9000 to 10 000 taste bumps (papillae) on top of the tongue—commonly called tastebuds. In fact, tastebuds themselves are microscopic and are housed within the papillae. The buds deliver messages to your nervous system and contribute to the sensation known as the 'sense taste'. With training and in concert with your other senses this can become a useful wine measuring system. Whereas your eyes use one nerve to transfer messages to the brain, delivering rapid identification, the sense of taste uses two nerves that are very flexible and diverse in their jobs of recognition.

In order to taste something, a flavour must exist in solution form, which is done through the production of liquid by our salivary glands that bathe the taste receptors in our mouth. The total tasting experience is made even more pleasurable as the retro-nasal process allows you to simultaneously smell the wine while it is in your mouth.

There are three types of papillae that recognise taste on the tongue. The most common taste papillae at the front of your tongue are the 200 to 300 fungiform papillae, linked to salt, sour, sweet and possibly savoury. The second group are the foliate papillae, which are ridged-shaped grooves on the edge of your tongue, that contain a total of about 1300 tastebuds that also sense salt, sour, sweet and possibly savoury. The third group is at the back of the tongue, where we have eight to 12 circumvallate papillae that each contains some 250 tastebuds. Circumvallate papillae have varying chemoreceptor cells that are closely linked to the reception of bitterness. Circumvallate papillae are mushroom-shaped and their gills contain the receptor cells within the tastebuds. These mushroom-shaped support structures contain 100 to 150 taste-chemoreceptor cells, most of which are located on the underside of the papillae and are capable of detecting bitterness.

Taste on the tongue

Many books on wine use tongue maps to explain the tongue's responses, with neat areas indicating where you taste sweet, acid and so forth. This has been largely discredited due to recent research. These areas are sensitive to the tastes described but they can also taste other tastes, which makes a map with neat zones inaccurate.

However, a tongue map does serve a useful purpose, it encourages you to think of the tongue as having a front, middle and back palate for flavour and texture perception.

Map of the tongue

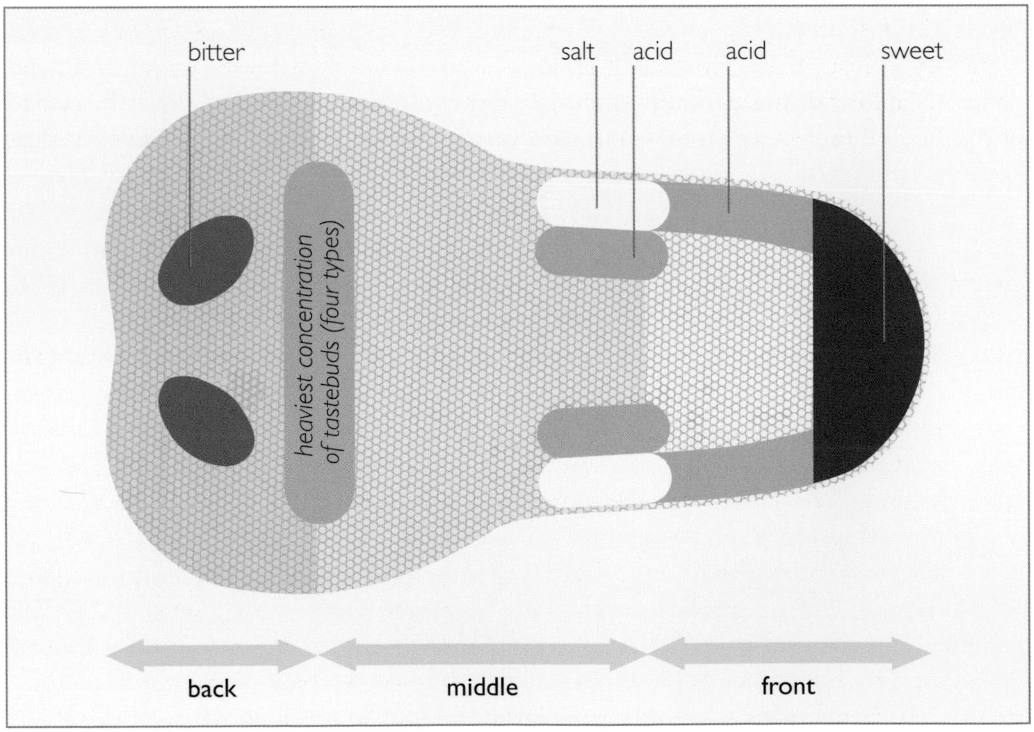

TASTING WINE

To professionals it's a seamless flow: judging colour leads to smelling the aromas through the nose, followed by taking in the basic tastes and examining the body, the mouthfeel and the aftertaste.

The synthesis of all these elements is flavour. It adds up to the tasting experience which allows us to judge memorable wine.

Tasting and flavour perception is a complex process. It involves simultaneous reception within the nose and the mouth: from picking up the glass to warming and swallowing the content in the mouth. This creates a rich mix of flavours that deliver on different mental and physical levels. Each taste receptor cell docks with molecules and opens a stream of charged particles that speed to the brain, delivering the taste message.

Stimulating the trigeminal receptors is also important for flavour perception. The trigeminal nerve serves the nose where the nerve endings are concentrated; it's our sneeze nerve when it gets assaulted by the likes of mustard or chlorine. These receptors are much more common than tastebuds and they respond to physical pressure, temperature and certain chemicals, in particular alcohol, which we may feel as a burning sensation that makes the taste pleasurable. In a complex pathway these nerves are stimulated in the same way as heat, hence the feeling of high-alcohol content as hotter than low-alcohol content. Chilling drinks naturally stimulates our coolness receptors and slows the activity of the alcohol molecules on these same nerves. So by cooling the alcohol the nerves can perceive little reaction, but too warm and they are over-stimulated by excessive alcohol.

How to taste wine

As opposed to drinking, tasting is an attempt to unravel a wine's character and, at certain levels, examine the relative concentration of different aspects of the wine. In a limited way your mouth is able to measure sweetness, acidity, bitterness, sparkling, waterness and temperature, and your memory can hold thousands of smells. The key to wine tasting as a hobby is concentration, focus and memory. This is made more piquant because we are not taught to taste and so we come to learn it socially.

Wine tasting involves seeing, smelling, sipping, and recording our perceptions with our mental language for future reference. The best tastings bring a sense of fun and articulation by attempting to express the essence of the wines under discussion. There is no right or wrong to personal taste. Drinking, eating and enjoying wine can be forms of tasting, but tasting really is a more serious business based on previous experiences.

The more we concentrate our brain on the task of tasting the more wine flavours make their lasting impacts on it; the more we focus on the process the more rewarding it becomes. Memory lies at the centre of the appreciation of almost anything, so our ability to concentrate and focus our first impressions in the context of previous experiences is an important part of the process. The art of wine tasting consists of concentrating on a glass of wine and focusing on its characteristics compared with other wines you have tasted. What are its special attributes? Does it taste better or worse than similar examples? Is the flavour familiar?

THE JELLYBEAN TEST *Pinch your nose and slowly chomp down on a jellybean three times, then release your fingers. Notice how the 'taste' floods into your mind as the vapours from chewing rise into your nose. This is the retro-nasal effect, or nose and mouth working to give you flavour or the total tasting experience.*

The following tasting procedure will assist you to develop your tasting skills—while not looking out of place in public—and is designed to help you to concentrate, focus and remember. As a starter kit for language I find a good way to sort the often-riotous ideas that enter my mind with each sniff is to follow the old adage: does it smell and taste of animal, mineral, vegetable or fruit?

In any wine tasting there are simple steps to follow. I call them the '6 S's':

- see
- swirl
- sniff
- sip and suck
- spit or swallow
- savour.

See

This is where the 'legs' come in—the legs inside a wine glass. A wine's colour and appearance tells us a lot, so first look at it in the glass. It should be transparent and bright whatever its style or age. Cloudiness in wine—as long as it's not simply caused by disturbing the deposit in a red wine—indicates a fault. Cloudiness means that the wine will have lost fruit flavours and may have gained some unpleasant ones. Lean the glass over to draw out the state of the wine's graduated colour from the rim to the heart. The depth of that colour can indicate fruit ripeness or age.

The imagery of tears in wine is interesting and people persist in believing that there is significance to them. Swirl your wine and look for the legs; this is the way the wine flows down the inside of the glass, which is supposed to reveal big distinctions in alcohol concentration and sugar richness. The myth runs that the more or wider the legs show within the glass as the wine runs down indicates higher alcohol or sugar content or both, but not necessarily higher quality wine. Now cover your glass of wine and see if there are legs present. They will dramatically decrease when wine is covered compared to when it's open. If there is no evaporation there are no legs.

Now uncover the glass and watch the legs form! In fact the legs have more to do with physics, the so-called Marangoni instability effect and the interplay between the wine's surface tension and alcohol content, than quality. Legs are due to wine being a mixture of alcohol and water—alcohol having a faster evaporation rate and a lower surface tension than water.

As alcohol evaporates faster than water it creates a meniscus above the wine, which enlarges the surface to volume ratio; this further increases the evaporation area and shifts the surface tension due to variations within the surface of the wine and a lighter concentration of rapidly evaporating alcohol where it touches the glass. The wine touching the glass follows the lower surface tension on top and forms thin tears, assisted by water's high surface tension on the sides, and crawls up the side of the glass until the force of gravity causes the wine to fall into the bottom of the glass. The physics requires larger variations in alcohol than we find in wine unless we are comparing table wine to fortified wine. Legs don't have any significance in judging wine quality or balance.

Swirl

Swirling the wine around the glass allows it to start to talk to you and prepares it for smelling. Swirling helps to coat the inside of the glass with wine and assists the alcohol vapours to lift the aromas to reveal the elements of the wine, such as fruit, age and oak.

Sniff

A smell lingers in your memory much more than taste, so by taking a clear sniff you can start to unlock your opinions. By focusing your mind on previous examples of the wine variety in the glass you are ready to take a good sniff by breathing in through both nostrils. Then by concentrating on what you have smelled, sort it for lightness or intensity, freshness or maturity, and mineral, animal, fruit, spice, flower or vegetable aromas. When you lock that mixture of smells in your memory it will help you to acquire the skill of identifying wines without having to check the label. Notice if the fruit aroma grows in power or complexity over time, as this is a good sign of a quality wine.

Sip and suck

A sip for tasting is done slowly. Take less wine than a mouthful for a drink and focus on your tongue and its receptors for sweetness or sugar, acid or sourness, salt and, in a few seconds, astringency, bitterness and heat from alcohol. Hold the wine in your mouth and roll it around inside to help gently warm it; this increases the rate of evaporation of fruit aromas and allows the layers of flavours to be revealed. Now turn up the volume of your flavour perception: gently suck a little air between your teeth and through the wine to magnify its flavours and introduce the more subtle flavours.

I find it fascinating how some wines will talk to you in a very direct manner, richly hitting and saturating all the pleasure spots rapidly and powerfully, yet one glass is enough, while another wine's aromas will unfold slowly and the flavours are shy but build over time to a crescendo, and makes reaching for more from the bottle easier.

Spit or swallow

Swallowing or spitting depends on the event. If I am swallowing then it's drinking and it's for fun! Spitting is the only way to go when you have a lot of wines to taste as it keeps your mental decks clear and focused on the flavour left behind in the mouth. Tasting and swallowing, with the contrary messages of concentration or pleasure, doesn't work, especially if notes are to be produced and used again.

The extraordinary spitting skill of some senior wine judges over remarkable distances is legendary. Delivering an accurate stream into a bin from a distance is a survival skill and art worth practising when it's going to be a long day. My advice if you want to take up the challenge is to practise in the shower beforehand.

Savour

After spitting or swallowing wait a good ten seconds to see what happens. As your mouth is saturated in wine a lot of flavour perception still goes on, so it gives you a chance to measure the length of flavour. Some flavours can be quite slow to emerge, about three to five seconds, and because of this you need to have that savouring moment with a wine to allow the full impact of all the flavours. One of the most important attributes of great wine lies in the aromatic and taste complexity and longevity of the finish or aftertaste. Look out for those tightly bound subtle wines that don't give you much up front but slowly uncoil in the seconds after tasting it; these wines are the most interesting.

The most important thing to take into account when tasting a lot of the same variety is the influence of adaptation; this means that if you taste the same flavour over and over again the flavour just gets blunted. For instance, the first slice of Christmas pudding always tastes pretty good, but by the third piece the taste becomes … well, unattractive; it is an indication that you are on the way past satiation and the taste has started to bore you. This is your body's warning mechanism; basically you have had enough. The loss of reward is based on a loss of need. The ability of skilled tasters to deal with this challenge is a mark of the art.

Oral traditions

I don't think you can learn about wine in isolation. It requires interaction with others to discover the language and real meaning of wine. Words alone cannot convey this meaning effectively without being accompanied by tasting. Tasting is a social activity that conveys

the oral traditions of received wisdom, and shared observation and description; hence it contributes to the modern point of view. Every individual has different levels of observation to contribute to the understanding of the whole wine.

A good memory is the key. As a complete novice at my first blind tasting I correctly identified my then current three favourite wines by winegrowing region, grape variety, vintage and winemaker. I was as surprised at my result as the winemakers were, as I could not describe the wine's character (flavour, alcohol, acidity) beyond their identity. Generalisations are dangerous as good wine judges are a diverse lot. Most are intelligent, thoughtful, strong characters, and not given to great flights of fancy; they are self-disciplined, observant and well-organised scientists and artisans. The best wine experts cover a wide range of abilities to discern and describe wines from all angles.

What you are looking for

There are lots of taste experiences that seem unique. The same wine does taste different from day to day. There are wines that nobody likes when they dip into them at home, but at the time when they were first tasted, in the company they were keeping, they were memorable. So much depends on when and where and under what circumstances the tasting occurs, and your experiences during such wine tastings. I guess a lot of the time it comes down to expectation.

Culture plays a role. The Romans, for instance, used to have a great taste for seawater mixed with sweet wine. They liked sweet, salty wines. Why? God knows. A more recent historic example is that the Victorian English regarded the ideal serving temperature for red wine as virtually ice-cold. So they drank all of their reds seriously chilled. One last thought—when drinking a homemade wine it might be quite passable or acceptable within a family context, but when you compare it to a commercial wine it tastes, well, distinctively different. So it is important to recognise that one of the biggest external factors that influence taste is the culture in which you live and the experiences you have had.

On offer here are some descriptions of aspects of tasting and some highlights in thinking from my generation of wine tasters, much of which resulted from the challenge of blind tasting to identify wines. What words do you use to express what you have just tasted? Initially there are those elements that make up the wine: sugar, tannin, acid, alcohol and water. Then there are the more cerebral expressions: bitterness, complexity, character, body or shape, and finish. The aroma chart will steer you in the right direction.

Sweetness

A special characteristic of the vine is that it can concentrate sugar at higher levels in its fruit than most other plants. It is also blessed with the ability to create fructose, which tastes nearly two times sweeter than glucose, as it reaches the final stages of ripening. The available sugars correlate to the final level of alcohol that will be in a wine. Yeast prefers to ferment glucose and therefore leaves the sweeter-tasting fructose behind; this makes the wine taste sweeter than the same amount of glucose would dictate. Quite often this level of sugar is retained in the winemaking process, or is added in the form of grape juice and concentrate to reach the required alcohol content.

Wine that tastes dry generally contains less than seven grams per litre (0.7 per cent) of sugar. The skill in noticing sugar content arrives at a threshold or sub-threshold level where it seems to make a wine taste fruitier and more pleasing. A well-constructed wine has a sense of immediate fruitiness and texture that most people will not perceive. When residual sweetness is required the art of winemaking avoids sugar standing out on either the front of your tongue (think of cheap sparkling wine as an example of where it goes), or as sweet on the finish (as cheap red wine can demonstrate).

Tannin

The word tannin derives from Latin roots that mean 'to bind together'. Wine tannins literally 'tan', as in how you make leather, by temporarily binding with the protein in your mouth. This constricts the tissue inside your mouth slightly, and gives you a drying and puckering sense of feel.

The scale of tannin involvement starts modestly with phenolics in aromatic wines, such as riesling and gewürztraminer. Any puckering on the finish in these wines is a negative. In this way a riesling with an astringent finish is said to be phenolic. Some wines, such as sauvignon blanc, are more phenolic as part of the varietal character. As white wines grow in alcohol content and body, some degree of tannin is used to help build a seamless body of texture. White-wine winemakers improve the texture of their wines by leaving a percentage of skin tannin from cloudy juice. Often they introduce it via oak fermentation or maturation, and then use ageing on lees to refine it. This leaves a characteristic creamy feeling in the mouth.

A richer texture—a sense of weight and full mouthfeel—is most often related to the level of tannins drawn from red grape skins and the oak barrels used for ageing. Deft handling will see the tannins contribute a silkiness, while more robust wines designed for long ageing will have a stronger, sandy tannin feel and astringency towards the back of the palate. It is worth comparing pinot noir or a young Bordeaux to a young Australian cabernet to see the differences in styles of tannin that exist. Vintage port marks the bass notes of tannin.

Acid

The prickle in the mouth that some people feel as a metallic effervescence and others as a neat tingle on the border of the tongue is the refreshment value that aids food friendliness, and has a vital impact on ageing. The vine is one of the few crops we grow that contains tartaric acid. As bacteria or yeast are not able to metabolise tartaric acid, it makes it a stable component in wine and an important contributor to the taste of it. Wine grapes on the whole carry more tartaric acid than table grapes.

Acids comprise about 1 per cent of wine. Acidity is a tangible taste and provides an insight into quality, region and variety, as grapes vary in their levels of acidity due to their varietal DNA and the climate in which they are grown. Riesling has a greater propensity for tartaric acid production while pinot noir is quite low in it. Harvest can be planned early to capture levels of the greener sharp malic acid to suit some styles. Weather and soil influence a variety's acid levels in the finished wine and very high acidity gives a stern sense of texture and bright, almost sharp, flavour—think champagne or sparkling wine.

Middle-ground acidity provides the lively progression and vivid brightness of flavour and freshness. Consider riesling, where the same level of acidity as in a red wine would make the tannins taste bitter. Varieties that are picked very ripe, such as shiraz, have less acid to balance the considerable tannins carried by fuller-bodied red wines. Low acid often gives a dull brown colour, soft flabby texture and a flat soupy sort of flavour. Some wines, such as fino sherry, manage to carry this well, making them the least acidic but still refreshing wine.

WINE IN FLIGHT *Air travel makes wine taste different. The low humidity makes the wine's aroma seem thinner. Our ability to develop saliva drops with altitude; this makes the tannins taste heavier and gives wine a firmer, drier finish. Without drinking any alcohol, a passenger will typically shed one and a half litres of water per eight hours in the air. Medium-bodied white and red wines with soft tannins work best in high altitude.*

Alcohol: the genie in the bottle

Alcohol content varies from 7 per cent in mosel—the German riesling with an almost watery, tart, character-filled grape sweetness to balance the searing acid—to 15.5 per cent in red table wines, and 21 per cent in some fortified wines. The balance between alcohol, acid, sugar and fruit elements of a wine is important.

The ability of alcohol to tickle our perceptions is not just linked to swallowing. It acts as the solvent for some aromas and transports others to our nose as it evaporates. It starts this process the moment we pour wine into a glass and then take it into our mouths. This is where the genie rises on the front of the tongue and we immediately start to unravel the relative sense of sweetness and body that alcohol creates along with sugar. Alcohol has a higher viscosity than water, and this makes it the major contributor to a sense of weight in wine, with the fullness increasing as the alcohol concentration rises.

White wines show how remarkably easy it is to taste differences in alcohol. They carry less extract and texture-modifying substances. Tasting wines at 8 per cent alcohol content in German riesling; 12 per cent in Australian riesling; and 13.5 per cent, often found in chardonnay or viognier, is great when you want to focus your attention on the front and middle parts of your tongue. That's where they hit the spot.

Alcohol is theoretically tasteless but in wine it is part of the sense of sweetness at the front palate and can be a fire at the finish. All producers aim for it to be a seamless and indistinguishable part of the wine with the exception of the brandy spirit used in Portuguese ports and Australian vintage-dated fortified wines.

Many producers aim for a sweet spot with 13 to 13.5 per cent, which gives enough body and weight without running the risk of higher alcohol (14 to 15.5 per cent) that creates a burning sensation or irritation of the mouth. The relative absence (around 8 per cent) of sugar in many German or Italian muscato wines gives them their delicacy.

Bigger reds, especially those made in the Barossa and with the United States market in mind, can easily reach 15.5 per cent alcohol. This gives them a sense of fleshiness on entry and they seem luscious with the alcohol-building fruit sweetness, but as they can carry less acid their ageing ability must be in question. Fruit varies in its ability to help wines carry their alcohol, so that it is a balancing act between fruit structure and alcohol content.

Watery

Next to alcohol water makes up most of the content in a bottle of wine. As alcohol and overall fruit concentration rise wines begin to change in density. The term 'watery' refers to a lack of body and sense of density across the palate, and a stronger sense of fluidity of texture unrestrained by body or acid. This is often linked to grapes picked from young vines or those that are overcropped.

Bitter

Anyone who has crunched into the seeds of a grape knows the mouth-shrivelling bitterness of grape tannin. It's also present in the skins of the grape but in a less concentrated form. Different grapes have more or less tannin inherent in their biological make-up. For example, pinot noir is thin-skinned and tannin-poor; shiraz is thick-skinned but tannin-rich.

Overextracting tannins will leave a bitter finish late in the flavour. Oak barrels will also add tannin in the winemaking process, as do a group of compounds that deliver vanilla and caramel. Tannins that are bitter or hard in the mouth are said to be unbalanced.

Complexity

Complexity is when you take a sniff or taste followed by another, and find the wine is subtly different from the first experience, even if it was only moments earlier. Complexity is the diversity of characters in the wine. On the palate it can seem layered as the wine unfolds different levels of intensity of differing characters.

Character

The character or personality of the wine is the overall sum of the elements that gives wine its over-riding uniqueness.

Body or shape

Master of Wine Andrew Corrigan quoted a recent survey from a UK market research company, which said that consumers thought full-bodied wines came from larger grapes!

The body you taste in wine starts with the tip of the tongue and alcohol. The sum total of the wine's weight and density on your tongue is the body. The effect of the wine's fruit profile as it flows across your tongue is how you detect the body and characteristic varietal 'shape'.

The shape takes its form from a differing sense of ripe fruit body along your tongue. The duration of body and residual taste is described as 'length'. The longer a wine's flavour persists in your mouth, the more interesting and the more food-friendly you will find it. The residual effect of body is the 'finish', which is examined by the wine buff at the end of the tasting experience, after swallowing or spitting, to give an overall sense of body and shape. It may be a sense of width that comes with some varieties, flooding the middle of your tongue but not finishing.

At first it is quite difficult to discern body and shape as the tasting experience seems to pass in a millisecond, but with time and focus you will find that it is a chartable process. This is what the palate charts on wine varieties in Chapter 3 are all about: a summary of the body of the wine, taking into account the changes your feel along your tongue. As you know, styles, varieties and regions have their own texture and characteristic shapes that add to the pleasure of tasting wine.

Big-bodied wines come from warmer climates. They possess a natural richness of flavour and structure that make them familiar to many Australians. Light-bodied wines mostly come from cooler climates and are more delicate in structure, while medium-bodied wines reveal their climatic origins with a crispness of acidity and brightness of fruit.

Fuller-bodied red wines are one of the delights of wine, as they are a veritable feast in the mouth with a coating of fullness and flavour. It is easy to be seduced by fuller-bodied wines as they initially make more of an impression on your senses; so it is a great personal journey to learn to find the beauty in wines with less body and often more interest in their delicate flavours and balance. Mostly you will find very soft red wines are full of front and middle palate flavour and body, but do not continue towards the finish (see below).

The trends for red wines have been to go for a stronger balance of fruit and tannin rather than oak. Leading-edge producers are currently trying to rein in their wines and bring more fruit freshness and complexity and balanced oak with more regional flavours and styles. Consumers are doing their part by preferring pinot noir over shiraz in some circles, which seems to be about body and tannin.

Finish

The after-effect of a tasting is the finish or the way a wine leaves your mouth feeling. The finish of a wine makes for its drinkability. For example, the classic combination of the

CEP
CEP

acids in white wine adds to the refreshment of your mouth and prepares you for the next mouthful; while in red wine a certain level of drying from tannins helps to pave the way for the next mouthful.

Finding a wine riddled with TCA (trichloroanisole) need not be the end of the bottle. Soaking food-grade cling film made of polyethylene into the wine will remove much of the TCA cork taint. Unfortunately, it also takes out other flavour constituents and reduces the overall flavour. But it's the best answer I can offer to save a bottle. Worth a try at home.

The perfect balance

In an ideal wine no one character should dominate. Acid, alcohol, tannin, sugar if present, grape and oak-derived flavours and textures would be seamlessly wed to be appealing and in harmony. The underlying balance of a wine should make you want to have another sip, at least, and add to the experience of the tasting.

When do you find the balance? Some people are quick to detect smells and some of us are slower to find the smells described. No doubt familiarity, practice and experience all play a role but some people are definitely more blessed than others in this region. Many wines don't immediately show their true selves; often time, aided by decanting, or just letting the wine sit in the glass, will allow it to settle and show its character. I have seen even quite modest wines at $15 a bottle requiring two hours to settle and reveal their fruit.

A common challenge comes when the same wine tastes different on a different day. While I have experienced this I have seen no research to indicate why other than to suggest subtle differences in our health, the glass, the level of humidity in the air, the cork containing the wine and the service temperature, all of which can influence wines on any day. I am very grateful to winemaker Philip Shaw from Orange for confirming that this was his experience too, allowing me some safe assurance that it is an industry-wide observation.

The effect of serving temperature

The effect of temperature on taste and aroma is a small book on its own. Most wines look much less than their best at the wrong temperature, yet this is maddeningly complex for an onlooker to decipher. Physics plays its part, as does the quality of flavour and aroma compounds contained in the wine. Physically, higher temperatures evaporate alcohol and subtle aroma compounds faster. So it's only quality wines that can take being served warm, but then it is very rare to serve a wine at over 20°C.

White wines perform better than red wines in outdoor conditions in Australia. An emerging group of low-alcohol, semi-sweet styles can really be served cold. Wines such as Italian muscato, German spaetlese and Australian muscato represent a sophisticated mid-afternoon sip. As the serving temperature climbs the sense of sweetness is magnified; and hence makes it best to serve a low-acid wine chilled. At low-service temperatures the sense of refreshment is enhanced and the volatility of aromas is reduced to the degree that most wines under 10°C will have lost their characteristic aromas. A budget white is best served very chilled, so that it dulls its aromas and flavours below 10°C and allows the wine to warm up in the glass.

Red wine tannins by contrast seem rounder and less astringent at higher temperatures, while lower temperatures increase their sense of bitterness, tannin and acidity. It takes skill to get a red wine to drink well outdoors in the middle of an Australian summer.

Essential guide to serving temperatures

Young champagne	Store at 6°C to 10°C Chill to 10°C to 12°C; allow it to warm to 15°C for enjoyment Must be served cold to minimise foaming when it's poured
Old champagne	Warm to 20°C and taste If it's good, continue. If it's not, serve chilled
Sparkling wines	Serve at 6°C to 10°C
Top quality chardonnay and complex whites	Serve at 14°C to 16°C
Young reds	Serve at 15°C
Older red wines	Serve at 18°C
Top quality rosé	Serve at 12°C to 14°C

A short list of wine faults

Yes, the list given on the next page is short! Most of the time you will not find a faulty wine. Over time and by drinking widely you will eventually find that different bottlings can vary. I have provided a few you might discover when wine tasting and their likely sources.

Key faults found in wine

What it smells and tastes like	Issue	Most likely cause
Vinegar or nail polish remover smell, low fruit intensity; aggressive dry finish	Grapes were damaged by hail, insects or birds	Fruit damaged prior to harvest or waited too long for pressing
Musty or rotting dank smell	Grapes had a degree of fungal infection and were partially rotten	Fruit damaged prior to harvest
Green vegetation, ivy-like aromas with a flavour of bitter herbaceousness, like crushed green leaves	Leaves and other foreign objects with grapes during pressing	Fruit damaged during harvest
Pungent herbaceous aromas and flavour	Under-ripe fruit and the grapes had immature tannins at harvest	Heavy shaded canopy or picked too early
Some herbaceous aromas and flavour	Grapes were roughly treated and poorly de-stemmed, de-stalked and crushed	Pressing
Smells leafy, green flavour or bitter; astringent finish	Grapes were pressed too hard, which extracts unwanted green tannins from the skins	Heavy pressing of white grapes
Overall unbalanced fruit flavour compared with dry mouthfeel and astringent tannins on the finish	Overextraction due to skins being in contact with must for too long	Fermentation techniques
Aromatic white wines with low-key green colour, flavour and slight astringent finish	Sunburned fruit from difficult growing season	Viticultural challenges possibly due to climate events
Light colour with thin palate structure and light-weight fruit	Inappropriate skin contact time	Overcropping, young vines or wrong fermentation approach
Smells of skins; taste lacks definition and texture seems soupy	Inappropriate pressings addition	Too much pressing of wine included in final blend
Fruity aromas with light colour and structure	Temperature was too low	Fermentation
Complex non-wine aromas, in extreme cases is pungent with earthy, horse yards, manure or low-level medicinal smells that can be appealing. However palate will be medicinal to metallic; wine fails to mature satisfactorily, developing stronger medicinal to horse aromas	Problems with barrels during storage	Brettanomyces, simply called Brett, is a strain of yeast with a powerful ability to contribute flavour. Liked by some at low levels but disliked by all at high levels. In small amounts it adds character; in large amounts it is considered offensive
Flavour of fresh dirt	Problems with barrels during storage	Dekkera is another wild yeast of the genus Brett; it comes from contaminated equipment and barrels
Smells of vitamin B extract	Yeast given additional nutrients to help finish ferment	Excessive yeast food addition
Fruit lacks aromas, smells of lees and tastes yeasty	Wine was aged on lees for too long	Winemaker's style attribute
Slight brown colour in whites and lack of freshness with a flat flavour	Excessive air in contact with wine prior to or post bottling	Storage and bottling issues
Tastes mouldy	Dirty or mouldy storage	Maturation

What it smells and tastes like	Issue	Most likely cause
Reds taste fruitless, stale or dirty	Old oak and/or excessive barrel ageing	Maturation issues. Poor barrel topping and sulphur use
Lacks fruit with otherwise excellent colour and often high alcohol on the label, yet fails to deliver fruit aromas and flavour despite huge texture and extract	Could be too young but may also be due to poor timing for picking grapes in a drought or picking overripe grapes past peak flavour with consequent loss of flavour	Harvest timing
Smell of rotten eggs	Hydrogen sulphide development from poor ferment	Breathing may reduce mild cases but wine is faulty
Smell of burnt matches with low-level fruit aromas and flavour. Can be positive at low levels in wines with complex fruit, oak and maturation aromas and flavour	Too much sulphur dioxide used at the wrong time in production	Can be a pointer to European wines, many chardonnay styles. If excessive marks a faulty wine
Smells of sulphur and tastes of sulphur on the finish	Indicates the wine has an especially low pH, probably marvellous acidity, and should mature satisfactorily. Too much sulphur was used at bottling	Cautious preparation for bottling, which happily may indicate a wine capable of long maturation
Heavy deposits in bottle; glass and wines may be cloudy in extreme cases, taste soupy and lack bright fresh fruit	Poor filtering or no filtering due to winemaker trying to meet market requirements or style	Check with winery, or consider decanting wine after careful storage
Wine possesses fruitless aroma or palate or is quite different to previous bottles	Random oxidation from variability in corks with some letting in more air than others, leading to prematurely tired bottles	Natural variation in corks
Taste of rotten cork	Bad cork	Contaminated corks
Wine that fails to live up to expectations based on previous bottles and once the cork is removed smells and tastes range from flat and fruitless to distinctly musty and damp cardboard	Cork has been tainted by trichloranisol. This compound is released by moulds that have been in contact with chlorine; while the incidence varies from 5% upwards, diam or screw cap closure is one way of avoiding this issue	Contaminated corks
Low-key fruit and very dry finish	Winemaker included a high proportion of tannins	Excessive maceration
No fruit flavour left; off colour	Wine has been subjected to oxygen or heat through poor storage	Extended storage beyond wine capacity or check for leaking corks and other signs of hot storage
Acid profile is sharp, tart, green, thin, like an unripe grape	Excessive acidity or volatile acids (vinegar), or too much ethyl acetate (nail polish remover)	Fermentation or maturation deviation
Smells subtly like someone left the gas on or of garlic or onion	Reduction. Sulphur dioxide combining with available oxygen in wine results in a smell of mercaptans	Wine preparation and presence of sulphides prior bottling, and low-dissolved oxygen in wine at bottling
Vinegar smell	Caused by volatile acidity from acetic acid. May indicate stuck ferment or poor storage prior to bottling	Fermentation or storage defect

1036
134

PUTTING IT ALL TOGETHER: VARIETY AND STYLE

Describing a wine by its variety of grape is the part of the three-legged stool that introduces the personalities we drink.

Choosing and planting a variety reflects our grape-growing and winemaking experiences filtered through current market acceptance. When varietals become successful we evolve styles to best show their attributes. However, varietal fads come and go, such as the Hunter Valley's affair with gewürztraminer, which is now limited to just two producers but was a major boom variety in the 1970s. Chardonnay has been more persistent.

In Australia there is general agreement among winemakers about the best winemaking style for most grape varieties. Our current styles are based on a mix of beliefs by winemakers about a certain variety and the necessary market acceptance. But varieties gain new expressions by experiments in their style—one of the most exciting aspects of the Australian wine industry is that our winemakers continually experiment with style.

Most of the time we refer to varieties knowing that they broadly conform to styles of wine; that is, a riesling is an aromatic or flowery dry white and extremely unlikely to be matured in new oak; semillon is a crisp dry white unless it is affected by botrytis. The mid-1980s experiments with long oak-ageing of semillon are a thing of the past, allowing us to have confidence in semillon or riesling as both a variety and a style.

Sometimes it is the style of wine that is as important. The following guidelines synthesise the styles of wine against the likely varietal culprits. Hopefully this will allow you to choose wines according to their style rather than variety. It's a useful guide, although no two wines are ever exactly the same so with a little bit of experimental drinking on your part you will, I'm sure, amend the list to suit your individual needs.

Sparkling wines

Generally speaking, sparkling wines have:

- an even release of beads of gas escaping
- pale, water-white to mid-gold colour, depending on maturity
- aromas from European spring flowers to the smell of pastry, and citrus to subtle butterscotch scents
- a delicate fruit flavour and lively acidity with long complex flavours; tannin textures and flavours, surprisingly, can also feature
- textures and acidity that are the most refined and detailed of all wines
- an initial fruit weight that reveals warm climate
- deeper colour and firm deep flavours.

Vintage sparkling wines are generally drier than non-vintage ones. Prestige cuvées have the finest, most delicate textured, long flavours and lines of acidity. Prosecco from Italy is unique, as is champagne. New Zealand has a distinctive delicacy and Australian wines a complexity compared with others.

Crisp, dry, light- and medium-bodied white wines

Characteristically, these wines display:

- pale, green-tinged colours
- subtle aromas of green and red apple, fresh-mown grass, wet clay and pebbles, and nettles, salad greens, gooseberry
- crisp acidity
- tangy, refreshing fruit on the palate.

Typical of this style are young semillons from the Hunter; Tasmanian sauvignon blanc; cool-climate riesling from Canberra, New Zealand and Germany; chablis; and Italian pinot grigio.

Aromatic or flowery, dry white wines

In these dry whites, look for:

- vivid green-gold colour
- aromas of nectarine, figs and honey; hay to smoky tangy citrus notes with pinot gris; Southern Comfort-like peaches to ripe muscat and roses in viognier; lychees and Turkish delight from gewürztraminer
- a palate with similar powerful aromatic flavours, vary in body from light to delicate to robustly perfumed and weighty.

Typical of this style are viognier from the Adelaide Hills and Yarra Valley, gewürztraminer from the Adelaide Hills and central Victoria, pinot gris from Victoria and Orange, and riesling from Tasmania, the Clare and Eden Valleys, central Victoria, Orange and south-west Western Australia.

Full-bodied white wines

The fashion for big, fully ripe, yellow peach-coloured chardonnay is passing and in its place viognier holds its exotic head up to the guillotine of public taste. Lashings of intense nectarine chardonnay fruit are often now encased in increasingly subtle oak and winemaking refinements using lees. These show:

- a full body, with varying degrees of acidity
- a range of textures from the slick to the syrupy
- intense fruit varying from restrained to high octane
- moderate acidity that helps accent the body.

The chardonnays in particular benefit from the oak's toastiness, while viogniers are coming to grips with the rich fruit and solid texture of this impressive variety. Chardonnays of note come from Orange, Margaret River, the Adelaide Hills and the Yarra Valley. Viogniers from Adelaide Hills and McLaren Vale provide the stuff of this dream. Other examples are aged semillon and marsanne.

Rosé wines

Made from red grapes but left for a short time with the colour-giving grape skins, the best rosés have the refreshment of white wine with the body of a red. Specifically they have:

- variation in colours: from pale pink made from cabernet, red-brown from pinot noir to deep opaque red from grenache
- aromas of red fruits and berries
- few tannins
- soft acidity.

Lighter wines such as pinot noir in the Yarra Valley and Mornington Peninsula are the most exciting and will be more delicate and textural with red fruit aromas. Heavier examples from Margaret River cabernet have richer, leafy flavours, while the Barossa grenache has almost red wine flavours and occasional dry finishes.

Fresh, fruity, soft-finishing, early-drinking dry red wines

This is red wine in its juicy simplicity, ready young, with:

- sweet primary fruit aromas of blackberry, cranberry and cherry
- sweet, slippery red fruit characters
- smooth, softly textured bodies
- supple finishing that is softly tannic and aromatic
- low tannin.

This type of wine is likely to come from large-company winemaking at affordable prices using grenache, merlot and shiraz varieties, all featuring typical style.

Medium-bodied red wines

Internationally this is classic red wine territory, particularly in Bordeaux where structure, as a result of long maceration times, gives these wines length and appeal. The good quality young wines can show:

- restrained, ripe blackcurrant and mulberry fruit
- firm structure, even texture, noticeable finish
- long-shaped palate, firm, tannic backbone, complex oak and tannin.

Structure is everything and the quality of the tannins, especially from cabernet in the Yarra Valley, Margaret River and Coonawarra, often provides the framework for these long-lived styles. Also seek out varietal blends from the abovementioned regions based around cabernet, merlot, cabernet franc and malbec. Best shiraz in cooler climates come from the Mornington Peninsula, Yarra Valley, the Adelaide Hills, Eden Valley, Mudgee and Orange. Paradoxical examples are from the Hunter Valley and under the St Henri label, which impress with their volume of flavour and sleekness over time.

Spicy, full-bodied red wines

Vine age is important for these styles of wines. the Barossa Valley and McLaren Vale make a speciality of them due to their old vines. Shiraz is the typical example and these wines offer Australian winemakers a lot to experiment with, including:

- a range of flavours with the spicy imprint hovering in the background
- inky black, red colouring due to volume of fruit
- prominent oak with American oak and increasingly French oak in more refined examples
- an enormous dollop of sweet fruit ranging from intensely ripe sweet cherry to blackberry flavours—they can almost resemble Cherry Ripe bars in extreme cases with their balance, luscious sweet fruit and dark chocolate oak
- enormous volumes of velvety tannin balance the fruit sweetness
- early drinkability with an ability to age well.

Great examples are durif from Rutherglen and zinfandel from McLaren Vale, which add their alcohol lash to their black liquorice and leather characteristics. Penfolds' RWT and Grange, and Kalleske's Greenock are textbook examples, while McLaren Vale's d'Arenberg, Fox Creek and Songlines make a good contrast.

Sweet and botrytis wines

Australia's got it all: from the delicate 7 per cent alcohol of Moscato d'Asti through to the mass market; off-dry sweet wines made from the light muscat or traminer grapes with all the market variations of delicate and sweet fruitiness to varietal botrytis wine and full-on ice wine. Suitable for pairing with main courses through to the more luscious candied pineapple, mango and crème brulée, botrytis semillons and rieslings with their intense fruit and botrytis personalities show:

- sweet and delicate fruitiness with apple pie, apricot, peach and tropical flavours
- liquorice texture
- wide range of sugar content, but finishing dry with complex flavours
- length of flavour with acid freshness.

The 7 to 12 per cent alcohol range and 30 to 210 grams of sugar is fine so long as there is enough acidity to balance the sweetness. From cask traminer riesling through to New Zealand semi-sweets, such as Danny Schuster, and the botrytis De Bortoli Noble One or Lillypilly's varietal editions, the range is breathtaking in scope. Great international editions are tokaji from Hungary, Alsace vendange tardive, sauternes, auslese, beerenauslese, *eiswein* from Germany and Austria and ice wine from Canada.

Dessert wines

Australian wood-aged dessert styles carry between 18 and 21 per cent alcohol with ease, the finest being clustered around Rutherglen and made from muscat or muscadelle (the old tokay). They display:

- awe-inspiring intensity of aroma, freshness and bright colour
- luscious concentration of fruit and sugar for drinking without a meal
- complex flavours free from harshness or heat.

Many of the old-established wine regions, such as Griffith, and the Barossa and Swan Valleys, produce these wines with remarkable personality. Good ones are still cheap compared to the pleasure they provide. Try to find an international example to compete.

Dry sherry and fortified wines

Characteristics of these wines include:

- their deceptively pale appearance
- an oily lick as you swirl the glass
- a powerful bouquet of almonds and savoury seaside in sherry
- classic baked-in aroma of mediera
- a bone-dry texture with no sense of acid.

Good examples are fino and manzanilla sherry from Spain.

Tawny fortified wines

Most of these wines are made from shiraz grenache with a lashing of mourvedre grown in warm to hot regions without irrigation. These wines have:

- a colour of tawny brown
- hints of chestnut, mature wood-aged with distinctive nuts including traces of walnuts, raisins and rich caramel-like aromas
- a shape that is sweet on entry but dry on finish.

The best are Seppelt's Para and The Pinnacle, the rare centenary-release bottled at 100 years.

chapter 5

Buying wine with confidence

If you can spit people will take you seriously

ALEX GILSON

Bottle shops can be intimidating places. Industry research shows that many consumers avoid them or minimise their time there, just grabbing whichever bottle they recognise and heading quickly for the checkout.

Adelaide-based research found that most people spend on average 12 seconds choosing a bottle of wine and are most influenced by grape variety and price; they are not very loyal to label, region or brand. White wine drinkers are apparently loyal to chardonnay and riesling; red wine drinkers, being a more contrary lot, are less loyal to any particular variety but are influenced by price.

Some people do purchase based on label, reassured by murmured rumours of good wine. Then there are those who spend only below $7.50 or only above $17.50—a price-loyal bunch! I assume many wine drinkers think price is a good guide to quality on the basis that the more you pay the more you get. Unfortunately it is not always the case that more money equals more pleasure in terms of better personality, style and quality. Most wine under $7.50 is produced by large wine companies, but owing to their superior economies of scale the wine may be technically faultless yet lack individual personality. In the realm of the more expensive wines those from smaller producers may be over-priced and can disappoint, although on balance they may be much richer in personality and style.

It appears true that a good many consumers are confused by what they are drinking. They want to be educated, but don't have time for the retail store environment and mistrust gimmicky labels. The internet, telephone sales companies and wine clubs have picked up 10 per cent of retail sales by responding to this phenomenon with more information or better personal service. In the end though there is really only one way to know whether a wine is good by your standards: buy a few bottles and taste them blind. This way you can determine if they are as good as the packaging indicates.

WHAT'S IN A LABEL

So what does a label tell you?

First, you look at its design. In these cynical times it's easy to dismiss design but a huge effort goes into creating emotional connection through labels; a smart label gets attention and builds awareness—at least for the first bottle. Producers who care often have labels that arouse notice; they are individual in style. These can be reliable guides to the contents. Sophisticated label designs can reveal much about the company's beliefs about wine, while labels for affordable wines aim for a straightforward relationship with consumers. The information about name, price and quality of contents builds a badge of substance with the effort going into nurturing brand reputation and hopefully repeat purchases.

During the glut of the early 2000s, some wines punched above their weight. They were often much better than cleanskins at the same price. But like cleanskins they benefited from the lower demand for premium grapes, allowing cheaper, high-quality wines to appear in lower-priced labels. Sometimes the labels also claimed a piece of meaningless geography that was unrelated to the origins of the wine.

Labels do indicate quite important information, though, such as the name of the producer, variety of the wine (see Chapter 3), probably the region in which the grapes were grown (see Chapter 1), the alcohol content, standard drinks, and perhaps a blurb about what the wine tastes like or about the winemaker and their philosophy and style for making the wine (see Chapter 2). Of most importance for purchasing purposes is the vintage of the wine, because wine vintage is a wonderful indicator of the finished drop.

Vintage

As a wine drinker, once you have understood the connection between region, climate, variety, conditions of growing season and variations in winemaking, you can understand the idea of vintage variation. For the best guide to vintages I recommend the website for Langton's Wine Auctions and Exchange (langtons.com.au) or, when available, purchase their *Fine Wine Guide* for a good regional overview.

A vintage review is a huge generalisation, as anyone linked to the land will certify that 'you can not make a broad statement in agriculture'. So I think it is better to trust your favourite winemakers to produce interesting and delicious wine that reflects the region and the season, regardless of the conditions. A good producer will have adapted how they have grown, fermented and matured the final wines to create a recognisable vineyard or blended style as they will not release wines that are inferior.

Reading a wine label

Australian labels operate from the perspective that if a claim is made it must be true and offers producers the opportunity to avoid saying anything misleading by not making claims. As a result of this labels can have a lot of meaning if producers so wish; in reality labels with high levels of disclosure tend to indicate high quality producers.

The logo represents the owner's intentions (mission statement) and cannot be a duplicate of another company

Estate may be a trademark or a designation of origin; if this also appears on the back label it means that the variety was grown on the estate and this becomes an enforceable claim

Any claims about the wine must be correct and terms are limited by international law to convey stylistic meaning

A term such as 'reserve' is not protected and the brand owner should explain how it is used to distinguish the wine. At least 85% of the stated variety must be in the bottle

99% of barcodes do not change with vintages, except for premium bottlings

Indicates at least 85% of the wine is from the country disclosed

DANBURY
ESTATE
Reserve Chardonnay
A very attractive complex French oak nose with a fresh nutty character. The soft palate eases into a creamy texture and long complex finish of peach and dried herbs. A wine that will age for years.
Grown Vintaged and Bottled
at DANBURY ESTATE
Blossom Grove Lane
COWRA NSW 2794
ISBN 978-1740459792
9 781740 459792
Product of Australia
Approx 7.4 std drinks
12.9% Alc/Vol
Preservative 220, 300

The claims given here are all enforceable; it indicates that the producer is looking after the wine to the best of their ability and control

At least 85% of the wine content must be from the region stated; the vintage must be from the same year of harvest

Average amount of wine in a bottle over a bottling run must be disclosed

Alcohol volume must be accurate to within 1.5% plus or minus; number of standard drinks is calculated by volume in litres: (0.75) × alcohol % × 0.789

Preservative and fining agent codes must be disclosed for consumers

Wines will change over time, sometimes dramatically. Vintages that have received rave reviews in the past or have been judged as classics can, and often do, fall over. Critics have been known to be wrong and producers within a region can avoid shortcomings that may have affected others. My advice is to take vintage charts and classifications for what they really are—a guide. They're certainly very helpful, but I think Leanne De Bortoli of De Bortoli Wines summed it up well when she said that a good producer doesn't make apologies for seasonal differences, but they do ask that you appreciate the nuances this can bring to the wine.

BEST VINTAGES *1996 was a brilliant vintage. The whole continent enjoyed warm, even sunshine and some extraordinary wines were produced. There were some pretty spectacular wines in Europe, too, so the Maker smiled on everywhere that year. Smaller crops, cooler conditions and an Indian summer in 2002 led to fruit-rich and refined wines, especially riesling from the Clare and Eden Valleys and Victoria.*

According to Tim Flannery, Australian scientist and commentator on climate and global warming, the world's weather changed in 1976 and has since become warmer and drier. The summers of the 1990s and 2000s seem to have been significantly hotter than those of the 1980s and this is reflected in the wines produced from these vintages. The onset of drought became struggling times for vignerons in the years 1999, 2000, 2001, 2006 and 2007. I can remember a great wine coming from this period, a 2000 Hunter shiraz, easily the best Hunter shiraz I've had for many years.

Climate change is going to hurt the wine industry faster than many other businesses, as we have relied on long trial and error to create the household names that people accept today. Vines in Burgundy are planted so they run east to west to make the most of the sunshine, but during the 2003 drought period they showed the impact of too much heat. The berries on the eastern side of the vines shrivelled up to little burnt currants, while the fruit facing the western slopes came in sound and round and whole.

White wines from vintages in hot years can show initial promise with rich, round perfumed fruit, but their lower-level acidity can see them blow out and become flabby and blowsy as they mature. Burgundy is in a dilemma—their grapes used to ripen in the cooler September period but now they are ripening in the hotter month of August giving a more alcoholic style with less fine aromas.

Cool summers allow vines to retain higher levels of acid and their aromas. This results in white wines that are very lean and tight when they are young, living a long time and developing more flavour (providing there is sufficient flavour in the first place) as they age. But cool vintage red wines may lack the weight, presence and palate texture of warmer years. They tend to lack structure, tannin richness and complexity of flavour and will be inclined to mature early or badly.

Snapshot of Australian vintages in the last 50 years

2007	Heat, drought and frost reduced national crop levels by 30 to 50 per cent, making it a very early, very small and ripe year giving wines richness and high alcohol.
2006	The coolest growing season in Margaret River in the history of the region meant very late picking. Appealing wines from eastern seaboard cool regions, while the rest suffered heat and dry conditions.
2005	Terrific year for shiraz in southern Australia and for riesling in Clare Valley; all areas of Tasmania produced outstanding wines; chardonnay was good to excellent in many regions and outstanding in Beechworth, Victoria.
2004	Average to above-average vintage in many areas; Margaret River produced exceptional cabernet sauvignon, shiraz and chardonnay. Pyrenees cabernet and shiraz also stood out, as did Grampians shiraz and Gippsland pinot noir.
2003	Drought in Hunter Valley produced superb, concentrated reds.
2002	A distinct personality because of a cool summer with a burst of warmth to speed things up at the end of the growing season. This combination enabled the production of elegant wines across most of Australia except the most southerly regions. They may not be the most long-lived wines, nor do they have quite the generosity and juice of better vintages, but they definitely have a real personality unique to that year: for example, a pepper and spice character to the South Australian shiraz.
2001	Warm conditions gave powerful concentration to top Hunter Valley wines with character; conditions favoured the Victorian inland regions and Margaret River, as well as many good wines from other regions.
2000	Fabulous Hunter Valley shiraz.
1990s	This decade started with a pair of elegant years, 1990 and 1991, while 1996 and 1998 came in with strong quality offerings across a wide part of the land. The year 1999 was viewed as a sleeper in warmer regions like the Clare and Barossa Valleys for reds. A scorching summer in 1997 brought forward the picking period; it was so hot that it virtually cooked all the grapes that didn't get brought in on time.
1980s	Saw both 1982 and 1986 (exceptional Coonawarra wines) deliver the goods across Australia, while 1980 and 1988 were near rivals. But 1983 was one to avoid with a combination of all things bad, including heat and drought.
1970s	Both 1974 and 1976 were widely acclaimed. Warm growing seasons produced a number of very rich wines, which have aged well, with 1971 and 1975 offering the second-best tier.
Pre-1970s	I have great wine from Coonawarra in 1962 and 1963; from Victoria in 1952, 1953, 1955 and 1957; and from the Hunter in 1943 and 1945, if you can find these wines at auction.

2002
ON-BRESSANDES
GRAND CRU

CRACKING A BOTTLE

Who took the cork out of my lunch?
W.C. FIELDS

Of course the label is not the stand-alone characteristic of wine packaging.

The label must be affixed to the bottle, but does the shape of the bottle matter? And what about the material used to seal the bottle?

Bottling history

Down through the years pulling a cork has had a magic of its own. The earliest reliable record of vintage wines comes to us from Roman times. Then, wine was not bottled as such but came in amphorae: large clay vessels with a volume capacity of around 27 litres. An amphora was identified by marks showing the age of the wine and the year of the consul—this practice marks the predecessor of today's capsules and labels. The seals were a mixture of cork, clay and pitch or pozzolana (derived from volcanic ash). Pozzuolana, in the Italian spelling, proved remarkably durable; modern-day divers have recovered amphorae from Roman shipwrecks and found corks still in place, and doing their job well. Thankfully, the Roman fashion for blending sweet wines with salt water did not last as long.

From the Roman period until the seventeenth century, wines, along with nearly everything of value, were transported in barrels. The business of wine was not well developed and most wine was either light-bodied and drunk within a year of production and near its place of production, or extremely sweet and capable of ageing and transporting to further climates. Bottles during this time were generally used as jugs to convey wine from the cask to the table, serving as a decanter.

The earliest wine bottle was made around 1650; it was globular with a long tapered neck, the so-called 'shaft and globe'. From 1650 to 1685 the neck became shorter and by 1715 the neck had become increasingly shortened and the body wide and squat. After 1740 the shape gradually became less rounded, the sides more vertical and the body more elongated. By 1770 the bottle had assumed a more cylindrical shape suitable for binning. Wine was still shipped in barrels and then bottled by merchants and consumers because they possessed the necessary capital to subsidise the cost of corks, bottles and storage; they also reaped the benefit of value adding!

The first recorded, modern-bottled vintage wines originated from Bordeaux: Château Chalon in 1774 and Château Lafite in 1787. The first recorded bottled port was produced in 1775. The use of bottles led to an awareness of ageing, the critical feature being that the ability to age meant bottled wines could be sold for more money than other types of wine. Vintage port was a major beneficiary of this and owes its creation to the development of bottles, as they provided an inert container and oxygen-free environment to allow the brandy and residual sugar time to marry and mature.

The development of champagne also required a reliable stopper and strong glass bottle. As English bottles were of more uniform quality than French the first 'foaming champagne' was created in England around 1650 and refined over the next 200 years by the French. And so began the fashion for matured wines and how the wine industry started to broadly look as it does today.

Over the centuries a variety of materials have been used as stoppers, including wooden bungs, linen, hemp, parchment and leather, which may have been soaked in oil and sealed with tallow, pitch or plaster. As early as the sixteenth century Spanish corks were used as stoppers and tied down to the lip on the neck of the bottle.

In 1681 the catalogue of Gresham College London makes the first reliable reference to a 'cork scrue' or 'steel worm' for the drawing of corks out of bottles. Early corks were elongated cones, most of which projected from the bottle and were tied to the lip. They could be grasped by hand for removal. The first patent for a corkscrew was taken out in 1795 by the English clergyman Reverend Samuel Henshall.

A method of bottle opening in the eighteenth century was known as 'breaking the neck' of the bottle, especially if it had a long neck. Not generally recommended in polite society, it means scratching around the bottleneck with a sharp pointed instrument. The top is then tapped, breaking off cleanly. This procedure known as 'cracking a bottle' is still used today with a different device.

Considerably refined in the nineteenth and twentieth centuries, we still talk of 'cracking a bottle' although now with so-called port tongs. These tongs are heated to red hot in the fireplace and positioned around the neck of a port bottle, clamping it tight where the thermal differences neatly crack it and allow the removal of the top and the neck with the cork intact.

Originally the ring on bottlenecks was used to tie corks down for transport. Later they evolved to provide a handling point for automated bottle production. Early bottles were hand blown from one piece and were flat bottomed. Punts, or the dimples on the bottom of bottles, evolved for ease of production. The end of the circular blown glass was reversed by being pushed into the bottom of the bottle. This also provided greater strength to the base of sparkling wine bottles.

Lead capsules evolved to prevent corks being attacked by vermin, especially rodents. Then during the nineteenth century the wealthiest French regions added their own local touch by creating bottles representative of their terroir and wine style. First was the bourguignon from Burgundy, followed by the champenoise for Champagne and the flute from Alsace.

Range of bottle shapes

The bottle shapes in Australia for wine are not a reliable guide to the varietal make-up of the contents.

Old wine in new bottles

Bottles have a long and noble tradition of service to the wine industry, and although cork is now under some pressure as the preferred closure no-one has developed a serious rival to glass. While a bottle happens to hold a nice amount for two people to share at a meal, its size is probably more closely related to the standard breathing capacity of the glass blower rather than to any gastronomic or medicinal benefit. A standard bottle holds as much wine as air in the lungs of a professional glass blower of the late seventeenth century, so becoming the template for the 750-millilitre bottle we see today. But it is an example of how wine, a gift from the universe, neatly matched up the needs of the consumer. Though I would say that there is a benefit in larger-sized bottles, especially magnums for champagne.

Magnums are a statement. They speak of large gatherings, festive occasions with lots of friends or a special event and they help make the celebration flow a little bit longer. I am especially drawn to magnums of champagne as this wine always looks at its best in this form. Magnums can sit for years until the right occasion appears for them to introduce their own brand of magic.

Magnums age more slowly, and there are those aficionados who believe that magnums never really develop as they are supposed to. I don't believe that there is a wine style, apart from sherry and maybe tawny port, that can't benefit from a bigger bottle. The problem is finding enough people to drink it once opened.

So where do magnums shine? They shine as recognition and celebration of something important. They shine when you find the year of a child's birth coincides with a good vintage. I know people who buy magnums of Hunter semillon, vintage port or vintage champagne that should last 18 to 21 years, provided that the corks hold. Now they simply wait for the right events to drink them!

Magnums can be a display of power, wealth or authority; they show their owners off, and they're quite glamorous. I'll never forget the sight of Len Evans, at well over 60 years of age, standing with a magnum under each arm at the end of the Brisbane Master Class saying, 'Come on then, who is going to drink these with me?' There is no doubt that magnums convey a certain level of authority and dignity.

Half bottles are not so convincing. I used to sell John Cleese a half bottle of claret for his lunch every day but somehow they don't seem to belong anywhere now except in air travel. The half bottle is not a great shape as wines don't age well in them and they're costly to produce. On the other hand, half bottles of sauternes, claret or champagne (in an emergency), for example, make a lot of sense when just a glass each for two is sufficient.

The rise of the single adult family will see the rise of the tetra pack and cask wine. There is nothing wrong with casks and the wine industry has not finished exploring the opportunities they provide. The Canadians, for example, have set themselves the task of increasing their tetra-pack wine sales over the next few years because they have a problem recycling bottles and disposing of glass waste. We don't suffer the same issues in Australia, but casks have still found their place thanks to their price point and convenience. Casks and tetra packs are a highly efficient way of delivering the simple pleasure of a glass of wine. In times of oversupply, casks can contain good wines. Right now there are opportunities arising for the marketing of new wine in casks.

Cork and stelvin: the battle

The biggest and most opinionated battle in the wine world currently is between those who support using cork and its variants and those who challenge it in support of the screw cap or stelvin. It's a dynamic and epic battle, but one fact has emerged that might hand the crown over to the screw cap: convenience.

The wine industry is unique among consumer industries in that it has been necessary to own a special tool in order to get into the container (bottle). Whether the convenience of the screw cap translates into a downgrading of the special place that wine holds in the world, while cork-sealed wines maintain the high moral ground of superior quality, remains to be seen.

Screw caps are not perfect but then neither are corks. On balance, I think the level of imperfection in the former is considerably less than in the latter. Let's look at the 'for and against' of both methods.

The cork

The biggest downside of cork is contamination. The wine industry had to deal with a random 5 to 7 per cent of bottles having bad corks, thus tainted wines. That's a lot of randomness. Imagine the pharmaceutical industry allowing for this sort of failure percentage just because of a closure. I don't think so. Corks can be contaminated by moulds reacting with chlorine to produce TCA.

The presence of these gremlins is heralded by a scent like musty autumn leaves, cardboard and wet dog. Another, more insidious problem is random oxidation, the penetration of oxygen down tiny hollow fissures in the growth rings of cork. In this case, the cork pulls out beautifully and looks fine yet the wine is flat, lifeless and tastes older than it is. Some cork companies are going all out to remove the possibility of tainting by removing all the possibility of rot and not using chlorine.

There have been some interesting ways of dealing with the limitations of cork. While good corks can last up to a century, it is wise to re-cork bottles after 20 years. Penfolds Red Wine Clinic does just that. This Australian refinement invented by Adrian Read has developed in a unique way. Where some French companies simply pull out the old cork and replace it with another, Penfolds pull the cork out, taste the wine, refresh the quantity if needed (with an exact or similar vintage) and issue the bottle with a new etiquette or slip label stating that it had attended the clinic. Interestingly, the auction market has not responded to this positively, so the re-corked bottles sell for less than bottles with the original cork. The upside for us experienced in wine during these cork-conditioned times is that for those bottles where cork does its job, it is sheer perfection.

The cork report

Cork, a natural forest product, is one of the most stable forms of agriculture. First used by the Romans, its cultivation has been unchanged for hundreds of years. Wine corks can show 1000 per cent variability in oxygen permeability. This means that the amount of air allowed into each bottle can vary by 1000 per cent in the same batch of corks in commercially important priced wines.

Help is at hand for winemakers and the new Diam cork, which looks like it's made from chips of cork glued together, is more consistent than natural corks. Other cork complaints include:

- crumbling from cheap corks or wrong humidity during storage
- breaking: from old corks or poor storage where air-conditioning has dried the atmosphere
- dust in the wine, which is a side effect of bottling.

The major issue lies with a 'corked' flavour contaminated with TCA. It naturally exists in nature but is masked by bitterness in such plant foods as coffee. It is more noticeable in wines that have been in warm storage conditions, which makes low temperature storage a necessity.

The screw cap

Wine has been traditionally made with the cork in mind. For example, at its best the cork allows for a modest amount of oxygen to get into the bottle. Ideally, this happens very, very slowly in a very limited interface (the cork in contact with the bottleneck) under quite a lot of pressure (the cork is squeezed in tightly). Long-ageing wines are made with more tannin to accommodate and capitalise on this fact.

One difference with having screw-cap bottles is that the wine is always incredibly fresh. This will become more important with key red wines, which means that you will have to open them and allow them to breathe before drinking. We tasted some wines from screw-capped bottles one afternoon and they were quite different wines after they were left to breathe for three hours.

Screw-cap bottled wine changes the chemical balance; the winemaker does not need to anticipate this effect. The wine will not require as much tannin to protect it from oxygen. From the winemaker's point of view, this is particularly important for red wines where oxidation is a critical element in the process.

Another question mark over screw caps is how well they will age. Certainly they will not oxidise or age in the same way. They will age, but I doubt they will end at the same point as wine closed with cork. What will happen is the wine will lose some of its traditional waxy, toast characters and retain more vibrancy of fruit in whites. Consequently, we will need to develop new descriptions for wines under screw caps as they will develop differently.

Red wines will need to be made with less tannin as they will not need as much for maturation. Though it does appear that the Swiss are onto a solution. They have developed a cap with wadding and liner that allows for a little bit more oxygen to penetrate. This may alleviate the problem with red wine that has difficulty in evolving without some sort of oxidation.

Winemakers will need to accommodate for the limitation of screw caps in their art but wine producers will be able to confidently deliver pretty much every bottle in the right condition. The screw cap has dampened the sommelier's panache somewhat. It's hard to make the same flourish when cracking a screw cap as it is when removing a cork. Apparently, a rearguard action is being fought clandestinely against the screw cap by sommeliers of fine-dining restaurants in the United States and Europe, who are turning their noses up at the impostor.

Consumers of wine report that they prefer the screw cap because the bottle is now effectively a resealable container. Some people ask me whether the screw cap is just the same as vacuuming out the air with a pump—a common way of stopping unfinished wines. But the problem with vacuuming is that you pump all the fruit aromas out as well. And the teaspoon in the bottle of leftover champagne is just a charming piece of frippery. Put a stopper in the sparkling. This resealing does, though, lead to a different way of experiencing wine. For example, a wine opened one night will change over the period of time when the bottle is resealed. I have tasted a young, tannic, fruity bordeaux become a warmer, more aromatic wine over three nights later—a good sign that this vintage could be cellared for years.

There is no doubt that screw caps do slow down the ageing process, and as a result have given us a new challenge for understanding how wines develop. In my eyes, they have also led to the re-emergence of the decanter because so many wines absolutely need that breath of air to open up. In turn, screw caps have extended the freshness of wines, ensuring that we all get a better and more consistent glass. In restaurants, sommeliers find the challenge of a screw cap a little hard to manage within their concept of service and delivery of wine. But figures do show that the advent of screw caps has increased the drinking of wine.

In 2006, the average amount of wine drunk per person was 26.5 litres per year. Before this, the figure had stayed virtually static at 24 litres for over a decade. Aside from the fact that it appears more women are drinking wine and thus pushing up the average, it also appears that wine drinkers prefer the ease of a screw-cap bottle. Let's face it, a product that needs a corkscrew to open it is providing its own impediment to sales.

Without getting too much further into the vexed debate about cork versus stelvin, it does seem to be a fact that skills with a corkscrew are going to be less and less useful. But right now you still need to know how to use one with some facility, as cork will be around for some time yet. The future? A glass-lock stopper called a vino lock waits in the wings to replace the screw cap. But that's for another edition.

Before moving onto tasting, some discussion would be beneficial on a few 'specialised' methods of bottling and selling that are a feature of modern times: cleanskins, buyer's own brand and home bottling.

Cleanskins

The obvious problem with cleanskins is knowing what you are getting. A retailer may advertise that a wine selling for $5 normally goes for $20, but how do you know this is true? Other additional unknowns include the alcohol content by volume, the equivalent number of standard drinks, what preservatives have been added and who the producers are. Ethically, all this information should be available on the label for the consumer to read. But cleanskins generally don't have labels and get away with some cheeky descriptions on what passes for a label.

In the cleanskin market, though, there is a lot of basic wine with occasional great bargains, not the other way around. And consumers who know their way around wine can often buy a labelled bottle of wine that has won a trophy or two for just $6, which makes you wonder why you'd buy a cleanskin when you have access to a reputable labelled bottle at that price. But nevertheless the cleanskin market, at the time of writing, is growing for the same reason that a medalled bottle of wine can sell for $6: affordable quality associated with the wine glut and supply problems in the grape-growing industry.

There are two genuine types of cleanskin available. The first is the need to move quality wines quickly due to distressed stock, failed export sales, poor sales projections and lower budget expectations.

When winemakers look at amended forecasts they sometimes realise that they simply have too much wine on tap and are prepared to lower their prices for large sales. This wine is short-circuited from the normal selection process. It's no secret that the wine industry needs to empty tanks around harvest time and sharp retailers get in there and buy up the surplus. Add in an oversupply of grapes in a saturated market and cleanskins move from an occasional feature of a normal retail market to an everyday occurrence.

The second types are those made specifically for the cleanskin demographic. They're just cheap wines made cheaper by leaving the label off. They are certainly a feature of the mid-1990s because of the state of the wine industry—the huge, tax-driven plantings that took place in 1998–99 that are now bearing fruit.

But a bottle without a label is a frame without a picture—there's no identity. It hurts the wine industry because wine has become anonymous; you don't know who made it, often they are sold on where they came from, damaging the region's reputation, and on what it's made from, damaging the reputation of the variety. Cleanskins remove a really important level of communication, which is the label and all it signifies.

On a budget, a cleanskin seems like a good idea. But when you stop and think about it, it's like a cheap impostor of the real thing. Wine has an identity that supports meaning and dignity in the tasting experience. It has been very difficult for wine producers but this system doesn't provide much money for reinvesting back into the production techniques to create differentiation, it just gives access to volume retailing.

Buyer's own brands

Within bricks and mortar and even internet retailing there is a large number of brands that are exclusive to a particular outlet. These are often good, reliable wines. Buyer's own brand (BOB) wines are usually bottled under a long-term contract with a wine producer and can feature popular varieties and regions.

If you check the prices and position on the floor, especially if it is in boxes stacked on the floor in a shop, against other named brands, you can work out if it is exclusive to that retailer. Generally speaking, if a BOB is done properly you will see it as the lower-priced wine in a range of price points for the same variety, tasting panel notes and retailer quality endorsement.

Home bottling

Regarded by many as a thing of the past, home bottling has never really left the scene. A handful of producers make a speciality of it, although it has waned under the influence of increased prosperity, wine casks, improvements in bottled wines and the rise of cleanskins.

But table wine producers Tinlins in South Australia and Huntingdon Estate in Mudgee, New South Wales, have continued the tradition; while in Victoria Pizzini in King Valley supplies Italian varietals and Yilleena Park in the Yarra Valley supplies home bottlers on a bigger scale. To home bottle fortified wines you will need to go to the Buller family at Rutherglen in Victoria for bulk sales of fortified muscat and reds which have been the mainstay of student parties for years.

TASTINGS

As we differ so much in our ability to detect aroma and flavour, tastings conducted by knowledgeable observers are a vital part of learning, particularly as wine has a strong oral tradition.

There is no substitute for tasting and talking about the same wine with a group. Unleash your curiosity and ask questions, that's how you learn! Approaching a tasting for the first time is daunting. Plan on writing notes and spitting everything! Remember that it's about what you like, so speak up about what you like and why. Better to form an opinion, make a decision and learn from drinking it than not. Whatever system you use to rate a wine, remember the discipline of scoring wine encourages you to form an opinion and gives you a quick overview and a useful insight later into what you thought.

Most tastings are not formal, everyone is standing around tasting the wine. This setting is easy to cruise in and out of. The best consumer tasting for unlocking the meaning of wine, though, is a seated affair, with a period of time to allow note taking before a discussion of the wines is led by a knowledgeable expert. These tastings are great fun, part philosophy, part autobiography and part weather report, mixed with a lot of humour. They allow for the transmission of the subtleties of wine as great winemaking is not technical but about observation, timing and care.

A series or group of wines to be tasted is often called a flight. I have no idea why this term was given, but a number of ways to conduct a flight tasting are: blind, horizontal, vertical and vertizontal.

Blind tasting

Blind tasting is a cornerstone process, much loved by the Australian wine industry for assessing wine quality with the terms of reference relating to the quality vintage, variety or style of the wines under examination. You are given no clues, just a bottle in a bag, or better still, a single glass and the chance to divine the contents and describe or rate them as closely as possible.

Horizontal tasting

This refers to a common feature among the wines being tasted, such as different producers from the same vintage. This allows the quality of different properties or regions to be measured.

The best use of bad wine is to drive away poor relations

FRENCH PROVERB

Vertical tasting

This is a comparison tasting of different, often succeeding years of the same wine to reveal differences in the vintages.

Vertizontal tasting

This tasting includes wines from different producers of the same variety across different years. It provides a rare opportunity to taste a wide cross-section of wines generally from a common district.

Wine options game

This blind wine tasting game was invented by Len Evans and employs multiple choice questions led by a quiz master. It turned out to be a great tool for training and I had the good fortune to discuss the game with Len one day and discovered its origins.

In the 1960s Len had guests over for lunch and they were reluctant to leave. He presented them with a wine and asked them its origins, telling them if they didn't know, they had to leave. They were knowledgeable and were able to correctly identify it with great speed. In frustration, Len introduced optional questions and requested a payment to continue to participate. Eventually one winner emerged and the guests finally went home. Len said that later when his wife went to move the pewter with the change in it she could barely move it!

The game Len developed from that afternoon gathering involved serving the wine 'blind'. It relied on the taster to correctly identify the answers out of three options, while the quiz master (Len) could use the optional answers to confuse or aid the participants.

ENDORSEMENTS AND RECOGNITION

When I say 'endorsement' I mean acknowledgment and applause from industry experts and associated bodies.

From the consumer's point of view, this translates to friends, wine reviews, wine shows and awards. Increasingly, wine shows are becoming regionalised, recognising the variety and region, thus emphasising and supporting the peregrination of the wine tourist. So, for example, Hunter Valley semillons, Clare Valley rieslings, Barossa Valley and McLaren Vale shiraz, and the pinots of Mornington Peninsula, Yarra Valley or Tasmania are all now known marques without quite being appellations in the European sense. From a purely mercenary, marketing point of view, it's a good idea as it helps inextricably entwine varietals and regions in the minds of consumers.

A better understanding of the system of accreditation requires an understanding of the wine critic and wine show, as well as the point system used to rank wines.

How to read wine reviews

I have the greatest respect for Australian wine writers who can entertain, inform and stimulate my interest after 35 years of reading them. In my mind Australia has many of the best wine writers in the world, recognised for their high principles, insight, knowledge, understanding and sheer professionalism. But it's no easy job being a wine writer, and seriously it's not all glamorous meals out.

The crushing weight of samples arriving daily takes hours to unpack and organise into tasting flights or groups. One journalist I spoke to admitted he devoted different rooms in his house to different varieties in order to keep control of the torrent of samples.

Wine writers are advisers to drinkers, not judges of what drinkers should or should not drink. Long ago they realised that their pages were too valuable a resource for consumers to publish criticism and the public is better served by the recognition and explanation of interesting events, high-quality regions, new wines or producers. It's criticism by omission.

Any person who is looking for advice is best to apply a bit of psychology to a wine writer's analysis and understand what types of wine the particular reviewer prefers. Having an understanding about your local or favourite wine writer's taste can save you time and money (as can a good retailer or website, see later in this chapter).

Read several reviewers and you will quickly get the gist of what's going on. Any score allocated to a wine in a review is based on experience, hopefully framed by honesty and transparency of process. At the bottom of all wine critiques lies the challenge of interpretation. Description is based on impressions and all impressions are interpretations framed by the taster's experience and preferences. The score is just a guide as it's the opinions put down in words that make reading about wine interesting when delivered in a literate and articulate way.

Surprisingly there is an inverse relationship between increasing wine consumption and the need for and amount of wine information required which has seen a reduction in the amount of newspaper space devoted to wine in recent years.

ROBERT JOSEPH, LEADING ENGLISH WINE WRITER

Reading wine scores

While I don't believe scores are the most important part of explaining wine or quality, they do provide a point of reference against other wine reviews from the same writer. There are a number of quality scoring systems based on the journalist's need to quickly express information of a current competitive status. Some publications use scores of: 5 stars; out of 20 points; and out of 100 points; these being the three most common systems.

Using stars allows readers to focus quickly on the author's view of a wide range of issues and summarise them concisely.

The 20-point system holds court in most wine show circuits and with a number of reviewers. Through practice and experience it provides a shorthand language of quality. When used by a wine judge the 20 points is divided into:

- a maximum of 3 points for the appearance of the wine
- 7 points for the aroma
- 10 points for the palate.

You add these together to get your score out of 20 and it obviously points towards the taste being more important than the colour.

I am hopeful that the 100-point rating system used by several wine-consumer publications will disappear before too long in favour of explanations on quality, wine style and character.

One common complaint made is that the American idea of good wine, which has been typified by this 100-point system, is too narrow. There is considerable evidence that it does Americanise Australian and French wine by favouring the fruitier, higher alcohol, lower acid and more forward wines common to California and Australia over the traditionally drier and more astringent tastes of old Europe, such as young Bordeaux or Rhône and Burgundy.

The 100-point system carries its own logic:

- 95–100 points: exceptional character and pretty often pricing as well
- 90–94 points: outstanding exemplary wine in every respect including price
- 88–89 points: full of interest but in reality closer to everyday than special occasions
- 85–88 points: good to pretty average, technically sound with a modicum of class
- 80–84 points: generally pretty average.

Numerical rating is an aberration whose time will surely come when people understand that it misrepresents what winemakers and their companies do. It is a shorthand overview that misses the interesting details such as wine style or character and value for money. Time-poor people will continue to support this system as they do not have the time to know why and how a wine was made. But a little learning does more to heighten appreciation of a wine than any point score possibly could.

At the 2006 Masters of Wine Symposium, James Laube from the *Wine Spectator* discussed this topic. He revealed the processes involved in his thinking about evaluating a wine and awarding it a rating of 92, which he sees as his opinion. Consumers have been led to believe that if Laube thinks the wine is worth a 92, then the consumer should think so too, as a consequence of reviews being repeated and used as sales aids. Laube and other users of the 100-point system do not intend that their opinion should dominate the consumer although retailers and marketers find it easy to sell wines based on this view.

Wine is a challenge to our discernment because without elaborate language and studied appreciation it would not find its special features transmitted. The language of a well-written review helps turn drinkers into judges. Hysterically raving fervour and enthusiasm are no substitute for clarity and reasoning.

In summary, my advice to approaching a review is to:

- read a selection of journalists until you find some you like and trust
- identify if you agree with them by tasting their selections
- remember they make recommendations based on their palates
- understand a retailer you trust can be just as good
- appreciate that price is less reliable than good advice.

Wine shows

Wine shows give awards irrespective of price, region, availability or distribution. There is a view that wine competitions are primarily public relations events to attract attention to wine. Successful extension of the awards provides public exposure and a marketing advantage. It has been one of the best ways by which an unknown winery or a little known region can achieve public acclaim. The recognition can significantly affect a

The Royal Agricultural Society
OF VICTORIA.
HIGHLY COMMENDED
H. T. C. WOODFULL, Secretary
THE ROYAL AGRICULTURAL SOCIETY
OF WESTERN AUSTRALIA INC.
ROYAL SHOW 1955
SECOND PRIZE
Secretary
ROYAL
MELBOURNE
SHOW
1960
The Royal Agricultural Society
OF VICTORIA.
Second Priz
Awarded to B. SEPPELT & SONS LTD. (C 24).
Exhibit CHAMPAGNE TYPE.
The Royal Agricultural Society
OF VICTORIA.
First Prize
Awarded to B. SEPPELT & SONS LTD. (B 5).
1960 VINTAGE.
Exhibit MUSCAT - any sugar strength.
Class 861 No. 123
H. T. C. WOODFULL, Secretary
THE ROYAL AGRICULTURAL SOCIETY
OF WESTERN AUSTRALIA
ROYAL SHOW 1956
THIRD PRIZE
ROYAL
MELBOURNE
SHOW
The Royal Agricultural Society
OF VICTORIA.
Commended
H. T. C. WOODFULL, Secretary
THE ROYAL AGRICULTURAL SOCIETY
OF WESTERN AUSTRALIA INC.
ROYAL SHOW 1955
FIRST PRIZE
Section
Class
Exhib. No.
Secretary
The Royal Agricultural Society
OF VICTORIA.
HIGHLY COMMENDED
Awarded to B. SEPPELT & SONS LTD.
Exhibit DRY WHITE (Hock, Moselle and Riesling types).
Class 870 No. 514
H. T. C. WOODFULL, Secretary
ROYAL
MELBOURNE
SHOW
1960
The Royal Agricultural Society
OF VICTORIA.
First Prize
Awarded to B. SEPPELT & SONS LTD. (B 4).
1960 VINTAGE.
H. T. C. WOODFULL, Secretary
THE ROYAL AGRICULTURAL SOCIETY
OF WESTERN AUSTRALIA INC.
ROYAL SHOW 1955
SECOND PRIZE
Section
Class
Exhib. No.
Secretary
The Royal Agricultural Society
OF VICTORIA.
Second Prize
Awarded to B. SEPPELT & SONS LTD. (CH 16).
Exhibit DRY RED.
Class 883 No. 463
H. T. C. WOODFULL, Secretary
THE ROYAL AGRICULTURAL SOCIETY
OF WESTERN AUSTRALIA INC.
ROYAL SHOW 1954
THIRD PRIZE
Secretary
ROYAL
MELBOURNE
SHOW
1958
The Royal Agricultural Society
OF VICTORIA.
Commended
Awarded to B. SEPPELT & SONS LTD.
Exhibit CLARET
Class 867 No. 306
H. T. C. WOODFULL, Secretary
THE ROYAL AGRICULTURAL SOCIETY
ROYAL SHOW 1954
SECOND PRIZE
The Royal Agricultural Society
OF VICTORIA.
The Royal Agricultural Society
OF VICTORIA.
ROYAL

winery's and region's reputation and media reports of these awards significantly influence people far beyond those attending the public functions when the awards are handed out.

In Australia, the seven capital cities agricultural society wine shows emerged in the nineteenth century as part of wide-scale agricultural exhibitions aimed at recognising and communicating the most recent improvements to the breed for cereals and livestock. The wine shows are very competitive environments, constantly searching for improvement, and are a major force in raising Australian wine standards. There is a wine show protocol run by the Australian Society of Viticulture and Oenology which addresses five major areas:

- audit protocols
- judge impartiality
- trophy judging
- wine show standards
- use of medals as well as establishing a national register of judges.

The admirable Australian Wine Show is designed for winemakers and is not a unified system that can communicate well to consumers. It is refined and sophisticated and offers considerable intellectual input on an agreed format and language. The wines are judged by peers, mainly other winemakers who act as technical judges. They examine grape quality and the winemaking process. Increasingly, though, sommeliers are invited to comment on style. The numbers of shows and wines to be judged does put pressure on the availability of top judges at all times. The introduction of overseas guest judges allows these wine professionals to experience the system at work by participating in it, and is doing much to raise the international standing of wine shows. The Australian wine show system is under challenge however, with its most likely rivals being purely local or regional wine shows or shows that only allow entry to finished wines ready for sale to consumers.

There are a number of non-capital city national wine shows (accepting entries from across Australia) run by regional agricultural societies, including Cairns, Cowra, Griffith and Rutherglen. The greatest growth in wines shows has come from the needs of grape growers and winemakers from single regions or groups of regions to receive professional feedback and advice without travelling far from home. Approximately 50 Australian shows or competitions focus purely on local areas. They vary in scope from a single region to a number of contiguous regions in what is now officially known as a zone. Adelaide Hills, Orange, the Clare Valley or Mt Barker in Western Australia, are good examples of these shows; and they allow judges to dwell on the finer aspects of the wines by restricting the range of distractions.

The Mornington Peninsula, Murrumbateman and Bathurst all run cool climate shows. In particular the Mornington Peninsula is distinctive among these as it accepts wines from around the world. Warren Mason's Sydney International Wine Competition calls on judges from the United States, the United Kingdom and New Zealand, with Australia in the minority as both technical and style judges. This competition has an original touch as style judges look beyond the technical aspects and taste them with food to grant its highest award, the Blue-Gold medal. According to one judge, accepting a position at this show can result in gaining three kilograms in weight in a week!

There are particular themes, such as tri-nations (for example, South Africa, New Zealand, Australia—like the rugby!) and small winemakers. Some focus on a single variety (for instance, Hyatt Canberra International Riesling Challenge and Great Australian Shiraz Challenge), while the Australian Alternative Varieties Show examines emerging wines, such as arneis, vermentino, tempranillo and sangiovese. Small makers are a speciality at Stanthorpe, Queensland, with the Australian Small Makers Show, or the Sydney-based Boutique Wine Awards; Canberra has the excellent Winewise Small Vignerons Awards, and has the New South Wales Small Winemakers Show based at Forbes.

Recent developments in the show system have been aimed at increasing the quality, knowledge and understanding of the judges. These include tutorials for young tasting talents which used to be led by the late Len Evans and ensured a solid international perspective at the highest quality levels. Longer standing tasting education, such as the Wine Assessment course at Adelaide University, helps to build the solid experience and wide-range exposure that is required for non-winemakers to make a contribution. Prior to these you had to have a great palate if you were a non-winemaker to get a head start and would need to know someone in the industry as well.

The wine show system does not award first place prizes unless a specific trophy exists. The closest it comes are trophies for the best wines judged from a number of classes. Overall it provides for collective placing groupings based on their points.

Typically very few wines, generally less than 5 per cent, win gold medals and only 30 to 45 per cent will win any award. Statistically it is as good a system as we can get. Of course this is provided that there is a sensible number of wines, approximately 120 to 140 judged per day undertaken by three experienced judges with no knowledge of origin or maker but knowing either style or variety or both and using their experience to record individual scores. At the end of the session the final rankings are awarded.

As three judges are involved, the actual score sometimes looks like the size of the 20-point system:

- 55.5–60 from three judges means individually they awarded 18.5–20 (gold medal)
- 51–55 from three judges means individually they awarded 17–18.4 (silver medal)
- 46.5–50 for three judges means individually they awarded 15.5–16.9 (bronze medal)

From a winemaker's point of view, in reality a bronze medal should be attributed to a sound everyday wine; while a silver-awarded wine has interest, and a gold wine should have defined fruit quality of character and be worth pursuing.

FINDING WINES

An awful lot of wine or a lot of awful wine!

LEN EVANS

Finding wines on any Top 100 list can be a challenge.

A multitude of commercial reasons, such as change of vintage, distributors or pricing-effect availability, can make it a frustrating search. With thousands of wines produced in Australia each year, and a few thousand more imported, there just isn't enough room on retailers' shelves and restaurant lists for all of them. So it's easily possible that your local doesn't carry the one you've read about, in which case you need to be canny in your search method.

A good wine retailer should be bottled

Selling wine is just like selling any other highly technical product, it is a specialist occupation. These days, however, the advent of chain stores has eaten up many smaller boutique retailers and tended to push the wine offerings back to a lowest common denominator: price. It's a formula for the democratisation of wine at one level with the risk of dumbing it down at another. Price wars can create bargains but often the businesses with the bargains are not going to have a wide range of wines.

When retailers or producers engage in battles for market share, consumers win in the short term through cheaper prices on a featured few. Longer term, the overall business no longer offers new and exciting ranges and it has become difficult for the wine industry to continue work with the trend of the last few decades: increasing wine quality for the same price.

One of the major issues producers have with liquor chains is that they have enough buying power to muscle into the production side of the industry and ultimately dictate what should be produced by selecting from a narrow pool of wines and almost telling consumers what they should buy. Despite the richness and creativity of the world of wine, retail chains often keep recycling the same old labels and varieties, leaving it all a bit bare and dull for the consumer. The other problem is that fine wines, besides being rare and expensive, require a high level of staff knowledge to meet the demands of an appreciative clientele, willing and able to pay for the care and attention that goes into their making.

A broad truism about the current situation is that the big retail chains are selling big company wines while the small retailers are selling small boutique company wines. So inevitably you have to search for interesting wine retailers who know their way around wine to sell you a more interesting bottle. There are some retailers who are determined to walk a middle course and not let their customers pay too much, but who are still committed to delivering good and interesting stock. These are the retailers who are trying to combine a good deal with discovery. Seek out these guys because they are keeping the world of wine lively and authentic. One such group is the Alliance of Independent Fine Wine Merchants.

Many retailers use tasting panels to create information to inform, educate and entice their customers. Wine show medals and wine reviews in newspapers and magazines are also useful. Another way retailers can distinguish themselves is to buy wines that nobody else has. This often means they have to import them so that there is no other competition for the label. Watch out for these on offer, as they can be acquired at quite good prices.

Looking further afield

Many wines never make it to retail stores. They can be made exclusively for a restaurant, wine club or the cellar door. Some sell so quickly that any review of the year's best wines could include wines no longer available, despite the best attempts of journalists to check availability in advance of their publication. The top publications will publish a list of importers and retailers, but what do you do if the publication doesn't carry a list? Here are some tactics to increase your opportunities.

For the less expensive wines which may be made in larger volumes, look to large stores such as BWS, First Choice, Vintage Cellars and Dan Murphy's. If you can't find that one wine you really want, ask your local manager to order it in for you; it will only take a few days, although you may have to purchase a case of either six or 12 bottles. Some are willing to let you buy the one bottle as they might take a punt that the excess bottles will sell. The next port of call will be the internet and perhaps wine auctions, clubs, societies and cooperatives.

Quality online wine retailers

auswine.com.au	A retailer with good comments
backvintage.com.au	
thegrapeunknown.com.au	A quality cleanskin supplier
winedirect.com.au	
winestar.com.au	Run by Melbourne wine retailer Bert Werden, this is a site with a mission and plenty of feedback; the offers are good as well. Kept lively by quality contributors

Wine blogs

Wine blogs are a growing international phenomenon with several Australians contributing to the scene. The writing style and tasting notes can be variable so it's best to check the ones that appeal to you. They allow for quick cross-referencing of what's hot and who is doing well.

The aim of many sites is to become subscriber-based over time and to that end this is a dynamic and growing area. What follows is by no means a comprehensive list, but these sites appeal to me.

Wine blog sites

aavws.com	Australian Alternative Varieties Wine Show website for a look at the new and upcoming grapes appropriate for growing in Australia
acehighwine.com	Mixes wine reviews and poker from the amiable Max Veenhuyzen in Perth
camwheeler.com	Appellation Australia's blog
classic.com.au	Franz Scheurer Australian Gourmet—Pages is a newsletter on the former chef's views about what's to be eaten and drunk. It is very knowledgeable and up to the minute on fine dining, spirits and wine
jeremyoliver.com.au	There is a yearly subscription but the site opens a Pandora's box of exciting and relevant information. Whatever you are looking for about wine might just be on Jeremy's site!
pinotisland.com	Tasmanian-focused, a one-stop site
pinotnoirista.com	All things pinot
quaff.com.au	Perth-based Peter Forrestal provides weekly updates on what tastes good from his considerable experience
torbwine.com	Reviews by Ric Einstein (The Opinionated Red Bigot)
vinosense.com	News and views from Sydney-based Dave Brookes
winefront.com	Award-winning journalism by Campbell Mattinson and extraordinary contemporary insights make this a must read. You will save the subscription fee in the first six months
winorama.com.au	Gary Walsh works and tastes hard to keep his site up to date
winosandfoodies. typepad.com	A food and wine blog, this New Zealand-based site is run by an Australian and should not be missed

Auctionablity: Dust on labels causes decay making clean labels the most prized examples of a good cellar.

ANDREW CAILLARD MW, DIRECTOR, LANGTON'S WINE AUCTIONS

Auctions

Some investors enjoy purchasing wine via online auctions, others at live auctions. Whichever avenue is taken, many bargains can be found if you know what you are doing. If you are going to buy at auction, then you need to inspect the wine first. It's not rocket science, but there are some things you need to know.

- Look for unbroken seals and unbroken boxes.
- Check if the wine is old and/or rare, and check the reviews.
- Inspect fill heights—a bad bottle will have low fill height, be dirty and dusty, and have an almost oily finish.
- Check how the wine has been stored. A good bottle that has been well stored will have an intact label without staining and the glass will look quite clean.
- It's always hard to tell what's going on with the cork, but if you can, find out if the wine has been stored in air-conditioning, which tends to make corks horribly dry and brittle.

Remember that an investment cellar doesn't usually see the light of day until it is sold, because it's not about handling or even drinking the bottles. So wine that has been well cared for in an investment cellar will look good.

Auctions are also one way to buy cheap wine during times of glut, perhaps the most efficient from a consumer's point of view. It's very much 'buyer beware', simply offering wines and making no claims of quality control or indeed selection. Smart buyers can buy nearly anything at prices well below retail. It is worth remembering that retailers do taste the wines they sell and as a result they are guardians of consumers' wallets and palates. But take the costs of bricks and mortar out of the retail price and the prices really do tumble. If there is a tasting beforehand then auctions do offer affordable reliable drinking.

The Sydney-based Grays Auctions (graysonline.com.au) have recently introduced online wine selling. Surplus stock from retailers is offered, as well as stock sourced from wineries and wholesalers at prices 50 to 80 per cent lower than retail. There are no reserve prices and bidding can start as low as $10 a case. Other notable sites include these five.

Online auction sites

cellarit.com	Not an auction site but good site for buying, selling or cellaring
langtons.com.au	The biggest range of wines for auction in Australia
oddbins.com.au	Adelaide-based wine auction company
sterlingwine.com.au	Perth based with monthly auctions
wineark.com.au	Cellaring business with top local and imported wines

Old and rare wines

If you are lucky enough to inherit old Uncle Bruce's cellar and, even luckier, you find that you have a clutch of early 1950s French, or perhaps mid-1960s Grange and maybe mid-1990s Margaret River red wines, what are you going to do? How do you do justice to these rare bottles?

The first thing is to pick up the sexagenarian geriatrics very carefully and stand them up to see where the fill lines are in the bottles. If they are looking a bit low tide (wine in the shoulder not the neck) then there is going to be a problem with oxidation from then on. I would not buy old wines if the fill height had fallen below the neck.

The wines can be valued by comparing the prices given on Langton's website (langtons.com.au) but I would suggest that you drink them (with me as a guest of honour) with some mildly flavoured meat dishes. It would be a fun thing to talk to a local chef and give them the headache of working out what to serve with them, as many chefs and sommeliers have experience and can imagine what will work for what you've got.

The best way to keep old and rare wines is in their original boxes. An original, unbroken box is best from the collector's point of view. Second best is the original tissue paper in which the bottle was wrapped. And a pristine label is highly prized.

I have great faith in the Langton's website for sourcing or selling fine old wines. You can get online valuations and if you have sufficient quantity, then you can contact them for an inspection. Or contact this author!

If you buy an old bottle from overseas, then you need to appreciate that it is not going to like air travel. The best way to transport it is to:

- cling wrap it in order to protect the label
- bubble wrap it generously
- put it in a wooden box with a sliding top.

Once it's in its sarcophagus, find some safe space in your hand luggage. When you arrive at the other end give the bottle some resting time—a chance to recover from the journey—before drinking.

The general rule is that transporting old bottles of wine is not good for them, so the closer you can get them to their original storage centre the better. A bottle of old claret from a great French vintage, like 1945 for example, found in Australia will probably not taste the same as the same bottle that was bought in France close to where it was made. The next best thing would be to buy it somewhere like London, where it had been moved to one cellar and not moved thereafter. And so on. Movement definitely does interfere with the maturing process but is unlikely to affect the price.

Another rule is that the bigger the bottle, the more robust the wine is likely to be. So a jeroboam will be a bigger but better investment than a standard bottle every time.

Wine clubs and wine societies

If you are uncertain of your own judgment and want advice and affordability, help is at hand. Wine clubs and societies employ skilled tasting panels of professionals and seasoned buyers who take known brands and buy significant quantities of them, often at sharp prices. Some producers don't mind at all because it is good business and good advertising. Mixed dozen regional offers put together by an experienced tasting panel will bring you a selection of often unknown brands.

Wine clubs can be great sources of information, entertainment, wine culture and education, and I think they are really useful. At the end of the day you learn by tasting, reading and listening, and so a wine club with all these things is going to enrich your experience of wine drinking and life. They also offer the chance to enjoy special travel offers to wine regions, which is not a bad thing at all! A wine club can also be a powerful resource. Some clubs allow you to ring up and check what food goes with the wine you choose, or can facilitate a check on BYO restaurants.

When thinking about joining a wine club, look for the following opportunities:

- Travel offers to join groups visiting wineries
- Dinners in good restaurants
- Face-to face-meetings with winemakers
- Active education events with expert visitors
- Entertainment programs
- Tasting events
- Detailed newsletter
- Selection of wines with known and unknown labels.

Cooperatives

A long-term friend of the wine lover is The Wine Society (winesociety.com.au), Australia's only wine-consumer cooperative, wine-buying group. The society has become one of Australia's leading direct wine marketing organisations through selling shares to members.

Through an expert selection panel and experienced buyers, the society plays an important role in both selecting and purchasing wines at realistic prices that keep consumers coming back—to the tune of over 52,000 current members. And by the way, you can leave your shares in your will for the next generation,

A bottle of wine begs to be shared;
I have never met a miserly wine lover

CLIFTON FADIMAN, NEW YORK TIMES, 8 MARCH 1987

POLITICS AND WINE

For reasons best understood by accountants and the government, tax legislation introduced in the 1970s was responsible for Australian producers concentrating on fast-maturing vintages.

The net effect of tax laws imposed at that time was to impoverish the culture of older maturing wines in Australia. So while the wine industry likes to take claim for the development of gorgeously drinkable young wines, the reason behind it was that the federal government gave us a big kick in the butt that forced us to get on with it.

The 1990s saw another tax change that again reshaped the landscape of wine production in Australia. Tax concessions were offered for the planting of vineyards—unusually, without the wine industry wanting these concessions or asking for them. The result was a mass over-planting of vineyards and a glut of wine. Those vineyards are not only in nice, warm, kind, generous regions where grapes grow regardless, they are also in cooler climate areas where the grape can be only as good as the way it is handled. The resultant falling prices have been disastrous for the industry and were only corrected by the drought cycle in 2007.

HOBOS AND HEROES

I am indebted to Jeff Collerson, wine writer for Sydney's *Daily Telegraph*, for some of what follows. I just love a good wander down the annals of time.

My birth year, 1956, was a very important year in the history of Australia and the history of wine. With the birth of me (and Mel Gibson), Australia's population reached 9.5 million. Circular Quay railway station opened. Poker machines were legalised. Bob Menzies was prime minister. And Barossa Pearl was created for the opening of the Melbourne Olympic Games. The drink became an immediate best-seller. Around the same time Cold Duck was released. It was a sweet sparkling red that was a big hit but unfortunately nearly killed off a lot of halfway decent sparkling shiraz producers.

Whatever happened to Barossa Pearl, Cold Duck, Spumante and Sparkling Rheingold? Or Passion Pop, Mateus Rosé and Sparkling Riverland Gordo Moselle? The changing tastes of a generation have consigned some dear old classics to the rubbish bin of history. Some of them are still around but they are not the huge hit they were. They were wines of their times; especially sparkling wines, because in the mid-1950s people were very familiar with beer and the sparklers were not a bad comparison. And for many years very sweet wines dominated the wine market.

While Barossa Pearl was phenomenally successful, its sibling, Pineapple Pearl, was not. Launched in 1959 in an attempt to capitalise on Barossa Pearl's success, it tasted pretty bad and came in a pineapple-shaped bottle encased in a cellophane bag and had a passing resemblance to a hand grenade. To my great regret, I never bought a bottle to add to my collection. It flopped, but it was the forerunner of the wine coolers of the mid-1980s.

Mateus Rosé, first made in 1942, seems to go on and on. There is a permanent market for it although it has shrunk and the bottle does not appear so ubiquitously on windowsills or dining room tables under the candelabra as it used to. Ben Ean was born in 1959 and became a child of the 1960s, offering freedom in the form of a lightly fruity fresh white wine.

The wine cask was refined from a fruit juice packaged by Tom Angove—owner of Angove's, the long-established winemaking company in Renmark, South Australia—and patented by his company on 20 April 1965. Its impact as a convenient package has been dramatic in democratising wine and creating an important market that accounts for 50 per cent of wine sold in Australia. Its thus cheap, robust, easy-to-transport container allowed wine to be sold more cheaply and, with the two-litre cask, introduced more premium wines.

In the mid-1970s most cellar doors in Australia were still selling more fortified than table wines. Tyrrell's winery had 18 different ports, sherries and other fortified wines, alongside 11 table wines and nine sparkling wines. The most popular line for them was the fortified Blackberry Nip, a snip at $18 a dozen.

The early 1980s Top Five sellers were Kaiser Stuhl Summer Wine, Seppelt Great Western Champagne, Leo Buring Leibfrauwein, Ben Ean Moselle (so-called 'benzene' as in the fuel), and McWilliam's Sparkling Bodega. In the 1980s we learned to make white wines better and red wines fell out of fashion. By the late 1980s the chardonnay phenomenon had really taken hold. The top-selling wines were: Woodley's Queen Adelaide Chardonnay, Houghton White Burgundy, Wyndham Estate TR222 Traminer Riesling, Woodley's Queen Adelaide Riesling and Jacob's Creek Chardonnay. By the way, these rieslings weren't really a riesling—they were a white wine made to present a lot of crisp acid style that could be mistaken for riesling if you didn't really know. The grapes used were trebbiano or sultana or anything pretty ordinary.

We've come a long way in sophistication. We are now quite knowledgeable and quite demanding. We now buy wine by the region, grape variety and maker; we know a bit about age, technique and wood, and we show preferences for the type of closure on bottles.

chapter 6

The wine lifestyle

The simple pleasures in a glass of wine

BERNARD STEPHENS

It's always busy and no-one really has time to speak to anyone else in our house, so we decided to have a family get-together at least once a week to discuss things over dinner.

As a treat my wife and I open a special bottle of wine. We are not alone in what has become a common household ritual. Welcome to the time-poor noughties. As the occasion is special, so should the wine be. The more you understand about wine the better able you will be to select the right wine, not necessarily the most expensive, for such occasions and in the process increase your drinking pleasure.

Wine, like art, can be appreciated at various levels. At its best, wine appreciation fits in with a heightened sense of existence in a particular time and place. At another level it is a symbol of the countryside, embodying the best attributes of a place, interpreted through the three-legged stool of variety, vigneron and the mix of climate and soil. Wine is cherished for its flavour, acid and alcohol, unravelling as a taste messenger of mysterious faraway places. It is an accompaniment to our memories of people, places and events.

People live in different taste worlds and wine similarly has at least a few taste worlds at work. There's the world of the opinioned, cultivated, sophisticated connoisseur, who knows through experience and/or training and/or family what happens and should happen with wine; this person brings a great body of knowledge to every sip. Then there's the taste world of somebody who wants to know, and who views the consumption of wine as a passionate hobby that is an extension of their enthusiastic pleasure and joy in being alive. Or there's the taste world of someone to whom wine may be an irregular treat. This person may not know much about wine but knows what they like, and will enjoy their treat anyway and feel that it celebrates some special moment in life. Even without these different profiles we now know that wine tastes differently to each individual. Subtle differences in our DNA dictate the specific way in which each of us experiences the sense of taste.

It is important that the coming together of people should be marked by something special and wine is capable of being that special thing if it's used well and wisely. Take for example, champagne. I had a marvellous aunt who always said that if the occasion was important enough for you to come, then it was important enough for French champagne—although not every occasion we met was necessarily a champagne occasion.

A JOYFUL PART OF LIFE

The simplest side of wine drinking is that it softens the hard edge of existence.

The simple pleasures lie in a glass of wine. It can open our eyes and minds to the true delights of the company we are keeping. The food tastes better. The wine tastes better because of the food, ideas form and fly and humour finds its home. It is this subtle entwining of very pleasurable experiences in a moment that is the birthright of any wine drinker who imbibes moderately or sensibly.

More recently in our cultural history, wine drinking has gone hand in hand with tourism and the desire for authentic experience of another world. One small example is the wine tours run in the Barossa Valley for visitors who want to see 100-year-old vines. People get a kick out of seeing them and hearing the tales of people and the forces of nature. That wineries are often in beautiful places undoubtedly adds to the joy, as well as the stories—the epics—that are told as part of each region or vineyard or vine's history.

Having a wine cellar is like having an art collection. The main difference is that bottles are meant to be shared and enjoyed. Hence most people who have serious wine cellars have a tremendous generosity of spirit and love of life and people. Rarely are such collections put together for investment purposes.

ANDREW CAILLARD MW

In another way, the tale of authentic experience is told in individual preferences for different varieties or regions or colours. In this way, the art of wine appreciation can allow expression not only for the grower and maker but also for the drinker. The culture of wine gives an interesting opportunity for the manifestation of individual style.

The world, and hence the culture, of wine has changed inexorably. Many more vines picked up their roots and marched south over the equator during the last 50 years (especially evident in the last 15 years), and we have seen the expansion of the Southern Hemisphere's vineyards. This new direction is a new language evolving: the language of variety and region rather than the language of soil or terroir.

Today in Australia, the culture of wine is more likely to be about a Barossa Valley shiraz matured in oak, consumed from a specially designed Riedel glass, rather than a bottle of Côtes du Rhône drunk out of a tumbler with a baguette at the side of the vineyard from which the grapes came. Although the latter experience is something many of us in the 'new world' hanker for, and would pay thousands of dollars as tourists to replicate, it is part of another world, another culture and, perhaps, a step back in time.

WINE ETIQUETTE

I was talking to an old Master of Wine on a long trip between vineyards and the topic came to vintage port.

I was amazed to discover that in certain circles in the United Kingdom old wine traditions still resonate. In case you are caught in the situation with a vintage port decanter in your hand beware the 'Widdershins', which means to 'send wine around the table the wrong way', that is anti-clockwise. Should the port come to rest near you, you are likely to hear the person next to you ask, 'Do you know the Bishop of Norwich,' and have it explained later that he is a 'terrible chap who won't pass the port!'

Well, those phrases are a bit in-the-know, but there are just some basic things about what to do with wine and how to serve that will help everyone enjoy their evening without committing a faux pas.

Breathing

Opinions vary about this topic and every bottle is different. French-educated wine people will be reluctant to decant red burgundy for fear of destroying its bouquet, while in Bordeaux they will open the wine some hours before.

The advent of screw caps has increased the need for a decanter to allow the wine some air and a chance to breathe, as wines in these bottles seem to arrive tighter, brighter and appearing more bony in body straight after the twist. Decanting gives them a slosh of air; they soon round out and seem more in balance with improved texture and mouthfeel. I have seen high quality Chilean wines requiring five hours to show their best form and they were under cork! Overall I am cautious about opening old wines too early, and prefer to open them later, closer to drinking to allow the wine to open in the glass.

Decanting

This is increasingly needed for everyday wines sealed under screw caps, and it is vital for older wines with sediment. Screw caps reduce the oxygen ingress into wines as compared to corks, and hence have increased the wine's youthful freshness of flavour and tightness of structure. This makes decanting necessary for most wines to open them up with a little air.

For wines with a sediment I would take great care to stand them up for a few days before serving, and wipe the top of the bottle to remove as much of the mould and wine exudate as possible. If I am too lazy to decant I take great care to pour for everybody else before filling my glass, knowing that the sediment-laden wine will lack aroma and flavour. I will decant if the cork has crumbled and is floating in the wine.

Decanting, especially for older wines, requires a steady hand. I always tip the first pour out of the bottle down the sink, as it is surprising how many first pours seem to be tainted in the neck of the bottle, in particular because of the cork. You only loose about 30 millilitres. Then I pour the wine steadily into the decanter, which I have checked beforehand is scrupulously clean. I watch the wine as it flows into the decanter, and aim to avoid emptying the bottle completely. I leave some wine in the shoulder if it's a claret bottle.

I have not found filtering the wine with coffee filter papers to be very quick or effective, but if you absolutely must get the last bit of wine out of the sediment and you have a lot of time it's worth a try with the last sediment-laden portion.

President Richard Nixon was a great lover of Château Margaux and in his day at the White House determined that all wine was to be served in decanters. During his tenure decanters would contain Margaux at his end of the room and another wine for those at the other end of the table! His view was that they would never know!

In the Victorian era, it was customary to pass the decanter of wine around a table from left to right without letting it touch the table until it was all poured. It was designed to prevent anyone from taking too much wine because it meant that everybody at the table had a very real understanding of who had just taken the wine and how much was poured before it was passed.

Alcohol and leading an interesting life

Studies have shown that people with good diets tend to drink alcohol more frequently but in less quantity. The opposite is true for those with poor diets, who tend to drink less frequently but binge when they do. Alcohol and health is a minefield but it seems these sorts of studies emphasise what we already know instinctively—that there is a very strong argument to suggest that the moderate consumption of alcohol is part of an interesting lifestyle with interesting food, whereas binge drinking denotes a lifestyle of someone who is disinterested in life and therefore food quality so they just tend to eat whatever is on offer, and probably drink rubbish with which to wash it down. In short, if you are interested in food and wine and life then you are probably less likely to overindulge in a destructive way.

Accessories

The first and most important wine accessory is your unclothed palate. Then you will need an education and a library; this book is a good start. Wine appreciation courses are great. There must be 100 basic courses run for every single advanced wine course. I don't really

recommend doing an advanced wine course until you have a thousand or so bottles under your belt—not bingeing on them, I might add. You really need to taste and appreciate those one thousand bottles.

The next essential tool is still a corkscrew. To my mind the simpler the better. I don't endorse anything large and bulbous, and certainly not the infernal, cheap self-tapping sort that have spread like a contagion and often lose one of their arms, rendering them useless. You really want one that fits neatly in the corner of your top drawer and doesn't take over.

After choosing good glasses and managing to get the bottle open, the next most important accessories are an understanding lifetime companion, a keen interest in food and wine, a good digestion, a great memory and an exercise regimen to accommodate the whole lot. The greatest of all would have to be a good partner. He or she should have similar views on drinking as you. Heaven forbid that you end up with a partner who doesn't like Australian shiraz—woe is thee! And worse, if you end up with someone who doesn't drink!

An English Master of Wine, upon passing his exams (which he achieved very smoothly), promptly became an analyst of the flavours and textures of different teas thanks to an overflow of marital wrath incurred during the run up to his exams. He set out to win his near teetotal wife back by sharing a good three months tasting tea with her until her approval rating rose to the level where he could resume his wine lifestyle with some harmony.

TOAST *refers to a hunk of toast that was served floating on glasses of ales to sop up and filter out sediment and floating yeast. It was served on top of fortified wines for the same reason, as even the most heavily fortified wines were habitually murky. They were often served hot, like an alcoholic soup, with the hot toast floating on top. It was also common at one stage to serve hot wine mixed with an egg, and egg whites are still used today to remove protein haze from wine and soups.*

Order of service

The ceremony of serving and drinking wine is a part of what enables the experience. Wine is a shared ritual of release and relaxation, of food and company. How and what is served will vary from the commonsense of service temperature through the ceremony of cellaring, maturing and decanting, to the finely honed skills of blind tasting. There is a formal order of service for wine but unless the host is practising a highly traditional and refined culinary manoeuvre, possesses superb glassware and is serving suitably reverential and knowledgeable guests, you can get away with a number of variations on the rules.

Broadly speaking, there are really three ways of serving the three classes of wine—aperitifs, main course wines and dessert wines. Generally, the rule is light before dark and dry before sweet. The most important thing is to get the wine to the table at the right temperature after getting enough air into it to do it justice. When it comes to aerating wine, the fundamental rule is that the more expensive wines of the world need more breathing than the less expensive ones.

Old wines should generally be served early in the meal and drunk relatively quickly. These are not wines that should sit as they've been lying down for a long time. If you are deliberately serving a special and very old bottle of wine, then it would be a good idea to make that the focus of the evening. This means choosing a dish that has subtle but complementary flavours without heavy spice to overwhelm the wine.

Some dessert wines can be served as aperitifs because the enormous whack of sugar and quite high level of alcohol stimulates the appetite. So, for example, you could start a meal with great indulgence by serving a glass of sauterne and a traditional foie gras. The sauterne served in this way would make champagne look like lolly water.

The temperature at which the wine is served is the crucial factor. A good bottle can deliver a mediocre experience if served at the wrong temperature. Too chilled is as bad as too warm. Let's deal with red wines first.

Serving red wines

Generally, as red wines warm up their aromas grow. Low temperatures tend to emphasise bitter and harsh textures, whereas high temperatures reduce the textures and flatten everything out. For red wines the optimum temperature is around 15°C, which means in Australia red wines often get too hot. Think about it; the ambient temperature in summer can easily reach between 25°C and 35°C without any trouble and that is too warm for a glass of wine to sit around for too long.

Even the best red will lose aromas as the heat and lower humidity conspire to dissipate aromas. It then becomes a thin, textureless drink that exhibits only the most dominant of its flavours, not much aroma other than alcohol, and very little tannin. It often happens at the end of a barbecue when you can least remember it—the reds become as mono-dimensional as the conversation. By the time they've reached around 20°C, they're gone. So chilling reds in summer is a good idea. They will warm up fairly quickly in the glass, especially if you pour little and often in big glasses.

There is a good argument for serving some red wines a little bit colder, especially if they are old and have lost a lot of their tannins and acidity. I have tried this with Barossa shiraz that should have been drunk a few years before they were opened and chilling did the wines a favour. Similarly there's a good argument for serving some very young red wines with grippy, tannic, over-dry characteristics a bit warmer. This will flatten out some of the roughness. The warmth will be more forgiving.

MULLED *is the English term for beverages served warm or hot. The Germans called it Glühwein (glowing wine); the Italians, vin brulé (burnt wine); and the French, vin chaud (hot wine). It is usually red wine heated up with spices, and sometimes honey added. When wine went old, this was the way to make it drinkable again. It's not experienced much these days, unless you're skiing in the European Alps where it seems to still hold sway.*

Serving white wines

White wines should be chilled, but not for as long as some people think, with the exception of champagne and sparkling wines. It's okay to chill a white wine quickly in the freezer—encase it first in a wet tea towel, which will reduce the temperature even more efficiently.

As with red wines, the cooler the wine the less its aroma shows and the more the acid will stand out and mask the sugar. The ideal scenario for the thoughtful host is to serve the wine, say a riesling or sauvignon blanc, both very aromatic wines, very cold. But serve small quantities frequently in large glasses; in this way the wine will warm slightly and the aromas will burgeon—they grow in the glass.

In general, keep white wine in an ice bucket while it is waiting for the next round of filling. Champagnes and sparkling wines should be served really cold, and if possible into chilled glasses. This allows the drinker to capture as much of the sparkle as possible and to sip slowly, which in turn allows the temperature to rise and release the flavours that are most apparent at white table wine levels.

How many wines should be served at once? At formal dinners I like to serve two different styles at the same time with each guest having two glasses. This prevents me becoming endlessly boring about the subject of wine and also allows people to taste and give an opinion of their own. It's the sort of thing that can get the night off to a good start. Of course I can't guarantee by the end of the night that a forest of bottles won't have sprouted all over the table, nor that people will be tasting in any sort of order; but then most guests seem to count that as a highly successful evening!

Temperature: the crucial element in serving wine

Style of wine	Ideal serving temp (°C)	Refrigerate to serving (hrs)
Light sweet wines	5–10	4+
Light (aromatic) dry whites	8–12	2
Light reds	10–12	1.5
Sparkling whites	6–20	4
Sparkling reds	10–12	1.5
Medium-bodied dry whites	10–12	1.5
Medium reds	14–17	–
Full sweet whites	8–12	2
Full dry whites	12–16	1
Full or tannic reds	15–18	–

How to deal with 'off' wine

Screw-cap bottles virtually annul the need for the ritual opening, sniffing and tasting that accompanies the opening of a new bottle. Some people find this a bit scary to do in a restaurant and don't really know how to tell if a wine is on or off, anyway.

First, it is quite possible for wines that are corked to have become oxidised or to be 'off'. Remember that it always pays to have a look first, then sniff. The appearance of wine gives a lot away. The worst thing you can see in a freshly poured glass is cloudy, crusty, soupy-looking liquid.

If you decide that the wine is corked or oxidised, then the problem can be handled with delicacy. I generally say, 'I don't think this wine is as the maker intended.' Most wait staff are swiftly apologetic and rush off to find another bottle immediately.

However, there are some who are not as professional. I remember being on an international flight in business class where the flight attendant got very catty about me returning a glass of corked wine. The response came back, 'They all come with a cork in them!' My reply, 'But they don't taste like this', was disregarded. It was all very unpleasant and hopefully instructive of a previous time and place.

So what to do? Repeat the mantra I have just given you; then firmly, but gently insist that the wine be taken away before others taste it; and ask them to take it up with the wine sales representative who is in charge of the label.

Giving wine

Taking wine to someone's house as an offering or contribution can be tricky, especially if you don't know what they are preparing. How are you going to determine what is appropriate? There are a number of rules that I go by.

First, never take a bottle of wine to someone else's house that you wouldn't be happy to drink yourself. Other people are not a dumping ground for crap. However, if you decide to bring a bottle that is extremely precious and special to you and you really want to drink it, I would suggest that aside from ringing ahead to ask, while you are passing the bottle across and shaking the host's hand, you should mention that sharing a taste of this wine is going to add to both their and your experience of the night.

Of course the host has the inalienable right to choose the wines that will go with the meal so, if for some cosmically profound and unknown reason they don't serve your wine after a strong hint that they should, then you are required to keep your mouth shut. Discretion is the better part of valour. If, in the first place, you think there is a danger that the wine won't be opened and you are desperate to taste it yourself, then don't take it there.

A tip for the perfect host: if someone indicates that the bottle of wine is special, then it is gratifying for the guest to receive some appreciation. At least have a look at the label to pay service to the thought. And ask if it is to be tasted at this event or whether it should be put away. Here are some other no-no wine gifts when you are a guest:

- Cheap wine is out of order unless it is a joke.
- A funny-shaped bottle, unless it contains something special and pertinent to the occasion, probably doesn't give the right message of care, consideration and thanks to the people who are having you around.
- Cleanskins don't cut it, even if they are good ones.
- Sparkling water is not on.

Apart from that very special bottle, what else can a guest bring?

Sparkling wine is always good because no-one ever has enough sparkling in their life. If you really want to make a mark, a bottle of champagne or vintage champagne if the budget will stretch that far.

A good bottle of red is always welcomed. I have a number of bottles in my cellar that were given to me at Christmas time by various uncles and aunts who are now deceased; I have written the year of the gift on the label and every now and then I open one of these bottles and remember the person who gave it.

If you can give a bottle with a story that is also a good idea. This comes back to knowing something about the variety and/or the region of the wine; mentioning this can be of interest, even if it is not a bottle that is consumed on the night. Similarly, offering something that is not in general commercial distribution is a very thoughtful gift.

Just as very few people have enough sparkling in their lives, most people don't have enough sweet wine either. Maybe they will drink it or maybe they won't, but most people don't have a lot of it and will appreciate the thought.

Think about the occasion. Is it a dinner, a christening, a drinks party, a lunch, a picnic? And who are you trying to impress? Is it the boss or the bank manager, the next-door neighbour, or a long-suffering old school friend?

The other critical factor for consideration is the weather. There's not a lot of sense taking along a macho dry red to lunch on a hot summer's day, unless it is to be put away for later. A perfect match would be a good pink sparkling for drinks before dinner on a balmy night.

GROG *comes from a mixture of rum and water called 'grogram', served by the British Admiral Edward Vernon to his men in 1740. It quickly came to refer to any mixture of spirit—rum, cognac, kirsch or whiskey—served with boiling water and sugar.*

GLASS RULES OR THE MASTER GLASS

It is important that you **hold your wine glass by the stem** for one very good reason: you avoid overheating the glass and thus the wine.

The other reason of course is that after you've patted your greasy fingers all over the wine glass bowl, the glass looks foggy and it needs more work to clean!

And yes, it is also important not to overfill the glass. Wine should be poured in relatively small amounts so that the contents of the glass remain at the right temperature and can be refreshed, so each sip is fresh. Drinking is not an Olympic skolling contest, so there's no need to pour heaps into the glass and gulp it down quickly. Approximately 150 millilitres would be sufficient.

One of the great things about the past 30 years has been the realisation, particularly from the mid-1990s onwards, of the importance of glass shape. Thirty years ago a thistle glass represented the standard wine show glass. There was a major breakthrough with the International Standards Organisation wine glass which swept through Australia in the early 1980s. It had a handsome shape and was a highly effective benchmark of wine glassware.

Then in the 1990s Georg Riedel strode onto the Australian scene like a missionary and we all were stunned to discover that different shaped glasses could considerably enhance the drinking experience. Riedel taught us that the shape of a glass could influence the balance of wine flavour and highlight the varietal characters of a wine.

In the 1950s Georg's father, Claus Riedel, devised the theory, now reasonably widely accepted, that a glass enhances the perception of a wine's flavour and therefore increases the amount of information we can find in the wine. It can change our perception of the length and character of the flavour, acid balance, and seems to make the aftertaste last much longer; this in turn alters the finish of the wine and of course your memory of it.

Now we know that the variety of the wine is an important element in the mix of shape and size of a glass, but this realisation was a huge leap forward. It acknowledged that wine glasses could be finely tuned instruments that lifted the quality of wine.

A good wine tasting glass needs three key features:

- It needs to be an appropriate shape.
- It has to hold a suitable volume of wine.
- It has to have the right diameter of the rim.

Glassware makers that you should look for and can rely on are Riedel— recognised as probably the masters of fine glassware—Spiegelau and Schott Zwiesel, which also perform exceptionally well. Be guided by your own sense of style. You don't need to take the glasses too seriously, but having a large and a small wine glass bowl and a decent champagne flute will definitely go a long way towards improving your drinking pleasure.

As the shape of the glass is critical for a wine's fruit and balance, experience will teach you which bowl shape will protect the fruit and put it at the leading edge of the wine. This is particularly important for Australian wines where we tend to have big, leading fruit flavours with acids and tannins coming in later. As the sweet fruit taste tempered with acidity is a wine's primary pleasure glasses which can maintain this progression of flavour are going to be the most attractive. It's a hard-wired mammalian response that we are going to prefer the floral, the sweet, the ripe—it defines what's best in our world. The glass shape that protects this fruity taste is going to do the best for the wine because it will please most of us.

As I have mentioned, when you pour a glass of wine the glass should be only a quarter full. This is why bowl size is important. So when it comes to glasses, bigger is definitely better. It's not a question of volume, it's a question of sensual delight. A bigger glass allows you to pour a decent amount without overfilling it; and a large bowl will allow the full aroma and flavour to develop.

Swirl, don't shake, the wine around the glass by holding it at the stem (which should be long and elegant) and then sniff and taste at leisure. The bowl has a magnifying effect on a wine. The larger the bowl the greater the chance to segment and layer out all the aromas.

The diameter of the rim is critical because it determines how far you will have to tilt your head back and thus determines the speed of the flow over your palate. The slower the flow the better; and the flow seems slower from a wider-rimmed vessel. The fact is that some wines will be wonderful whatever you drink them from, but most wines benefit from being presented in good glassware that is a pleasure to both hold and drink from.

A master class on wine glassware explains the following all-important seven elements when choosing glasses.

Transparency

There are two common glassware types:

- Soda glass, sometimes called crystalline: When you ping it with a fingernail it sounds like a brick.
- Lead crystal: I heard an opera singer strike a note and watched the wine glasses on the table start to vibrate at the Australian Opera Auction in 2006.

Transparency is important to first impressions, helping the wine to look like it's alive and kicking in your glass. It needs to look good and that's the reason they have a stem, so you don't put your greasy fingers on the bowl.

Soda glass tends to throw a grey hue. Lead crystal has, depending on the quality of it, a very slight hue to it that can be a slightly grey, steely colour (lead crystal is the clearest material to work with in terms of clarity). Of course glassware should be clear and crystal is the best. Ornate crystal glasses with their myriad diamond cuts or colours don't deliver the goods.

Shape

There are two important things for the shape: the actual globular nature—an oval nature, egg-like, or whether it's got a more open edge—and the lip. The teardrop or tulip shape tends to present the wine in the best fashion. This is when the glass is narrower at the top than it is at the waist.

Different shaped glasses will deliver the wines straight onto different parts of your mouth. Holding the wine glass by the stem, tilting it and bringing it to your lips causes you to hold your head in a certain position to deliver the wine. The shape of the bowl, the width of the bowl and the cut of the rim will dictate where the wine falls on your tongue. Directing wine onto different parts of your tongue will change the apparent impressions of fruit, acidity and tannin in order to bring out the best of the wine you are drinking. Because no wine glass is ever filled more than a quarter to a third full this allows for the evaporation of alcohol to help lift the aromas and flavours out of the wine; so the wine starts to develop a much more attractive bouquet as a result of the proportion of wine to the glass.

Rim

The lip of a great glass is cut, not rolled. A rolled glass lip is similar to what a tableware tumbler looks like—quite thick and rolled over. A good wine glass lip is cut and has a really crisp clean edge to it.

Size

The size of the glass should be about as big as you can store. Glasses with larger bowls make swirling wine easier. The swirling wine releases volatile aromas that are important indicators of the quality and character of a wine's personality. Bigger glasses for red wine suit their richer alcohol, complexity and structure. Finer and more delicate wines can take a smaller glass. Small amounts of wine can be kept refreshed easily to keep them cold; also smaller volumes don't warm up as quickly in smaller glasses, so you can refresh the contents often giving a much better flavour experience.

Thickness

The fashion right now is definitely for thin glassware. A good glass will ping when you flick it and can be very thin. There's been some marvellous technology in development by glassware manufacturers to provide thin but robust glasses—double firing is one such method.

Range of glass shapes

The other big development is marrying the bowl to the stem in a single seamless flow, which gives you a much stronger and more vibrant glass. This can be seen in the new Riedel 'Grape@Riedel' series.

Stem

The stem is really there to give you something to hold so you don't wrap your hand around the bowl. It also allows for all of that gorgeous posing.

Durability and value

Durability is a serious challenge, with fine lead crystal having some vulnerability. I prefer to link the cost of my wine glasses in terms of the cost of my wines. I believe that a good wine deserves to be served in a good glass, and I feel that the pleasure derived from that first mouthfeel of good wine comes from taking it from a fine glass.

It seems that the innovations in glassware has continued unabated for more than 20 years now. I'm not sure if there is now a timeless design but I think there are still new ideas coming through.

CLINKING GLASSES *apparently evolved in Italy from the brilliant yet gruesome Medici family, who invented an odourless, tasteless poison that could be added to wine. The tradition developed that when a toast was called the guests would stand in a circle and clink glasses. At the same time each person tipped a little of the contents of his or her glass into their neighbour's, so that the whole circle effectively shared the same drink. This shows either supreme trust or supreme stupidity, depending on which way you look at it!*

Cleaning glassware

To clean good crystal glassware you should use plenty of hot water. You don't really require detergents unless you need to get rid of the fattiness of lipstick or meaty paws. To dry, hang them or stand them upside down if you can. But when storing (see below) stand them right side up. The most important rule is to use them often.

Certainly as an informed consumer you want to ask the question: Are my glasses dishwasher proof? Lead crystal turns milky as a result of mineral salt reactions in dishwashers, so the glasses become opaque and dull with time with the wrong soap. I don't put my wine glasses in the dishwasher, preferring hand washing instead. If you really couldn't be bothered to hand wash, lay the glasses in the dishwasher on their side so that there is less likelihood of breakage in the machine.

No doubt the most common problem with stemmed glassware is beheading them during cleaning—that's when you are rather too vigorous with your tea towel, and through twisting you behead the stem from the bowl. The way to dry these large crystal glasses is to hold the bowl in your tea towel and then wipe and polish, drying the stem separately from the bowl. By doing so you will greatly enhance the durability. The other secret is to wash them in the morning.

Storing glassware

Think carefully about storing your wine glasses. If they are not used every day, a wine glass is in danger of becoming neglected, foggy and dusty. In order to make the most of a wine glass, it needs to be kept clean and refreshed. The best way of doing this is to fill it frequently with wine.

Don't store wine glasses bowl down—unless they are on racks and are used every day—you'll only risk chipping them and the rims may pick up tastes from the surface they are stored against. Store them upright; bowl to the heavens and preferably in a cabinet that closes.

Also make sure that your wine glasses are pristine. Traces of dirt or soap are all going to have an impact on taste, and they tend to cancel out the fruit and knock the acid around. So clean glasses, please.

I once met the CEO of a wine company on a plane who related his priorities when he moved himself from Melbourne to Sydney. After having arranged for his cellar, his suits and his shoes to be packed, he personally packed his glassware. We were on a red-eye from Tokyo to Sydney and I was not about to question him deeply about this but it seemed to me that he had his priorities in admirable order.

WINE STORAGE

When I was working at Rosemount Estate, it fell to me to sort out the winemaker's wine cellar because they had been a little too squirrel-like in their storage of the company's fine wines for over a decade.

Sadly, some of the oldest vintages had been stored in conditions that were little better than a hot shed. However, on a subsequent tasting, it appeared that well-made wines from good vintages weathered this treatment in storage and taught me an important lesson: good wine can hold up quite well no matter what you do to it. That's taking out of the equation a big variable like a rotten cork.

Some essential rules about wine storage follow. Put the wine in the cellar if you have one. If not, then leave it in its box and find a place in the house that is cool and dark (sunshine leads to changes in temperature as well as fading labels), and not subject to too much temperature variation. The less variation the better off your wines will be. Ageing curves for stored wines will be faster at higher temperatures and lower at lower temperatures. So if you are laying wine down for your children then you need to get the storage conditions right.

Wine corks need humidity—above 80 per cent is necessary. I find that some people who are serious about their wines will air-condition their cellars but they don't always humidify them. After about five years in a very cool but dry environment, the corks are in danger of drying out, which means that they can break off halfway up when you remove them. Not a good look with a cherished bottle of wine.

Much is made of wine cellars but very few people have them. A cellar to my mind is a concept. It is really about being interested in seeing what happens when a wine ages. So a cellar could comprise only a sundry six bottles. It's more about the motivation. When constructing your own cellar, you need to consider what exactly you are going to store and why. I find that most people underestimate the amount of bin space as opposed to rack space. In Bordeaux and Burgundy, most cellars store much of their wines in bins rather than racks as they afford more space. Personally, I think a great big wooden table is a must.

If you are going to have a genuine, bona fide consumption cellar then you will need more racks and shelves. If it is predominantly an investment cellar then you will need more bin space. One of the best ways to get the humidity right is to put in a rubble floor over the cement with a decent drainage system. Then, when the air gets too dry, it's a matter of throwing a few buckets of water around. That's another technique I learned from the Bordeaux winemakers.

For the serious punters the best book on the topic of cellaring is James Halliday's *Setting Up Your Own Wine Cellar* (Angus & Robertson 1989).

chapter 7

Matching wine and food

I cook with wine, sometimes I even add it to the food!

ANONYMOUS

IT'S A THEORY

Good quality food and wine literally lift the amusement, experience and education of the activity.

Good food stimulates your tastebuds and you get more from your wine. Food has weight like wine—light, medium and heavy—and this needs to be balanced with the structure of its accompanying wine, for the wine to drink well and match the dish. There is a good case for familiarity and knowing the food or wine thoroughly to awaken subtleties in each, but that is just one of many different theories on how to match food and wine.

Native theory

The native theory has some very high profile exponents in the restaurant business. Put simply, it argues 'if it grows there, it goes there'. So if the game for your dinner comes from a certain region, then the best wine to accompany it grows in the region. This is the oldest and most traditional rule for matching food and wine.

When you are in places like Europe where they actually produce food and wine in roughly the same spot it is a charming idea. It is definitely one way to achieve a cultural harmony in food and wine but I don't think that it is the only way or even the best way to achieve a qualitative perfect match. In the middle of a big modern city with modern urban values it can't be anything more than an ideal as life is not that serendipitous. But you really can't go past a lot of the classic old food and wine matches—Rhône with rich red stews; a good bottle of Bordeaux with chateaubriand; or a good bottle of Volnay with roasted meats.

Regardless of region, balancing flavours is central to French food and wine philosophy. Subtlety and harmony are predominant themes. This sits nicely with the delicacy of so many of the French wines and suits many French dishes which tend towards a clever merging of flavours. These are matches made in heaven.

This is completely different to the Australian experience, though, where our full-blooded Australian wines can accompany a big bowl of fabulous Thai food, which can in itself contain eight or nine different flavours. We don't mind our wines' powerful tastes—we welcome contrasts as much as we appreciate harmonies. There are a lot more modern marriages available with new world wines, starting with the basic shiraz with steak or kangaroo; a good bottle of cabernet merlot with rabbit; or a riesling with whiting.

The native theory has never really been easy to achieve, even in the days when regional trade was restricted and wine was difficult to transport. There were always exceptions to the rule due to the relative scarcity of great wine. We can see the native theory with its inevitable exceptions still gloriously at work in France for instance, in the very acid wines of Burgundy. There is really no sweet dish native to Burgundy because there is nothing sweet that will make a good chardonnay or a good pinot noir taste better, all they can do is rob from it. So the desserts of Burgundy are nearly non-existent; you'd have a piece of cheese.

So 'if it grows there, it goes there' has its moments but the underlying belief that for some reason a fish caught from a particular harbour is going to be best supported by the wine growing in the hills above it relies too much on serendipity.

There is a notion that cold white wine numbs the palate, and there have been occasions in France when I have been drinking those cold, high-alcohol and acid-impact wines and the joy I am expecting with my first mouthful of red hasn't been delivered.

Cause and effect of matching

American Tim Hannai, a Master of Wine as well as a chef, has thought and eaten long and hard to arrive at a more sophisticated theory of food and wine matching. And like all good thinkers, he has introduced a couple of new ideas too. For Hannai cause and effect are central. Some foods make your wine taste milder by reducing the flavour of the wine, which may or may not be a good thing. Some foods make your wine stronger, which means that the flavour of the food may enhance or strengthen the flavours of the wine. Again this may be a good or a bad thing, depending on the balance you are trying to achieve. For instance, sweet food accentuates wine's acidity and tannin. A glass of cabernet served with a rich chocolate pudding is going to taste bitter and astringent. On the other hand, acid food or cooking veal with verjuice will complement a wine's acidity and make it seem richer and mellower.

Under this idea, if you want to do yourself a favour with a wine that needs a bit of help (that is, it's too acid), then go down the acid path—high citrus, tomatoes, high-quality verjus (early-picked grape juice), salt or fat will hide acidity or bitterness. Or, go for high protein and a fair bit of fat—meat and gravy will make an acid wine much more mellow in its effect on your tastebuds. In a more humble setting try meat with a dab of mayonnaise.

Bitterness in vegetables, herbs, spices or burnt food will increase the bitterness of a wine. So if the wine tends to dryness or bitterness, then trick the palate with high acid or protein food, similar to the combinations for acid wine above. Saltiness in a dish will temper red wine astringency, that is, if you want to go that hard. Salted meat will have a softening effect and the overall taste experience will be more generous.

Spice is nice

Lyndey Milan and I discovered a concept that Lyndey calls inoculation. We were undertaking an experiment while preparing a presentation for a Brisbane Master Class in 1997.

We discovered that when spice dominates a wine's flavour, such as pepper in a Victorian shiraz, serving a dish with pepper in it will mute the spicy taste and allow the fruit flavours (in this instance, blackberry) to be more pronounced. Hence we inoculated the taster against the spice by adding it to the food.

The use of spices also opens a fertile field for bridging flavours (see below) and using herbs, such as mint with cabernet, nutmeg with pinot noir, or dill with young semillon, help the wine's flavours come out.

Matching intensity

There are some particularly Australian rules to the cause-and-effect theory. For example, a good many Australians always drink white wine with fish. I wondered why this wasn't regularly satisfactory for me until I met representatives from the guild of fishmongers in London. According to them, the rule is not to drink white wine with fish because fresh white wine often makes the fish taste fishier. They suggested young pinot as being particularly good with seafood, which was confirmed for me by an older Master of Wine, who suggested I match the colour of the red wine to the size of the fish—the bigger the fish the redder the wine. So with tuna you can really drink deeper-coloured pinot noir, which is an interesting rule that matches intensity.

Big-flavoured wine goes with big-flavoured food. Light food works well with lightly flavoured wine. Only serve good wines with great food and ordinary wine with ordinary food. Less assertive flavours should go together too. Ripe apple or pear, and white bread with cheddar cheese, and good company, go with older whites. And so it also follows that more complex wines should match or reflect the complexity of the food.

Think about the texture or viscosity of the food, which will determine whether the wine needs to cut through with a bit of tannin or acid. For example, a big oily meaty fish can be bolstered in this characteristic with a big peachy chardonnay; or you can provide a counterpoint with a piquant riesling. With a fatty duck, try a pinot noir that is rich in tannins, or a shiraz to pick up the sweeter melody of the duck. A louder, plastic-chopsticks type of approach is sparkling shiraz. A Vietnamese spring roll that has the sharp but delicate flavours of chilli and mint resonates well with a crisp white wine such as riesling, sauvignon blanc or pinot gris.

Beware whatever you taste after having brushed your teeth. Toothpaste will set off a very strange reaction in your mouth and reduce the flavour of wine.

Bridging worlds

Mental imaging and bridging are other concepts we use when talking about wine matching. It is much easier for some people to understand taste in terms of imagery—landscape or painting, for example. So, if I describe a wine as a van Gogh and food as the interior decor of the room in which you would display the van Gogh, you will get my drift. Or, if I ask you what sort of food you would serve with a wine that is like a steam train in a tunnel, you would probably instantly get the feeling of the robustness and directness of the wine's taste and the effect it has on your palate.

Bridging is a term I learned from chef Tony Bilson. He refers to it often when he talks of using sauces to bridge the wine to the food. For example, a marmalade of beetroot and orange juice served with duck and pinot noir will find both acidity and sweetness from the orange and pinot-like flavour in the beetroot.

There is no one way to approach the notion of bridging in food and wine matching. For example, chef Danny Russo in Sydney was asked to prepare a dish to go with a McLaren Vale Songlines shiraz that retailed for over $100. He prepared a dish with squab cooked simply with a few cherries because this was a red wine of superb proportions; so the semi-sweet cherries actually served to bring out the lovely fruitiness of the wine and made it sing. Danny had punctuated the fruit of the wine with cherry richness. At Circa in Melbourne the next day chef Andrew McConnell showed the answer was a combination of harmony and weaving. He used a touch of coffee in a veal reduction served with the most magnificent venison that was deliciously tender. So in the same wine he found the bass notes of oak and ripe tannins to hold the wine and food together.

Two different cities and two quite different ways, Danny Russo tied a knot in it by punctuating the fruit with the cherry and the richness of the tannins with the squab, whereas Andrew McConnell at Circa chose to weave the flavours by using the stock reduction with just a hint of coffee and bringing everything together. At the highest level of cooking there will always be different answers to the same challenge. One thing is certain, we've come a long way from the old days of serving mushroom-based sauces with our big smoky reds, once thought to be the epitome of building harmony and marrying flavours.

Classic simplicity

Another way of looking at wine and food matching is to cut through to an idea of classic simplicity, almost austerity. With this approach, you would choose the simplest preparation of food and the greatest bottle of wine and let them shine on each other. Some fantastic examples of this approach that work really well are:

- riesling and whiting
- sauvignon blanc and asparagus
- seared tuna and pinot noir
- rare steak and McLaren Vale shiraz
- a lump of hard, not too acidic, cheese and Coonawarra or Margaret River cabernet
- homemade garlic-rich aioli with cold prawns and fresh white baguette from the bakery, and aged riesling
- olives and almonds with fino sherry.

Each of these is a pinnacle in the taste maps of the world, providing the palate with gorgeous, gleaming clarity of flavour. So as you see, a really ideal match can be very simple: a great piece of meat or cheese and a great bottle of wine—and you let them both shine in their naked unadorned glory.

The key thing is simple, well-cooked food, without complicated sauces, made with quality ingredients that don't confuse the flavours. Complexity of flavours in the dish rather than a complexity of flavours all over the dish. The food supports the wine; it works time and time again because both the food and the wine are good. It's seen as a modern version of 'if it grows there, it goes there', but taking into account the elements included within the food and wine rather than the region.

Food and wine matches without doubt are a matter of personal taste. But never believe that chocolate goes with cabernet and remember that champagne was perfected late by French standards, so it is relatively loveless in food matches. However there are some sensational partnerships that most will agree with:

- chicken or lobster with chardonnay
- blue cheese with liqueur muscat

- oysters with champagne or young Hunter semillon
- rum-and-raisin-flavoured old Australian fortifieds with good, rich, chocolaty, strongly flavoured foods—made in heaven.

If you were tasting champagne in France, God forbid having coffee in the morning. The French maintain, through long experience, that coffee numbs your palate. Well, French coffee would, and many in the wine trade advise not to drink coffee before indulging in champagne because it will impede your enjoyment.

Seasonality

For me wine and food matches are quite seasonal. The first match is that cold seasons suit older white wines as well as older red wines. The corollary of aged white wine is that you don't have to serve it as cold as young ones. So if a riesling variety of white wine is to be drunk at around 10°C or 11°C, let it warm up a little bit more to serve for winter and you'll find that its personality will come out.

In winter the fuller chardonnays, viogniers and other rich wines, such as Rhône blends, marsanne and rousanne, meld to give you an opportunity to indulge in a higher alcohol level that provides warmth to the palate, your tummy and your mind.

Winter, I think, also suits oak, but there's a big exception when you've got chilli in the dish, it's all a bit too much. Oak is like seasoning in cooking and normally the seasoning is not the main flavour—oak should never be the main flavour either. Most often there is a symbiotic relationship between the fat in a dish and oak tannins in red wine. One of the great drivers is that fatty dishes help you appreciate dry red wines by making your palate slippery, and thus chemically softening the tannin. Fats react with the most active elements in grape and oak tannins, which tame their ability to dry your mouth. This increases the sense of ripeness and fruity flavours and brings a sense of the warm ripe fruits of summer to your mouth, even in winter.

In summer time it pays to drink the young, fresh, light and crisp wines. The pinnacle 'white wine meal' is probably still fish—though in the Northern Hemisphere there are a number of white wines you can almost serve with lamb.

The wine should be eaten; it's too good to be drunk

JONATHAN SWIFT

CULTURAL MOMENTS

Theories about **wine matching** don't stop at the door of ideas.

Oftentimes they are inherited from classic cuisines, and then moulded into a new shape. By looking at a couple of these theories we can see some interesting examples of matching food with wine. The French are undoubtedly the masters at weaving flavours, but I think the Italians are pretty good at it too. And Asian food, being perhaps the biggest style of eating in Australia, shines new light on these older cultural theories.

French food

If we take classic French dishes, most of them work towards a harmonious combination of blending and balancing the intensity and the mouthfeel so the food merges into one dreamy, often creamy, flavour and texture. The trick with these dishes is to match the flavour volumes and textural qualities of the wine with the food. The shape of the wine in your mouth should match the shape of the food, the volume of flavour of the wine should match the volume of flavour in the food, and the texture of the wine should match the texture of the food. Then everything works like the slippery effect of a silken sheet—it is very, very sensuous and refined.

The idea of weaving flavours comes with sauces. Within French cuisine there are at least three classic sources of fat: butter, goose or pork fat, and olive oil. Each of these provides its own separate form of cooking, which in turn allows you to more easily think about the flavours in the food to choose the right wine to go with it. The thing about French food is that the sum total of the plate is the blending together of every flavour on that plate, which is then unified by the sauce.

The French unified flavour, bringing it all together on one plate in one style, remains the pinnacle of fine food for many people. It is also a very happy match with fine wine. The only problem that arises is when you start to get more robust flavours coming out. How do you balance it all in these cases?

Balance is a curious thing, perhaps best described as opposites attract. When flavours become more strident with spicy food, the answer is not to chase that volume of flavour and go head to head with it. You need to provide a strong contrast to balance wine and food; for example, a sweet wine will balance an acidic food.

The notion of balance and harmony is at least trying different wines with the same dish until you discover what works. For example, I've discovered, and still think, a big

coconutty, oaky Australian shiraz is going to do reasonably well with a soft fruit-style duck curry with coconut in it. This is more or less the classic wisdom. But the other view would be if it's a big coconut-flavoured dish why not just go for something slightly sweet that mirrors the sweet image of coconut: light, bright and refreshing. So in chasing balance you can try and balance dishes, but sometimes you will find that equals repel and become virtual opposites rather than bringing themselves together.

Wine and cheese does not always please

The French had it intuitively right: if there is any red wine left mop it up with a little bit of cheese. Cheese flattens the flavours and fattens the texture of red wine, while dampening its aromatic fruit and oak and tendencies to astringency. Expensive pinot noir, shiraz, cabernet and other full-bodied red wines served with cheese taste fatter and flatter with the all loose flavour.

There might be useful insight here. While some food makes your wine taste stronger, some food will make your wine taste weaker and maybe if you've got to get through that last glass of red before you head on to the next course anything that reduces the flavour of the wine could be an advantage. The French have always understood this. The strongest flavoured cheeses will have the greatest effect, although even a mild cheese will help.

The protein in cheese binds both the tannins and the flavour compounds in wine and makes them hard to taste. The fat of the cheese also coats your mouth, particularly the tastebuds, so it helps mask the flavours and makes it harder for the wine to get a hold of your tastebuds to make an impact.

If you want to take it to a higher level you have to be very careful because I think some cheese and wine pairings are truly horrible. It's very rarely I've come across a strong blue cheese that has a happy fit with wine. Strong blue cheeses should be left to their own resources and Rutherglen muscat.

Italian food

Italy is awash with over 2000 grape varieties producing strident acidity, grippy tannins and gentle flavours. Italian wines seem to physically cleanse the palate as well as irrigate it. It's as if the whole tasting experience has been wound up a notch or two in almost operatic vividness.

Italian food delivers vitality in its flavours; any country that can make a ripe tomato salad a satisfying main course has a lot going for it. Distinct from French food, Italian food can have individual elements of intensely flavoured food on a plate, which may cause matching wines other than the local versions a bit of a challenge.

The quality of Italian vegetables and fruit gives Italian food a striking distinctiveness that the French, in the case of fruit especially, often choose to smooth away with butter, cream or sugar. Anthony Miceli, winemaker medico from Mornington Peninsula, serves his barbecued eggplant over polenta and matches it with pinot gris or pinot noir. He finds the creamy, bland nature of the polenta highlights the subtle, smoky edge of the barbecued eggplant, and the combination needs a relatively subtly flavoured wine. The marriage bodes well.

Asian food

I remember the first Master of Wine to tutor me in London took up tea tasting when he needed a break from wine. He became an absolute expert on all sorts of different teas and we used to talk about such things as fermented black teas, which he described as being fatty and cheesy. So texture matters in the cuisine of tea cultures as much as flavour and viscosity. You can see this in Chinese food; they love texture and offer a vast variety, from jelly fish to shark lips and backwards.

When matching wine with Chinese food it's as much about getting texture as actual flavour, so the viscosity or oiliness of the food and the drink—the degree of softening of the tannins—is blended. This is a vital key. The Chinese have traditionally drunk tea with their food to achieve this because they do match well.

Teas also match the spicy chilli, ginger or lemon verbena flavours of Thailand and Malaysia, foods which have traditionally been eaten with fruit juices as an accompaniment. The fruity flavour of teas and juices is the important element here. In the wine industry we have until recently had a low view of fruit-driven wines like sauvignon blanc, simple rosés or unwooded chardonnay, but Asian foods seem to have changed this.

Acids are very important in Asian cuisine. There are a lot of acids in wine—lean acids like tartaric and malic, and even occasionally ascorbic acid, which is vitamin C, often added as an anti-oxidant. Those characters dominate in sauvignon blanc and riesling and are part of the reason why they have that skinny mouthfeel about them. So the next step after the viscosity is to look at the acid, strength, texture and structure of a food.

A clever host could look at comparing and contrasting the wines with the food, which is a great way of making either the wine taste stronger or the food taste stronger. By setting up the contrast where you have got a big fatty dish, such as salmon, you can choose either to bolster that characteristic with a big fat pinot gris or a big peachy chardonnay, or provide a piquant counterpoint with sauvignon blanc or pinot noir. Sauvignon blanc, for example, has got a soursob oxalic acid character that would slice through the sweetness of the fish very quickly.

Similarly, for duck you can have pinot noir because its soft tannins give a beautiful mouthfeel and get a structural thing happening, or go with a shiraz with lots of soft tannins. Duck twice cooked with spices, dripping in a spicy coconut sauce, ripely flavoured because of the cooking process, is a heartfelt friend of a good pinot or a good shiraz. The loud plastic chopsticks-type approach would be a sparkling shiraz.

As mentioned earlier Vietnamese spring rolls have a very crisp, fresh flavour with a little bit of chilli and Thai mint. I think those flavours resonate best against a crisp white wine—riesling and sauvignon blanc—as well as a richer wine like pinot gris or the fatter chardonnay.

The Japanese have a rich tradition of saki and there is a wide variety available, but I don't see a big problem with matching Japanese food with wine. Pinot noir makes a happy marriage with this cuisine. Young fresh wines are also called for here; riesling or semillon sauvignon blanc highlight the immaculate freshness of the little bit of salt in a lot of fresh fish. I don't think the bigger bodied wines—shiraz, cabernet merlot or zinfandel—would offer very much.

You don't have to cry into your beer if you are having a curry. Spicy food demands crisp white wines and smooth red wines, not barrel-aged or tannic wines. With strong chilli dishes you are dumbing the fruit flavours of the wine down but you find the exaggerated oak and acid flavours. A lot of spicy dishes react by highlighting the acids and making the oak taste hard and strong, and they'll react to alcohol as well, making the wine feel hotter than it is.

Asian food with its at once sweet, sour, spicy and hot flavours can be a challenge to match with wine, but the heat in most of these dishes comes from the chillies. The flavours that survive heat are both sweet and sour, which is why a crisp wine will work off its sourness within a dish and can cool your mouth after the fiery onslaught of something this hot. Because chilli is so hot it diminishes your perception of flavour. The capsaicin—the substance that makes chillies hot—takes the nuances out of your mouth by acting as a leveller across all flavours, so don't serve wines of high quality and great refinement. With these sorts of food serve wines that have plenty of power and grunt with bold flavours, which are often nicely and honestly made.

Great grapes for fiery food are riesling, muscat and viognier as well as, in the aromatic category, young New Zealand sauvignon blanc, Australian riesling, Italian pinot grigiot, and Alsace pinot gris if you can find one. Reds such as beaujolais, gamay, pinot noir (without oak) and possibly Californian zinfandel and fruity shiraz also work well. In general, though, don't think too much about the grape variety to serve with Asian food; rather consider a powerful wine that will overcome the numbing effects of strong chilli.

The wines you choose for these sorts of food will have to do a fair bit of lubricating. The hotter the dish the more cooling you will need. Cooling is best provided by something sweet. Nothing sickly sweet and syrupy, but a spaetlese or auslese riesling that will finish dry but pick up the lively flavours of the curry on the way through. This sort of wine actually mirrors the traditional Asian drink with food—a sweetly fragrant but dry-finishing tea.

A good idea with wine matching spicy food is to keep the alcohol down so that you avoid pouring fuel on the bonfire of flavours already going on in your mouth. If the wine is very alcoholic, it will heat up rather than cool down the overall effect in your mouth, so stay within a maximum 12.5 per cent alcohol.

Crazy but true, serve bubbles—anything goes better with sparkling, but sparkling wine by the physical action of the bubbles is cold and refreshing on your tongue. The sparkling character refreshes as well as being on the low side in alcohol. It's rare that you'd find sparkling that's going to hit more than 12 per cent so they tend to soothe the palate. At first impression sparkling red wines with sweetness might seem to work with spice but in my experience the tannins do not sit well and suffer from the chilli's magnifying effects.

Sparkling white wine could go very well with good quality Vietnamese or high-quality Thai food. I would want a spicy takeaway sparkling red to be very smooth rather than astringent. You can with a little bit of cunning find that the effervescence and sparkling red or white character will elevate an ordinary Thai takeaway.

Food and wine matching—some specifics

- As a general rule, food will dominate the wine.
- In a restaurant, look at the wine list first, then look at the food. After perusing both in that order choose food that suits the wine, not wine that suits the food.
- Some food will make your wine taste stronger, such as sweet wine and dark chocolate.
- Some food will make your wine taste weaker, such as young tannic red wines and medium-rare beef.
- The wine should always be sweeter than the food. This can be a real problem in some parts of the world. For example, in the United States bread can be very sweet and in New Orleans, in particular, they also cream and sweeten the butter. If you are trying to deal with a chardonnay as well … well, drink local or don't.
- The sauce will have the most influence on your success in matching food with the wine. You can only have two or three flavours on the plate and one in the glass. You need to decide which is the most important on the plate and then match it with the wine. So, if the wine is an alluring, young, highly oaked red, go for meat, as the protein will help to soften its tannins, as will any fat in the sauce; and have a sauce heavy in mushroom flavour to form a bridge between the woody and fruity flavours.
- Look for vegetable cues. For example, cabernet sauvignon often has red capsicum characteristics, so you might want to include a bit of red capsicum in the salad to bridge flavour.

SPUNTINO BAR
HALF
FULL
$14
$23
MOSCATO
STONE
WHITE PINOT
PINOT GRIGIO
PINOT GRIS

WINE LISTS

Wine lists are the business end of restaurants, as wine must contribute to covering their operating costs.

It is expensive to buy, store and serve wine. Very few wine lists are just slapped together, as most reflect the philosophies of the owner and of the restaurant respectively. Given we are spoilt for choice with the variety of wine available there should be no 'average' list, only great or boring ones.

On the boring side are lists put together by those who want a manageable and relevant wine selection to offer its customers without the work involved. Wines are purchased on implications for business profits and to reduce the time management spent on creating the list. Wine companies assist in compiling these lists by offering to print them as long as enough of their wines are included on the list to justify the costs. Unfortunately, these lists can have wines that don't match the food style on offer at the restaurant.

Great wine lists are a feast for the eyes and a famine for the wallet. They should explain the weight of each wine or body and not be wordy or condescending, offering perhaps short notes for each wine aimed at helping you match wines and food by a simple weight and colour compatibility.

Great restaurants offer a more complete service and give you full interaction with the staff, usually a sommelier. Sommeliers guide restaurateurs as well as the guests by caring about what is best for the restaurant and they take their role as the 'nose and tongue' of the establishment seriously to achieve the right balance. These wine lists show a diverse range of wines allowing patrons imaginative choices. You can pick them by their purposeful choice, their diverse structure and awareness of the wines of the world.

Most modern inner-city restaurant wine lists are small, constantly changing and feature a mix of the recognisable and moderately priced, often blending small producers with mainstream and cutting-edge wine varieties and styles. If a restaurant's dishes are typically light, fresh and aromatic, as in a fish café, the emphasis will be on zippier aromatics. If dishes are richer, thickly textured, complex and long-cooked, then weightier wines will get a bigger share. The challenge in these lists is for the wines to be relevant to the patrons as well as being fine wines that match the food.

The role of the sommelier

With the exciting diversity of food and range of wines available there is a definite need for highly articulate people who can take your senses to the next level, especially if you have planned a big night out. Before talking to the sommelier, think about what is most important—the wine, the food or the event. There's a lot of evidence to support the view that people are rewarding themselves for their time-poor lives by buying better bottles of wine when they go out. Either way the sommelier should definitely be able to help.

Some people complain that sommeliers are overbearing rather than adaptable and some diners report feeling intimidated into buying pricier wine following discussions with a sommelier, so they don't discuss their choice at all. But a good sommelier will be thoughtful, responsive and promotional. They are there to help you enjoy. A really good sommelier will have a sense of what you are going to eat and drink by the time you are ready to sit down.

COOKING WITH WINE

In many houses there is that old bottle of red or white wine with a cork sticking out of it sitting near the stove waiting to be used for cooking.

But there's an old adage about cooking with wine: if you can't drink it, why would you want to cook with it? I suggest that if you want to cook with wine, open a bottle that you would look forward to drinking, cook with it, and drink the rest. It creates a circle of enjoyment.

The only time you can get away with cooking with an old bottle of wine is when it is sparkling wine. Even if it has gone flat it will still be able to add a marvellous acid edge. In flat sparkling wine, there's usually plenty of acidity left, and not much sugar, so it can add a good, zesty, crisp crunchiness to a dish. Leftover wine from drinking needs to be stored in a half bottle in the fridge with a cork in it, at least then it won't oxidise as fast.

The classic cooking techniques that have wine as a core ingredient include: flambéing, glazing, deglazing, macerating, marinating and poaching. Consider boeuf bourguignon, coq au vin and osso bucco—they're all dishes to which wine is crucial. There's nothing like the scent of slow-braising meat in a wine sauce to make you salivate.

There are three drivers: alcohol, flavour and acidity. In the cooking process, alcohol releases and integrates flavours before it evaporates at fairly low temperatures; this takes away the alcohol flavour edge but leaves the wine flavour. As alcohol doesn't dissolve in

fat or water, it is especially good for deglazing pots and pans. The flavours inherent in wine means that the cook can often cut down on salt and other seasonings as well as oils when using it. Wine is fat free but has natural tannins that help to bind ingredients and assist in the making of sauces as well as providing acidity. Heating wine does not reduce acidity so quite acidic wines should be used with care in cooking. Avoid cooking with excessively oaky wines, as the oak may overpower everything else in the dish. Oak sticks out taste-wise and emphasises acid.

So how should a cooking wine be chosen? The first task is to assess the shape and structure of the dish you are preparing. If it's a gently flavoured dish, then don't choose a great big red that will overwhelm the other more delicate flavours. Similarly with rich and hearty dishes, there's no point in adding a delicate white wine. So the matching is pretty obvious: it's like for like, a harmonious marriage.

Some specific suggestions for cooking with wine are:

- Citrusy, zesty whites are ideal for seafood, shellfish and poultry.
- Poaching fish with a glass of white wine always seems to bring out the flavours of the fish more keenly.
- Crisp whites can also work well in vinaigrettes and salad dressings. But why stop there? Salad dressings with a little slash of gin can be lifted immeasurably.
- A glass of pinot noir is a fantastic adjunct to braised quail or duck.
- Pears are delicious when poached in red wine.
- Champagne works well in dessert sauces.
- Marinate oranges studded with cloves in white wine and brandy; experiment to find the best proportion, leave for about six weeks and then drain the liquor off to mix with soda water as a Christmas Eve aperitif.
- Serve Christmas pudding flambéed with brandy and a dollop of brandy butter.
- Add a tiny bit of amontillado sherry to soups to lend a more intense flavour.

Epilogue

FROM ARISTOCRACY TO MERITOCRACY: NEW WORLD V OLD WORLD

The unthinkable happened, California defeated Gaul and the French were aghast

TIME MAGAZINE

The past 30 years of the international wine industry could be described as the arrival of the blind.

I'm specifically referring to the arrival of blind tastings and the belief that the 100-point system for rating wines can provide enough information for consumers, judges and buyers about the quality inside a bottle of wine. The acceptance, use and importance of blind tasting results in different countries plays out wine's epic discussion: the role of nature and the power of place versus nurture and the power of man.

Blind tastings challenge the traditional European way of judging wines and the reputations they had developed. In France quality is primarily described by geography and framed by history. Initial awareness of regional wine quality led to reputations for places, which over generations of production have become historically defined and recognised less by variety and more by region. The use of vineyard classifications as quality clues reduced the label's emphasis on the property or producer.

On the other side you have quality based on the result of a blind tasting and the transcendence of man's nurturing of wine over the natural beneficial contributions of climate, soil and location. The best wine is defined by a tasting based on grape variety, not history; by producer rather than region; and by an example tasted once. As they say, 'it's what in the glass that counts'. This has been at the heart of the very important changes that have occurred since the 1976 tasting that has come to be referred to as the 'Judgment of Paris'.

When Steven Spurrier hit on the idea of holding a tasting in his Paris store with the best of Californian wines compared to the best of French wines during the bicentennial of North America he could not have seen that this tasting was to give legitimacy to the new world's wines and have ramifications that would still be felt 30 years later. Spurrier did not set out to humble the French. He appreciates French wine and has since admitted that he believed his tasting would prove French wines as superior. He was hopeful that the panel might be interested because they had little knowledge of the quality of Californian wines.

Steven Spurrier and his partner conducted a tasting of chardonnays and cabernets using a panel of judges from the crème de la crème of France's wine professionals. The tasting was blind; the labels were hidden to ensure objectivity. The tasting was held on 24 May 1976 at the Hotel Intercontinental in Paris; and the judges systematically awarded California wines ahead of France. In fact six of the eleven most highly rated wines in the tasting were from California yet the effect was a slow revolution. Time magazine coined the phrase the 'Judgment of Paris'.

The impact of the results ensured that new world wines had come of age and with it new ideas of quality and judgment. It was also a huge tick for varietal wine labelling and it seemed to suggest that ingenuity and technology together with a lot of hard work by producers meant that California had arrived in the big league.

It points to a great issue of blind wine tasting, which is that focus and concept is everything. Tasting a wine once in a blind tasting is not really a long-term endorsement of its quality; it says that it was the best wine judged by that panel on that day with that group of judges. Nor is blind tasting a judgment on longevity, although subsequent tastings have often confirmed the longevity and quality of the winning wines.

Blind tastings in effect under-describe wines. Judgments do not assess *typicité* (the typicalness of a wine from a particular region) or the longest lived wines either; rather, judges choose the greatest wine according to that panel of tasters on that day and on occasion may do no more than select overpowering freaks. For many of the people who make and sell these wines it becomes the measurement of power, and one of the sad effects of the 'Judgment of Paris' has been to see a cult based around blind tasting as judging quality at the highest level. This weakness has been addressed by some English international blind tastings by judging the wines both varietally (only the same variety, any region) and then regionally (only the same variety and region) to find the top wines.

The Australian wine show system also conducts blind tasting using panels of judges from different backgrounds within the wine industry. This has been described as similar to 'allowing the engineers of major car companies to test drive each other's cars prior to release and award them prizes anonymously'. Australia has done well from a shared sense of purpose and belief in wine shows to 'improve the breed', for it has led to the rapid dissemination of new ideas and a sophisticated industry.

Judges are attempting to move towards selecting wines with more finesse and detail and moving beyond those wines with raw power and concentration, even while tasting large numbers of wines each day and battling the anaesthetic effects of alcohol on the palate. Smaller regional shows with more homogeneity of wines seems to be the answer.

Wine shows have worked to determine the best regions in Australia, but it's still a work in progress. Australian capital cities wine show results are direct evidence that some regions are arriving at long-term dominance with their best varieties. Wine shows may struggle with the inherent fineness, subtlety and refinement that matters with fine wine, yet they remain vital tools in the armoury of a maturing wine industry.

But the 'Judgment of Paris' went on to have other meanings as well. It marked a turning point in the perception that quality wine only came from France. It galvanised the Californians and gave them a new sense of mission and confidence. The traditional notion that only the traditional great terroirs produced great wines was put under challenge because suddenly there were seen to be a lot more great terroirs than just in France. Quality could also come from wine described varietally and under a producer's brand. These new ideas of quality needed new ways to describe them, which helped the rise of published wine critics and the points system.

It's a huge pity that more varieties weren't included in the 'Judgment of Paris'. Australia had not been as slavish as other countries in following the European model, so while cabernet sauvignon was a matter of interest to us, we were also following our own local stars and making great shiraz, riesling and semillon at that time. Shiraz did suffer in the 1980s as the global fascination with cabernet distracted local winemakers—until they understood just how majestic the local shiraz was.

We have traditional varieties which we had adapted to the language of our country, but we hadn't quite arrived at a stage of having sufficient cabernet and chardonnay to compare with other similar varieties from around the world. Their absence meant the impact of the 'Judgment of Paris' was more muted in Australia, but the ideas were still potent. The notion that there were other great terroirs where a combination of technology and skill could overcome the limitations or the lack of reputation of a great district took hold.

It was also an endorsement of blind tasting as the best method to judge quality. Len Evans saw both sides of blind tasting and he realised that to play a good wine options game you have to have wines that are truly representative of where they come from—they must be the greatest wines from those places. If you choose wines that are less than top end you run the risk of muddying the waters and making it extremely hard for people to analyse them.

Len would agree that you have to experience the great wines to really know wine, and as the numbers of these wines have grown it remains that experience that enables one to assess quality. It would be a huge loss to the world if blind tasting became a sort of

Olympic competition, where just one great wine was chosen by blind tasting. We don't need or want this sort of quality assessment. The need is for a system that selects many wines which reflect the diversity of their upbringing and are made to the highest standards of quality.

Some American commentators claim that blind tasting is a very American idea, but the fact is that by the 1980s the Australian wine industry had been developing the technique for nearly a hundred years. Championing blind tasting and representing its assessments by numbers was part of the revolution brought to wine by Robert Parker. Parker's assessment of the quality of the 1982 Bordeaux vintage and the English wine trade's misjudgment of that vintage's quality cemented his place as the pre-eminent judge and broadcaster of quality and launched the 100-point system into the wine world.

The arrival of blind tasting had the effect of taking some of the finesse out of wine judgment. Blind tasting discounts a producer's or a region's historical performance. Originally, wine ranking in France had been based on pieces of land as well as prices, and the wines were grouped by quality, first growth and second growth. Suddenly you now had winners and losers, the modern world had arrived in the dear old foggy world of wine and the winners and losers came with numbers up to 100.

The overall impact of the arrival of the point system was to make consumer wine buying easier. Consumers, uncertain of their own tastes, found that they could trust wines judged by taste and marketed under taste terms, rather than relying on their own palate. Many people who couldn't tell the difference between sauvignon blanc and cabernet sauvignon suddenly became aware that wine no longer had to be expensive, French and foreign. That it could be local, lively and around the corner at the local bottle shop, but they needed a leading palate as a guide.

The media post-war trend of lifestyle food and wine writing was flourishing and the collective deluge of information made for the destruction of the old-class approach to wine. The association between France with upper- and middle-class knowledgeable clientele was slowly beginning to break down. People who knew little and were just beginning to educate themselves realised that anybody could learn about wine, that you didn't have to have a wine cellar or even have a lot of money to spend—the time was right for the points system.

The 'Judgment of Paris' had neatly pitted students against teachers as the Californians were using the same varieties as France and pretty much the same techniques. It finished off the era of attempting to emulate French wine and launched Californian winemakers out of the narrow intellectual concept of judging themselves against France. With no 'traditional' boundaries their harvest dates have become later and the wines have changed to become overripe, high in alcohol, low in acid and powerfully extracted. The focus for many producers is on achievement of massive youthful flavour and monumental power all aimed to make the biggest first impression on a drinker's palate.

Australia, blessed by the tyranny of distance and cursed by the shortage of great cabernet, was much more articulate about making different wines and doing wine in the traditions, heritage and styles that had been developed and were well known. So to a degree Australia and New Zealand benefited from being absent from the 'Judgment of Paris'; it left their respective intellectual heritage, beliefs and grape varieties intact.

This was to flow through as a benefit when our wine started to reach overseas markets. Bemused wine buyers in the 1980s have since revealed that during sales presentations they found the Californians would compare themselves to producers in France. According to the same buyers, Australian dialogue and logic was delivered with gusto with an Australian accent and derived from Australian experience. Australia found the English easy to understand, and they marvelled at us; and we learned to meet the challenges and demands of the English market. So we represented a version of wine less slavishly French and quite original in its own way.

The English search for our memorable wines and our struggle to meet their needs has taken the Australian industry through a turbulent time, with exports showing extraordinary growth from $10 million in 1990 to $3 billion in 2007. The export market has been challenging and informative. It has given some of our homegrown memorable wines a new audience and ensures that our winemaking is informed with a new sensitivity that constantly propels wine quality and understanding forward.

Australia's initial successes, however, created a 'value for money' perception that has trapped too many of us into becoming producers of a sea of varietal wines that taste, according to our critics, 'as if they could come from anywhere'. We currently struggle to wrestle the market's perception towards the increasing amount of fine wine we produce. Australia's successes have also led to changes in ownership, with a significant slice of the industry moving offshore or into publicly listed share companies.

Ownership is an emotional issue, for the family-owned wineries of the past have been responsible for much of the good and great achievements of the wine industry. Look to the post-war contribution of Penfolds, Hardys and Seppelt, or the Knappsteins, Brown Brothers, Tyrrells and more recently the De Bortolis, Taylors and Oatleys when managing Rosemount Estate.

Australia's leadership role doesn't seem to sit easily on our shoulders yet, with many export marketers aiming low in price and quality and the true potential of the opportunity in danger of being lost. The good in this is that many of our most memorable wines remain easier to buy in Australia than overseas.

The flip-side is that we need to make more wines of memorable quality and market them better. The fruit and the winemaking talent is there, yet we find wines priced at $50, $100 or even $200 hard to envisage; unfortunately, many of the best vineyards can only survive by producing quality at these prices. It requires a special breed of person to sell sophisticated, expensive wine; they need to understand the culture of their customers and their pleasures.

Wine is one of mankind's best friends, our fellow traveller for over 5000 years, and it shows the diversity of the perfection we have created. Yet for all the changes some aspects of wine remain the same. Wine mirrors our own story, with its birth, how its flavour comes from the vines and the people who make it, and how it reflects the place it is raised and matures, and, just like us, declines with age.

ACKNOWLEDGMENTS

from the author

This book was born following a discussion with Catherine Hanger, an author mate I have known for many years, who encouraged me to take the leap. To spur me on, she spoke to me at length, developed the structure, wrote the book proposal and a sizeable part of the first draft, and sold it to her agent—now my agent—Fran Moore, at Curtis Brown. I would also like to gratefully acknowledge the help of Sarah Price, Joanne Holliman and Sandra Davies for seeing words and ideas through to completion. Thanks to Murdoch Books for their thoughtful interpretation of a sketchy idea. At home, thanks to Jill for her patience, and Edward for sharing the computer with me.

In the wine industry, my thanks to those who mentored me through the early years: Mick Knappstein, Doug Collett, Max Schubert, Bernard Stephens, D'arry Osborne, Chris Hancock, Charles Taylor MW, Patrick McGrath MW, David Gill MW, Gabrielle Shaw MW, James Handford MW, Joe Thompson, John Gay, Ariki Hill, Rob Gibson, David Fatches, Andrew Caillard MW, Mark Baulderstone, Alex Gilson, Robert Hurst, Neil Hadley MW, Darren De Bortoli, David Haviland, Anthony Miceli, Philip Shaw and Jeffrey Wilkinson; and those inspirational characters Len Evans, Philip John, David Fatches, John Duval, Jim Brayne, Peter Wall, Stephen and Prue Henschke, James Godfrey, Bruce Tryrell, Andrew Moore, Jamie O'Dell, Jane Skilton MW, Andrew Stark and John Tomich.

Finally, for the enduring spirit of Australian wit and innovation, as exemplified by a group of engineering students from the University of Queensland who managed to get themselves into the *Guinness Book of Records*. Their feat—breaking the world record for accelerating a champagne cork to 41 400 kilometres per hour!

from the publisher

The publisher would like to thank all of the vineyards in the Barossa and Eden Valleys, the Mornington Peninsula and Mudgee who allowed us to take location photography for the book, including Andrew Harris Vineyards, Barossa Valley Estate, Chateau Tanunda, Crittenden, Eldridge Estate, Fernfield Wines, Frogs Pond Vineyard, Hickinbotham Winery, High Valley Wine and Cheese, Hill Smith Estate, Huntington Estate, Kenrose Vineyard, Langmeil Winery, Miceli, Montalto, Peter Lehmann Wines, Penfolds Barossa Valley Winery, Pieter Van Gent Winery and Vineyard, Pier 10, Port Phillip Estate, Red Hill Estate, Rolf Binder Wines, Stonier Wines, Seppeltsfield, T'Gallant Winemakers, Ten Minutes By Tractor Wine Co, Tuck's Ridge Winery, Whistler Wines, Willow Creek Vineyard, Wolf Blass Winery, and Zayat Restaurant and Vineyard.

INDEX

First published in 2007 by Murdoch Books Pty Limited

Murdoch Books Australia
Pier 8/9
23 Hickson Road
Millers Point NSW 2000
Phone: +61 (0)2 8220 2000
Fax: +61 (0)2 8220 2558
www.murdochbooks.com.au

Murdoch Books UK Limited
Erico House, 6th Floor
93–99 Upper Richmond Road
Putney, London SW15 2TG
Phone: +44 (0) 20 8785 5995
Fax: +44 (0) 20 8785 5985
www.murdochbooks.co.uk

Chief Executive: Juliet Rogers
Publisher: Kay Scarlett
Project Manager: Emma Hutchinson
Concept and Development: Catherine Hanger
Editors: Sandra Davies and Joanne Holliman
Designer: Heather Menzies
Photographer: John Fryz
Additional photography: p. 120 iStockphoto.com/Donald Gruener, p. 143 iStockphoto.com/Agata Malchrowicz, p. 260 iStockphoto.com/Eva Serrabassa, p. 281 iStockphoto.com/Angela Martindale; pp. 256–257 Getty Images
Illustrations: Genevieve Huard and Tracy Loughlin
Figure illustrations: Heather Menzies
Cartographer: Ian F Faulkner & Associates
Production: Kita George
Colour separation: Colour Chiefs Pty Ltd

National Library of Australia Cataloguing-in-Publication Data
Geddes, Robert.
A good nose and great legs.

Includes index.
ISBN 978 1 74045 876 4 (pbk.).

1. Wine and winemaking - History. 2. Wine and winemaking - Australia – History. 3. Wine tasting. 4. Food. I. Title.

641.22

Printed by Midas Printing (Asia) Ltd. in 2007. PRINTED IN CHINA.

a good nose
& great legs